T0330426

The Financial and Economic Crises

The Financial and Economic Crises

An International Perspective

Edited by

Benton E. Gup

University of Alabama, USA

Edward Elgar

Cheltenham, UK • Northampton, MA, USA

Published by
Edward Elgar Publishing Limited
The Lypiatts
15 Lansdown Road
Cheltenham
Glos GL50 2JA
UK

Edward Elgar Publishing, Inc.
William Pratt House
9 Dewey Court
Northampton
Massachusetts 01060
USA

A catalogue record for this book
is available from the British Library

Library of Congress Control Number: 2009943917

Mixed Sources
Product group from well-managed
forests and other controlled sources
www.fsc.org Cert no. SA-COC-1565
© 1996 Forest Stewardship Council
FSC

ISBN 978 1 84844 666 3

Printed and bound by MPG Books Group, UK

Contents

PART IV INTERNATIONAL REGULATORY ISSUES

Contributors

Masanori Amano is Professor of Monetary Economics at Chiba University, Japan. He graduated from the Department of Politico-Economics, Waseda University, and the Graduate School of Economics, Hitotsubashi University. He received a doctorate from Hitotsubashi University in 1989. He is the author of three books on monetary economics, business cycles and monetary policy. He has also published articles in international journals dealing with development economics and money and banking.

Apanard Penny Angkinand is a Senior Research Analyst in the Capital Studies group at the Milken Institute, Santa Monica, CA. She previously worked as an assistant professor of economics at the University of Illinois at Springfield. Her research specializations include banks, financial markets, monetary policy, exchange rates, financial integration, capital flows, emerging market economies and financial crises. Her research has been published in the *Journal of International Money and Finance*, *Open Economies Review* and the *Journal of International Financial Markets, Institutions and Money*. Angkinand received her PhD in economics with a concentration in international money and finance from Claremont Graduate University, Claremont, CA. While completing her PhD, she also held visiting scholar positions at the Claremont Institute for Economic Policy Studies and the Freeman Program in Asian Political Economy at the Claremont Colleges.

Chris Bajada is Associate Professor of Economics and Associate Dean (Teaching and Learning) at the University of Technology Sydney. He started his teaching career at the University of New South Wales, from which he holds a PhD. He has taught economics in a variety of undergraduate and postgraduate courses and his most recent teaching experience has been in applied microeconomics. In recognition of his teaching, he was awarded the University of Technology Teaching Excellence award and the Carrick Institute Teaching Award for outstanding contributions to student learning in higher education in Australia. His research is primarily in applied macroeconomics, with a special interest in the underground economy. He has worked with the Australian Taxation Office as a member of the Cash Economy Task Force and his research has attracted national publicity. He has published numerous papers and books on the topic, and has also served as a member of Council of the Economic Society of Australia (NSW Branch).

James R. Barth is the Lowder Eminent Scholar in Finance at Auburn University, Auburn, AL and a Senior Finance Fellow at the Milken Institute, Santa Monica, CA. His research focuses on financial institutions and capital markets, both domestic and global, with special emphasis on regulatory issues. Most recently, he served as leader of an international team advising the People's Bank of China on banking reform. Barth was an appointee of Presidents Ronald Reagan and George H.W. Bush as chief economist of the Office of Thrift Supervision until November 1989 and previously as chief economist of the Federal Home Loan Bank Board. He has also held the positions of professor of economics at George Washington University, associate director of the economics program at the National Science Foundation and Shaw Foundation Professor of Banking and Finance at Nanyang Technological University. He has been a visiting scholar at the US Congressional Budget Office, Federal Reserve Bank of Atlanta, Office of the Comptroller of the Currency and the World Bank. He is a member of the Advisory Council of George Washington University's Financial Services Research Program. Barth's expertise in financial institutions and capital market issues has led him to testify before the US House and Senate banking committees on several occasions. He has authored more than 200 articles in professional journals and has written and edited several books, including *The Rise and Fall of the US Mortgage and Credit Markets: A Comprehensive Analysis of the Meltdown* (2009), *The Great Savings and Loan Debacle* (1991) and *The Reform of Federal Deposit Insurance* (1992). Other recent books are *Rethinking Bank Regulation: Till Angels Govern* (2006), with Jerry Caprio and Ross Levine, *Financial Restructuring and Reform in Post-WTO China* (2007), with Zhongfei Zhou, Douglas Arner, Berry Hsu and Wei Wang, and *Global Banking Regulation and Supervision: what are the issues and what are the practices?* (2009), with Jie Gan and Daniel E. Nolle. Barth is the overseas associate editor of *The Chinese Banker*.

Navin Beekarry is a Barrister-at-Law, called to the Bar of England and Wales, and worked with the Attorney-General's Office in Mauritius until 2002, when his last position was that of Assistant Solicitor General. Thereafter, he established and headed, as Commissioner, the Independent Commission against Corruption (ICAC) in Mauritius from 2002 to 2005. In 2005, he joined the Legal Department of the International Monetary Fund (IMF) in Washington, DC, where he worked on anti-money laundering and combating the financing of terrorism (AML/CFT) and anti-corruption issues. He holds an LLM from the London School of

Economics and was a Visiting Scholar at Harvard Law School in 2009. He is presently Senior Anti-Corruption Consultant with the S.J. Quinney College of Law of the University of Utah, Salt Lake City, UT, on the Global Justice Project for Iraq.

James A. Brox is Professor of Economics at the University of Waterloo, Ontario, Canada. He is the author of more than 100 articles, books, book chapters, monographs, and technical reports on various economic issues, usually with a strong policy focus. He has been chair of the Economics Department at the University of Waterloo (1996–2005), President of the University of Waterloo Faculty Association (1984–86 and 1992–94), and Associate Dean of Arts for Computing (1989–90). He is currently President of the International Banking, Economics, and Finance Association (formerly, the North American Economics and Finance Association) and is managing editor of the *Journal of Economic Asymmetries*. He is an honorary life member of the Atlantic Canada Economics Association.

Joseph Cauthen is a Senior Financial Engineer within the Research and Model Development group of the Federal Housing Finance Agency (FHFA). He conducts financial and economic research and model development related to measuring and monitoring the solvency of government sponsored enterprises (GSEs).

Horst Gischer is Professor of Economics and Executive Director of the Research Center for Savings Banks Development (FZSE) at Otto-von-Guericke University Magdeburg, Germany, where he is Chair in Monetary Economics. His fields of interest include theory of financial markets, banking systems and new empirical industrial organization.

Benton E. Gup holds the Robert Hunt Cochrane/Alabama Bankers Association Chair of Banking at the University of Alabama, Tuscaloosa, AL, USA. He has lectured on the current economic crises for the US Department of State in Europe and North Africa. He is the author or editor of 28 books, and his articles on financial subjects have appeared in the *Journal of Finance*, the *Journal of Financial and Quantitative Analysis*, the *Journal of Money, Credit, and Banking*, *Financial Management*, the *Journal of Banking and Finance*, the *Financial Analysts Journal*, and elsewhere. In 2009, he was awarded the Midwest Finance Association's Lifetime Achievement Award.

Hikari Ishido is Associate Professor of International Economics at Chiba University in Japan. He graduated from the Departments of Economics and of Engineering, University of Tokyo. He has a PhD from SOAS

(School of Oriental and African Studies) at the University of London. Ishido is the author of a book on development economics, and several journal articles on international trade and development.

Hyeongwoo Kim is Assistant Professor of Economics at Auburn University, Auburn, AL. He joined the Auburn faculty in 2006 upon completion of his PhD at Ohio State University. His research focuses on theoretical and empirical models of exchange rates, optimal monetary policy in dynamic stochastic general equilibrium models, and empirical financial economics. His research has appeared in the *Journal of Empirical Finance*, the *Journal of Forecasting*, *Applied Financial Economics*, and the *Economics Bulletin*. He has presented his research papers at the NBER Summer Institute, the ASSA annual meeting, the MEG Annual Meeting, the Midwest Macro meeting, the KEA-KAEA International Conference, and the MEA annual meeting. He has served as a referee for *Applied Economics*, the *Chinese Economic Review*, *Empirical Economics*, the *International Economic Journal*, the *Journal of Money, Credit, and Banking*, the *Journal of Forecasting*, and the *Quarterly Review of Economics and Finance*.

Jungeun Kim is a finance PhD candidate at the College of Business Administration at Inha University, Korea. She obtained her master's degree in finance from the university.

Júlia Király has been the Deputy Governor of the Magyar Nemzeti Bank since July 2007. After graduating at the Budapest University of Economics, she was an applied econometrician at the Planning Office. In 1988 she joined the International Training Center for Bankers. She has been one of its CEOs since 1999, and one of its owners since 2003. She took part in the privatization of Hungarian banks (MHB: 1996; K&H: 2000) as a member of the board, and in the privatization of the Postabank in 2003 as the chair of the board. She holds a PhD degree in economics and she is an honorary professor at the Budapest University of Economics. Her special research fields are monetary policy and financial risk management.

Thomas Lutton is Principal Economist in Research and Model Development in the Federal Housing Finance Agency, Washington, DC. He also serves as a technical expert in bank supervision and early warning systems for the International Monetary Fund.

Katalin Mérő is Managing Director of the Hungarian Financial Supervisory Authority's Economics, Risk Assessment and Regulatory Directorate. Previously she was the deputy head of the Financial Stability Department of the National Bank of Hungary. From 1990 to 1997 she was Director of Strategy and Economic Analysis at K&H, a large Hungarian commercial bank. Prior to her banking career she worked as a researcher at the Economic Research Institute and Research Institute for Labour. She graduated from the Budapest University of Economics and received her PhD from the Budapest University of Technology and Economics.

Doowoo Nam is Associate Professor of Finance at Inha University, Korea. His research interests include banking and corporate finance. He has published in the *Journal of Applied Corporate Finance*, the *Journal of Risk Finance*, the *Journal of Emerging Market Finance*, and *Research in International Business and Finance*, and contributed to several books. He was formerly a faculty member at the College of Business of the University of Southern Mississippi. He has presented papers at various professional meetings and received the Best Paper Award in the financial institutions area at the 2001 annual meeting of the Southern Finance Association.

María J. Nieto has been Advisor to the Director General of Banking Regulation at Banco de España since December 2000, and during this time she has represented the Banco de España at working groups of the Basel Committee of Banking Supervisors as well as the European Commission. She has been a visiting scholar with the Federal Reserve Bank of Atlanta since 2004, and a contributor to the Center for European Policy Studies and the Center for Economic Policy Research. She has coauthored several articles on banking and regulatory issues that have been published among others by the *Journal of Banking and Finance*, the *Journal of Financial Stability*, *European Financial Management* and the *Journal of Banking Regulation*. She has developed her career at the European Central Bank (1998–2000), the Council of Economic Advisors to the Spanish President (1996–98) and the International Monetary Fund (1991–95), which subsequently hired her as a consultant on financial sector issues. She is a Certified Public Accountant (CPA), Instituto de Contabilidad y Auditores de Cuentas of Spain, and earned an MBA (finance) degree from the University of California, Los Angeles and a PhD *cum laude* from the Universidad Complutense de Madrid. She was recipient of the Fundación Ramón Areces Scholarship to pursue studies at the University of California at Los Angeles.

Peter Reichling is Professor of Finance and Director of the Research Center for Savings Banks Development (FZSE) at Otto-von-Guericke University Magdeburg, Germany, where he is Chair in Banking and Finance. His fields of interest include risk management, performance measurement, and rating models and validation.

Kyeong Pyo Ryu is a finance PhD candidate at the College of Business Administration at Inha University, Korea. He obtained his MBA degree specializing in finance and accounting from the Sloan School of Management at the Massachusetts Institute of Technology, Cambridge, MA.

Rowan Trayler is Senior Lecturer in the School of Finance and Economics at the University of Technology, Sydney. Prior to joining the faculty in 1987, he worked for 16 years in the finance industry. He has spent the last 11 years at Barclays Bank Australia Ltd, where he held several different management positions. Since joining the University of Technology he has been closely involved in teaching in the Master of Business programs, and is responsible for the coordination of the introductory finance subject in the Bachelor of Business. He has made contributions at a number of international conferences, has a number of journal publications in banking and finance and has written several book chapters in international publications. He is a co-author in the adaptation of a leading introductory finance text for the Australian market.

Preface

The financial and economic crises that began in the United States in 2007 quickly spread around the world. Like other financial crises in the 1980s and 1990s, real estate booms and busts, and excessive financial leverage played key roles. However, this financial crisis had some unique aspects to it. Equally important, the global impact of the crises varied widely from country to country. This book examines the causes of the crises in the US, and its impact in selected countries in North America, Europe, Asia, and Australia. The book also explores some international regulatory issues related to the crises.

The book is divided into four parts covering North America, Europe, Asia and Australia, and International Regulatory Issues. The chapters are written by academics, practitioners, and regulators. Unfortunately, there were no contributors from South America.

PART I

North America

1. Global financial crises

Benton E. Gup

1 INTRODUCTION

Subprime mortgages refer to high risk mortgage loans made to borrowers with low credit scores and other high-risk characteristics.[1] Another factor adding to their risk is that many subprime mortgage loans have adjustable rates of interest (adjustable rate mortgages, ARMs) that can change over time resulting in higher monthly payments. Subprime mortgage loans were packaged (that is, securitized) and sold to banks, government sponsored enterprises (GSEs, that is, Fannie Mae, Freddie Mac, Ginnie Mae), and to other investors throughout the world. The delinquency rate on subprime mortgage loans in the United States increased from 11.5 percent in 2005 to 21.88 percent in the fourth quarter, 2008.[2]

The high delinquency rates and subsequent foreclosures contributed to losses on subprime and other real estate loans. The losses caused a 'liquidity crunch' in August 2007.[3] Mortgage-backed securities became illiquid, and companies had problems borrowing funds. The liquidity crunch became widespread and adversely affected other markets. For example, French bank BNP Paribas halted redemptions on some of its funds because of concerns about mortgage values.[4] The losses and liquidity crunch also contributed to the Federal Housing Finance Authority (FHFA) putting Fannie Mae and Freddie Mac into conservatorship in September 2007.[5]

How and why did the delinquencies and foreclosures on real estate loans, and a deep recession in the United States spread losses around the world? And what caused the crises? To answer these questions, this chapter proceeds as follows. Section 2 explains how the crises became 'global'. Section 3 examines the causes of the crises. Section 4 examines what happened when the real estate bubble burst. Finally, Section 5 examines government responses to the crises.

2   GLOBALIZATION

Banks

Part of the answer to the first question about how and why the crises spread around the world is revealed in Table 1.1, which lists the world's 10 largest banks in fiscal year 2007. Eight of them are foreign owned. Crédit Agricole is the only foreign-owned bank in the list that does not own or operate corporate entities in the United States.

The Royal Bank of Scotland (RBS), chartered in the United Kingdom, was the largest bank in the world in 2007. The Royal Bank of Scotland Group owns financial institutions in Europe, the Middle East, Asia, and the United States. For example, it owns Citizens Financial Group, Inc., the fourteenth largest Bank Holding Company in the United States.[6] Citizens provided RBS with subprime loans.[7] Subsequently, RBS lost about $45 billion in 2007, which was blamed largely on subprime loans. This was the largest loss in British corporate history. Consequently, the British government injected about $59 billion in capital into the bank and it now owns a controlling interest in RBS.[8]

Deutsche Bank (# 2 on the list) is chartered in Germany. It owns Taunus Corporation, the eighth largest Bank Holding Company in the United States. It deals in mortgages and a wide range of other banking and investment activities.

BNP Paribas (#3) is chartered in France and operates in 85 countries. BNP Paribas owns BancWest Corporation – a holding company that

Table 1.1   World's 10 largest banks in 2007

Rank	Name	Assets ($ trillion)	Country
1	Royal Bank of Scotland (RBS)	3.81 T	UK
2	Deutsche Bank	2.97	Germany
3	BNP Paribas	2.49	France
4	Barclays Bank	2.46	UK
5	HSBC Holdings	2.35	UK
6	Crédit Agricole Group	2.27	France
7	Citigroup	2.19	USA
8	UBS	2.01	Switzerland
9	Bank of America Group	1.72	USA
10	Société Générale	1.59	France

Source: Global Finance (2008, p. 111).

owns Bank of the West and First Hawaiian Bank in the United States.[9] BancWest Corporation is the 22nd largest Bank Holding Company in the United States.[10] It operates in 20 Western and Midwestern states, Guam and Saipan. The banks also have offshore locations in Tokyo, Taipei, Taiwan and Grand Cayman (West Indies).[11]

Barclays (# 4) is chartered in the UK and Barclays Global Investors, Barclays Capital, Barclays Wealth and Barclaycard all operate in the USA.[12] It also operates in more than 50 other countries.

HSBC Holdings (#5) is chartered in the UK and has offices in 86 countries and territories around the world.[13] In the United States, it owns HSBC Finance Corp., which holds risky consumer loans. It has taken more than $40 billion in impairment charges. HSBC also owns Household International Inc., which holds subprime mortgage loans.[14] As of March 31, 2009, the book value of Household's assets was $90 billion, while their estimated market value was $57.5 billion.

Crédit Agricole Group (#6) is a leading retail bank in France and Europe. It also has 11,500 branches in 70 countries.

Citigroup (#7) and Bankof America (#9) are the only US banks in the World's top 10 banks. Citigroup operates in more than 100 countries and Bank of America in 23 countries.[15]

UBS (#8) headquartered in Switzerland, is a global firm providing financial services to private, corporate and institutional clients in all major financial centers. It has offices in over 50 countries.

Société Générale (#10), a French universal bank with a Corporate and Investment Bank that offers a product mix including derivatives and structured finance. The Corporate and Investment Bank operates in more than 40 countries including the US Société Générale which opened its first office in the United States in 1938.[16] Today, it has offices in 13 US cities.

The bottom line is that large global banks with operations in the United States and their participation in subprime mortgage lending facilitated the spread of those loans throughout the world.

Foreign Holdings of US Securities

Foreign holdings of US debt and equity securities increased from $4.3 trillion in 2002 to $10.3 trillion in June 2008.[17] Thus, economic shocks in the US were felt by investors around the world who held US securities. More will be said about foreign holdings of US securities in connection with 'Foreign investors and governments' in Section 3.

3   CAUSES OF THE CRISES

Population Growth and Urbanization

The population of the United States increased from 205 million people in 1970 to 306.9 million in July 2009.[18] The growth of the population is attributed to immigration, higher birth rates and longer life spans. The growing population moved into cities and metropolitan areas, mostly in the south and southwestern parts of the United States. The fastest-growing metropolitan areas are listed in Table 1.2.

Note that the table shows the *increase in population*, not the total number of people living in the metropolitan areas. The population in the Atlanta Metropolitan Statistical Area (MSA), for example, is about 5.1 million people. In the Los Angeles MSA – which includes Los Angeles and Riverside, the population is 13 million. In the Greater Los Angeles area – which includes nearby counties – the population is over 17 million. The important point here is that the large and rapid increase in population increased the demand for housing and the price of housing in those areas, which are some of the cities and metropolitan areas that had the biggest real estate booms, and the biggest real estate busts.

The increased number of women in the labor force is another demographic factor to be considered. In 1970, women aged 16 years and over accounted for 40.8 percent of the civilian labor force.[19] In 2007, they

Table 1.2   US metro areas with highest numerical growth: April 1, 2000–July 1, 2006

MSA	Population
Atlanta–Sandy Springs–Marietta, GA	890,211
Dallas–Fort Worth–Arlington, TX	842,449
Houston–Sugar Land–Baytown, TX	824,547
Phoenix–Mesa–Scottsdale, AZ	787,306
Riverside–San Bernardino–Ontario, CA	771,314
Los Angeles–Long Beach–Santa Ana, CA	584,510
New York–Northern New Jersey–Long Island, NY–NJ–PA	495,154
Washington–Arlington–Alexandria, DC–VA–MD–W. VA	494,220
Miami–Fort Lauderdale–Miami Beach, FL	455,869
Chicago–Naperville–Joliet, IL–IN–WI	407,133

Source: US Census Bureau News (2007).

accounted for 59.3 percent of the labor force. The key point here is that a family with two sources of income is likely to buy a more expensive home than one with a single source.

Government Policies

Laws
The population growth put pressure on the federal government to pass the following laws that supported homeownership:

- The Community Reinvestment Act (1977) encouraged banks to meet the credit needs of their communities.
- The Depository Institutions Deregulation and Monetary Control Act (DIDMCA, 1980) preempted state interest rate caps on loans.
- The Alternative Mortgage Transaction Parity Act (1982) permitted the use of variable interest rates and balloon payments.
- The Tax Reform Act of 1986 eliminated the tax deduction for interest expense on credit cards. This induced borrowers to use Home Equity Lines of Credit (HELOC), or second mortgages on their homes. The interest expense on mortgage loans is a tax deductible expense.
- The Taxpayer Relief Act (1997) eliminated capital gains tax on the sale of homes up to $500,000 for married couples. People cashed out home equity profits to buy additional homes/condos. The 'Snowbirds', that is, people living in the cold northern part of the US, bought a second home in the warmer south and western parts of the US, in places such as Florida, Arizona, and Nevada.

In addition to laws that encouraged borrowing, market rates of interest declined over the years. The contract interest rate on a 30-year conventional fixed rate mortgage peaked at 14.67 percent in July, 1984.[20] Subsequently, mortgage rates declined gradually over the years, reaching 4.81 percent in May 2009.

Government-sponsored entities
The GSE Federal National Mortgage Association (FNMA, Fannie Mae), the Federal Home Loan Mortgage Corporation (FHLMC, Freddie Mac), and the Government National Mortgage Association (Ginnie Mae) were chartered by Congress to provide liquidity, stability and affordability to the US housing and mortgage markets.[21] Fannie Mae was established as a federal agency in 1938, and it became a private shareholder-owned company in 1968. Freddie Mac was chartered by Congress in 1970, and

in 1989 it too became a publicly traded company. In 1968, Congress established Ginnie Mae as a government-owned corporation within the Department of Housing and Urban Development (HUD). It is still government owned.

FNMA packages (that is, securitizes) mortgage loans originated by lenders in the primary mortgage market into *m*ortgage *b*acked *s*ecurities that are referred to as Fannie Mae MBS that can then be bought and sold in the secondary mortgage market. FNMA also participates in the secondary mortgage market by purchasing mortgage loans (also called 'whole loans') and mortgage-related securities, including Fannie Mae MBS, for their mortgage portfolio.[22] Freddie Mac's operations are similar to those of Fannie Mae.

Ginnie Mae deals exclusively in loans insured by the Federal Housing Administration (FHA) or that are guaranteed by the Department of Veterans Affairs (VA). Other guarantors or issuers of loans eligible as collateral for Ginnie Mae MBS include the Department of Agriculture's Rural Housing Service (RHS) and the Department of Housing and Urban Development's Office of Public and Indian Housing (PIH). Consequently, Ginnie Mae securities are the *only* MBS to carry the full faith and credit guaranty of the US government.[23]

The Federal Home Loan Bank (FHLB) system was created in 1932 to provide funding for home mortgages.[24] Today, FHLBs provide funding to banks for housing, development and infrastructure projects. FHLBs are cooperatives owned by banks and other regulated financial institutions. FHLB advances to their member institutions provided an important source of funding and liquidity both before and during the banking crises.[25]

In 2005, the GSEs held about 50 percent of the securitization (packaged loans) market. The other half was held by private firms (that is, not government owned). Since the onset of the financial crises in August 2007, the private firms have been out of the market.[26]

Subprime loans
Privately owned companies, GSEs, and many other mortgage lenders tried to increase their profits by financing and/or acquiring lower-quality mortgage products, including subprime mortgages. Riskier mortgages have higher interest rates than prime quality mortgages. Subprime mortgages can be defined in terms of FICO® credit scores and other factors:[27]

- FICO scores of 720 and above: excellent credit;
- 680–719: good credit;
- 620–679: conditional credit;

- 585–619: high-risk credit; and
- 584 and below: very high-risk credit.

Subprime mortgages are loans to borrowers with low FICO credit scores. There is no standard definition of subprime. Nevertheless, credit scores below 680 are generally considered subprime. 'Subprime ARMs comprise only 6.8% of the total outstanding home loans in the US, but as of the 3rd quarter of 2007 they represented 43% of the loans involved in home foreclosures. That means that nearly half of the home foreclosures in the US were subprime loans'.[28]

Subprime loans also include loans originated by lenders specializing in high-cost loans and types of loans not available in 'prime' markets, such as 2/28 hybrid loans (interest rate is fixed for two years and then becomes adjustable). In addition, prime mortgage loans that are securitized along with loans that have low credit scores, high loan-to-value ratios, and high debt-to-income ratios are labeled 'subprime'.[29]

The alternative – *paper or Alt-A* mortgages – are mortgage loans that lack full documentation, or that have high loan-to-value ratios, or the borrowers have high debt-to-income ratios and the loans do not conform to the GSE standards. They are generally considered less risky than subprime mortgages.

Foreign investors and governments
Foreign investors and governments have played an important role in the US economy. In June 2008, foreign holdings of US debt and equity securities amounted to $10.3 trillion compared to $4.3 trillion in June 2002.[30] Japan was the largest investor followed by China. 'Belgium, the Cayman Islands, Luxembourg, Switzerland, and the United Kingdom are financial centers in which substantial amounts of securities owned by residents of other countries are managed and held in custody'.[31] Banks and other corporations can create 'special purpose entities' (SPEs) in offshore financial centers or elsewhere to take advantage of low taxes, regulatory benefits, and to isolate financial and other legal risks.[32] SPEs are called 'special purpose vehicles' (SPVs) in Europe. They are usually organized as limited liability companies or limited partnerships.

Table 1.3 shows that two countries, Japan and China, hold 65 percent of long-term US Treasury debt. This is a substantial increase over 35 percent of long-term US Treasury debt that was foreign owned in March 2000.[33] Japan and China also hold 45 percent of federal agency (that is, Fannie Mae, Freddie Mac) asset-backed securities (ABS). ABS are long-term debt securities backed by pools of assets such as residential mortgages, credit cards, and car loans. They include collateralized debt obligations (CDOs).

Table 1.3   Value of foreign holdings of US securities by country, June 30, 2008 ($ trillions)

Rank	Country	Total	US Treasury long-term debt	ABS
1	Japan	1,250	568	121 federal agency
2	China, mainland	1,205	522	369 federal agency
3	UK	864	45	
4	Cayman Island	832	25	193 corporate
5	Luxembourg	656	58	
6	Belgium	456	14	
7	Canada	441	17	
8	Ireland	400	12	
9	Middle East oil exporters	391	78	
10	Switzerland	314	34	
	World totals	10,322	1,684	1533

Source: US Department of Treasury (2009, Table 5).

Sovereign wealth funds are state-owned investment funds that buy stocks, bonds, real estate, or other financial instruments funded by foreign exchange assets. Abu Dhabi, Norway, Singapore and other countries used sovereign wealth funds to invest billions of dollars in Citigroup, Morgan Stanley, Merrill Lynch, and other financial firms.[34] The inflow of their investment funds provided liquidity that helped to fuel the real estate boom in the US.

Shadow Banking

The term 'shadow banking' is attributed to Paul McCaulley, Managing Director of PIMCO – a global investment management firm.[35] In August 2007, the beginning of the financial crises, McCaulley defined the shadow banking system as 'the whole alphabet soup of levered up non-bank investment conduits, vehicles, and structures' He went on to say:

> Unlike regulated real banks, who fund themselves with insured deposits, back-stopped by access to the Fed's discount window, unregulated shadow banks fund themselves with un-insured commercial paper, which may or may not be backstopped by liquidity lines from real banks. Thus, the shadow banking system is particularly vulnerable to runs – commercial paper investors refusing to re-up when their paper matures, leaving the shadow banks with a liquidity crisis – a need to tap their back-up lines of credit with real banks and/or to

Table 1.4   Personal savings and home ownership

	1980	1990	2000	2007
Personal savings rate as % of disposable income	7.9	7.0	2.3	0.4
Average size of new privately owned single family homes (sq. ft.)	1,740	2,080	2,266	2,521
Median sales price of single family homes ($)	64,600	122,900	169,000	247,900
Home mortgage debt* (bn)	$905	$2,504	$4,818	$10,509

Sources: US Census Bureau (2005, 2009), 1995: Tables 1214, 787; 2009: Tables 656, 929, 933, 1132. *Home mortgage debt (Table 1132) is from the Board of Governors of the Federal Reserve System, Flow of Funds Accounts, Assets and Liabilities of Households, Statistical Release H.8. Data are not adjusted for inflation.

liquidate assets at fire sale prices. And make no mistake: that is precisely what has been happening in recent weeks . . .[36]

Shadow banks are nonbank financial intermediaries. They include, but are not limited to, investment banks such as Bear Stearns and Lehman Brothers, hedge funds, private equity funds, structured investment vehicles (SIVs), and other organizations. By 2007, shadow banking activity exceeded the level of activity in the traditional banking sector.[37] The shadow banks contributed liquidity that helped to fuel the real estate boom. Some shadow banks also dealt heavily in MBS. Finally, shadow banks had excessive financial leverage that contributed to the crises. More will be said about excessive leverage shortly.

What the Data Show

The consequences of the population growth government policies and increased liquidity are shown in Table 1.4. Personal savings rate declined from 7.9 percent in 1980 to 0.7 percent in 2007. A large part of the decline in savings is due to individuals buying larger and more expensive homes, and incurring substantially larger mortgage debts. The price of new single family homes almost quadrupled, reaching $247,900 in 2007, and home mortgage debt soared from $905 billion in 1980 to $10.5 trillion in 2007. The mortgage debt also includes home equity lines of credit and other junior liens. Home equity lines of credit are a type of second mortgage on the home.

From 1980 to August 2007, commercial bank holdings of real estate

Table 1.5   Sample ARM comparison 2/28 ARM, $200,000 loan/30 years

Years/interest rates	Fixed rate 7.5%	Reduced initial rate 2/28 ARM 7% for 2 years then adjusting to variable rate
Years 1–2/7.5%	$1,598	$1,531
Year 3/10%	$1,598	$1,939
Year 4 /11.5%	$1,598	$2,152
Years 5 – 30/13%	$1,598	$2,370

loans increased from 14.5 to 33.6 percent of total assets.[38] The high concentration in real estate loans contributed to the failure of many banks. Gup (1999) found that high concentrations of real estate loans were a major contributing factor contributing to international banking crises.

Financial Innovations

Securitization
Securitization is a financial innovation that gained widespread use in the 1970s.[39] It refers to the packaging and selling of loans, such as mortgage and credit card loans. Securitization is a great financial tool when used properly. However, the improper use of securitized mortgage loans was the time bomb that set off the financial crises.

Some mortgages had little or no documentation (low-doc and no-doc loans), and were given to borrowers who could not afford them. To make matters worse, many of the mortgage loans had adjustable rates of interest. Table 1.5 illustrates the difference between the payments of a fixed rate mortgage and an ARM when market rates of interest rise. The ARM is initially given a low teaser interest rate for the first two years of a 30-year loan (2/28) to induce borrowers to use this method of financing. However, when market rates of interest rise, the monthly payments increase significantly. In some cases, the new payments exceed the borrower's ability to repay the loans, and the loans go into default.

Mortgage backed securities
Originators of the securitized mortgage loans got paid when they sold the MBS to other investors. The originators did not retain an equity interest in the MBS. This contributed to a *moral hazard* problem. Simply stated, the originators had no risk associated with selling high-risk–low-quality loans (that is, subprime loans) to investors. The more loans they sold, the more money they earned. As previously noted, the delinquency rate of subprime

mortgage began to increase from 11.5 percent in 2005, to about 21 percent in 2008. According to the Mortgage Bankers Association, the delinquency rate for all types of mortgage loans in March 2009 was 9.12 percent, the highest level since 1972.[40] The large foreign banks that were discussed previously acquired securitized mortgage loans, and they facilitated their distribution around the world. Thus, the impact of rising delinquency rates and defaults on mortgage loans that were originated in the United States was felt around the world.

The *lack of transparency* of complex MBS was part of the problem. Investors did not know exactly what they were buying, and the credit rating agencies did not correctly estimate the risks of these securities. Two plausible reasons why the credit rating models did not work well is that they were based on historical data that did not apply to subprime loans, and they made certain assumptions about future economic conditions. When neither assumption is correct, the models did not accurately reflect credit risk.

Credit default swaps

Because investors did not fully understand the risks associated with securitized loans, they bought *credit default swaps* (CDS), which is a form of insurance for MBS. The CDS market increased from about $6.4 trillion in December 2004 to about $57.9 trillion in December 2007.[41]

American International Group (AIG) was the major issuer of CDS. Its failure would have caused systemic risk in the financial markets. Consequently, when AIG got into trouble in September 2008, the Federal Reserve provided $85 billion in loans.[42] The loans have a 24-month term. Interest will accrue on the outstanding balance at a rate of three-month Libor plus 850 basis points.

Quantitative models

Mortgage lenders, insurance companies (that is, AIG), credit rating agencies (that is, S&P, Moody's), credit scoring companies (that is, Fair Isaac Co.) and others make extensive use of quantitative models in their risk management and rating systems. For the most part, the models were based on historical data that did not accurately foresee future events. According to Richard Fisher, President of the Federal Reserve Bank of Dallas,

> The excesses in subprime lending in the United States were fed by an excessive amount of faith in technically sophisticated approaches to risk management and a misguided belief that mathematical models could price securitized assets, including securities based on mortgages, accurately. These valuation methodologies were so technical and mathematically sophisticated that their utter complexity lulled many people into a false sense of security. In the end, complexity proved hopelessly inadequate as an all-encompassing measure of risk, despite

its frequent advertisement as such. The risk models employed turned out to be merely formulaic descriptions of the past and created an illusion of precision.[43]

Bank business models

Finally, as a result of the growth of securitized assets and brokered deposits, the basic business model has changed for some banks. The term 'deposit broker' is defined as any person engaged in the business of placing deposits, or facilitating the placement of deposits, of third parties with insured depository institutions, and a 'brokered deposit' is any deposit that is obtained, directly or indirectly from a deposit broker.[44] The ability to buy and sell both loans and deposits has increased banks' liquidity. One consequence of the increased liquidity is that the business model of banking is changing. It used to be 'originate-and-hold loans'. The new business model is 'originate-to-distribute loans'. Not all banks use the new model. Dependence on short-term funds contributed to the increased liquidity risk that was experienced in 2008. To avoid future liquidity crises, Federal Bank regulators sought comments on a proposed 'Interagency Guidance on Funding and Liquidity Risk Management' in July, 2009.[45] The proposed Guidance is consistent with the 'Principles for Sound Liquidity Risk Management and Supervision' issued by the Basel Committee on Banking Supervision (BCBS) in September 2008.

Excessive Financial Leverage

Many subprime lenders and investment banks were very highly leveraged. An equity capital ratio of 3 percent means that for every $1 in equity capital there is $33 in assets (that is, loans, investments, other assets). A $1 loan loss translates into a 100 percent loss of the lender's capital. Bear Stearns had an equity capital ratio of 3 percent. It avoided failure in March 2008 by being acquired by JP Morgan Chase.[46]

Some hedge funds have lower equity capital ratios, such as 2 percent. When highly leveraged borrowers default, the losses flow back to highly commercial banks. In 1999, the President's Working Group on Financial Markets said the following in its report on long-term capital management (LTCM), a hedge fund that almost failed:

> When leveraged investors are overwhelmed by market or liquidity shocks, the risks they have assumed will be discharged back into the market. Thus, highly leveraged investors have the potential to exacerbate instability in the market as a whole. . . . These secondary effects, if not contained, could cause a contraction of credit and liquidity, and ultimately, heighten the risk of a contraction in real economic activity.[47]

The equity capital ratio for Federal Deposit Insurance Corporation (FDIC) insured banks was 10.2 percent in the first quarter, 2009.[48] Although the equity capital ratio for banks is substantially higher than that of hedge funds, banks are still highly leveraged compared to nonfinancial corporations which have an equity capital ratio 58.6 percent.[49]

4 THE BURSTING OF THE REAL ESTATE BUBBLE

The real estate bubble burst as the delinquency rate for subprime ARMs soared from 12 percent in March 2004 to almost 28 percent in March 2009.[50] The foreclosure rate for subprime mortgages went from 1.3 to 6.9 percent.[51] As previously noted, they accounted for nearly half of the home foreclosures in the US.

Bank Failures

Rather than letting the largest US financial institutions fail, federal banking authorities arranged for Bank of America to buy Countrywide in January 2008 and Merrill Lynch in September. The government took over Fannie Mae and Freddie Mac in September, and the Federal Reserve invested in AIG. Nevertheless, the government did let Lehman Brothers fail in September 2008.

The government pushed mortgage service firms to modify mortgages to reduce the stress on banks and other financial institutions as the number of defaults on real estate loans and foreclosures increased. [52] As previously noted, nearly half of the foreclosures were subprime loans.[53] The mortgage service firms include Bank of America Corp., Citigroup Inc., J.P. Morgan Chase & Co., Wells Fargo, and others.

The number of FDIC insured bank and savings institution (hereafter called 'banks') failures increased from zero in 2005–06 to 25 banks in 2008, and 123 banks in 2009 (as of November 11, 2009). To put the number of failures in perspective, about 9,000 banks failed during the Great Depression of the early 1930s, and more than 1,600 banks failed during the 1980–94 period (see Table 1.6). The data also show that the number of banks has declined over the years, reflecting the consolidation and increased asset concentration of the banking system. In the first quarter, 2009, there were 8,246 FDIC insured banks.[54] Out of that total, 115 banks with assets greater than $10 billion held 78 percent of the total assets.

Changes in the following banking laws contributed to bank consolidation and increasing banks' geographic footprint and banking activities:

Table 1.6   Bank failures

Years	Number of banks	Number of bank failures
Great Depression – 1930s	14,146 (12/1934)	9,000+
1980–94	10,451 (12/1994)	1,600
1995–2004	8,976 (12/2004)	55
2005–06	8,681 (12/2006)	0
2007	8,533 (12/2007)	3
2008	8,305 (12/08)	25
2009	8,200	124 as of 11/20/09

Sources: FDIC (1995, 1997, 2009); FDIC Failed Bank List.

- The Bank Holding Company Act of 1956 allowed for the bank holding companies to acquire banks in other states.
- The Riegle–Neal Interstate Banking and Branching Efficiency Act of 1994 allowed interstate branch banking.
- The Gramm–Leach Bliley Act of 1999 (GLBA) permitted financial holding companies to engage in banking, selling insurance and securities, and other activities.

Colonial bank

The previously mentioned changes in laws and consolidation of banks helped to reduce the number of bank failures. By way of illustration, Colonial BancGroup, Inc. ('Colonial') was headquartered in Montgomery, Alabama. In 2009, Colonial was the 41st largest bank holding company in the US, and it had $26 billion in assets. It was the largest bank failure in 2008–09.

Colonial's strategy was to grow through acquisitions. During the 1981–2007 period, Colonial acquired 70 banks. It had 347 branches, with 197 in Florida, 90 in Alabama, 19 in Georgia, 21 in Texas, and 20 in Nevada in December 2008.[55] Most of the assets were concentrated in real estate loans: commercial real estate 34 percent, real estate construction 33 percent, and residential real estate 18 percent.[56] Florida and Georgia are among the states that suffered the most bank failures from real estate loans; there were also large real estate losses in Nevada. Colonial absorbed the losses from their branches. As a result of the losses, Colonial required additional capital, liquidity, and additional allowances for loan losses. In March 2009, Colonial signed a deal with Florida-based Taylor, Bean & Whitaker Mortgage Company for $300 million. The deal was contingent on Colonial receiving $500 million in Troubled Asset Relief Program (TARP) funding which it did not get, and the deal fell apart.[57] On July 22, 2009, Colonial consented to an Order to Cease and Desist by bank regulators concerning issues of capital, liquidity, allowance for loan losses, dividends, and other issues.[58] Announcing its second quarter 2009 results, Colonial said:

> As a result of the above described regulatory actions and the current uncertainties associated with Colonial's ability to increase its capital levels to meet regulatory requirements, management concluded that there is substantial doubt about Colonial's ability to continue as a going concern.[59]

It did not survive. On August 14, 2009, the FDIC announced that BB&T Corporation, based in Winston-Salem, NC, was buying Colonial's branches and deposits.[60] As of June 30, 2009, BB&T Corporation was the 18th largest US bank holding company, with $152.4 billion in assets.[61]

Had each of Colonial's 347 branches in Alabama, Florida, Georgia, Nevada and Texas been small independent banks, some of them could have failed as a result of the previously mentioned losses. Thus, consolidation of the banking system helped to hold down the number of bank failures.

Failure of six Illinois banks
On July 2, 2009, the FDIC closed six small Illinois banks that were owned by the same family, but operated as separate banks.[62] All of the banks invested in trust preferred securities that resulted in fatal losses. Had the banks been consolidated by the family that owned them, there would have been only one failure instead of six.

Spread of the Crises

The financial crises spread to the real sector of the economy. According to the National Bureau of Economic Research (NBER) the previous business cycle peaked in December 2007.[63] Subsequently, real estate values and stock prices declined. Consumer spending and industrial production slowed. And unemployment, business failures, and bankruptcies increased as the recession deepened.

As a result of globalization of the banking system, the subprime crisis spread to other countries as well. The following chapters examine the impact of the subprime/financial crises around the world, and how various governments responded.

5 GOVERNMENT RESPONSES

As shown in Table 1.7, there have been many domestic and international financial crises since the 1970s.[64] The causes of the crises varied widely – oil

Table 1.7   Selected financial crises

Year	Financial crisis
1973	Oil price shock
1980s	Latin American debt crises
1980s	US savings and loan crises
1990s	Japanese asset prices collapse
1994	US bond market crash
1995	Mexican economic crises
1997	Asian financial crises
1998	Russian default, rouble collapse, LTCM bailout
2000	Dot-com bust as technology, media, telecom sectors collapse
2001	September 11, terrorist attack. Payments system disruption
2001	Argentina's crises
2002	German banking crises
2007	US subprime mortgage crises – spreads around the world

prices, interest rate shocks, foreign exchange rates, dot-com bust, terrorist attacks, and others.

Government responses to financial crises include, but are not limited to monetary and fiscal policy, and the following methods for dealing with banks and other organizations:

- assisted mergers;
- bankruptcy;
- forbearance/waiting to see what happens;
- nationalization;
- payoff;
- providing long-term debt and/or equity investments;
- providing short-term liquidity and/or guarantees; and
- sell all or part of the organization.

The initial responses by governments are aimed at promoting economic and financial stability. The Emergency Economic Stabilization Act of 2008 (Public Law No: 110–343) was signed into law October 3, 2008. Title I, Sections 101 and 115 of the law authorized the Secretary of the Treasury to establish the TARP to purchase up to $700 million in troubled assets from any financial institution. Section 112, recognizing the international scope of the crises, instructs the Secretary to coordinate with foreign financial authorities and central banks to work toward the establishment of similar programs.

The second response was to pass new laws and regulations. The Credit

CARD Act of 2009 (Public Law No 111–24) was the first such law to be passed. It amends the Truth in Lending Act to establish fair and transparent practices concerning credit card and open-end consumer credit plans. It also directs the Federal Trade Commission to initiate rulemaking on unfair and deceptive acts or practices with respect to mortgage loans, loan modifications, and foreclosure services.[65]

Subsequently, Congress may address the causes of the problems. Credit risk from commercial real estate loans was associated with previous boom/bust financial crises (for example, Japan, Spain, Sweden, Thailand, the United States, and elsewhere).[66] Interest rate risk (for example, the US) and foreign exchange rate risk (for example, Argentina, Russia, Thailand) also contributed to previous crises. Subprime residential real estate loans are at the heart of the economic crises that began in the US in 2007. Securitization of those loans helped to spread the crises around the world.

NOTES

1. Subprime loans can be defined in terms of FICO credit scores and other factors that will be discussed later.
2. 'Some Delinquency Measures Tick Upwards in Latest MBA National Delinquency Survey', Mortgage Bankers Association (2008), Press Release, September 13; 'Delinquencies Continue to Climb in Latest MBA National Delinquency Survey', Mortgage Bankers Association (2009), Press Release, March 5.
3. Getter et al. (2007).
4. Cecchetti (2009).
5. Ben Bernanke, Chairman, Board of Governors of the Federal Reserve System (2008a). More will be said about GSEs shortly.
6. Top 50 BHCs (as of March 31, 2009), National Information Center, available at: http://www.ffiec.gov/nicpubweb/nicweb/Top50Form.aspx (accessed June 24, 2009).
7. Winnett (2009), Also see: Armistead (2009).
8. The exchange rate was 1 US dollar to 0.6 pounds sterling in June 2009.
9. BNP Paribas, http://usa.bnpparibas.com/en/home/default.asp.
10. Top 50 BHCs (see n. 6).
11. BancWest http://www.bancwestcorp.com/Home/index.htm (accessed June 24, 2009).
12. Barclays, available at: http://group.barclays.com/Country/1231781206400.html.
13. HSBC Global Site, available at: http://www.hsbc.com/1/2/.
14. Muñoz and Mollenkamp (2009).
15. Citi Annual Report (2008), Bank of America (2009, p. 7).
16. See the following website for additional information: Société Générale Corporate & Investment Banking, available at: http://www.sgcib.com/about-us.
17. US Department of Treasury (2009, Table 1).
18. US Census Bureau (2004); US Census Bureau, US POPClock Projection, available at: http://www.census.gov/population/www/popclockus.html (accessed July 18, 2009).
19. US Department of Labor, US Bureau of Labor Statistics (2008).
20. Board of Governors of the Federal Reserve System, Selected Interest Rates, Statistical Release H.15.
21. As previously noted, Fannie Mae and Freddie Mac have been under conservatorship, with the FHFA acting as conservator, since September 6, 2008.

22. Federal National Mortgage Association (2009, p. 1).
23. Text from Ginnie Mae, 'Who we are . . .', available at: http://www.ginniemae.gov/about/about.asp?section=about.
24. For additional information about the FHLBs, see their web page: http://www.fhlbanks.com/.
25. Bech and Rice (2009, A63, A71).
26. Bernanke (2008b).
27. FICO scores are a product of FICO™. For additional information about FICO, see http://www.fico.com/en/Company/Pages/default.aspx. See http://www.myfico.com/Default.aspx and http://www.myfico.com/crediteducation/ for information about FICO scores. Prior to March 10, 2009, FICO was formerly known as the Fair Isaac Corporation, see http://www.fico.com/en/Company/News/Pages/03-10-2009.aspx.
28. myFICO (2009).
29. Demyanyk (2009).
30. US Department of Treasury (2009, Table 1).
31. Ibid., pp. 8–9.
32. Bertaut et al. (2006).
33. US Department of Treasury (2009, Table 2).
34. For a listing of Sovereign Wealth Funds, see the Sovereign Wealth Fund Institute, http://www.swfinstitute.org/funds.php; see also: Ellis and Wong (2007); Bennhold (2008).
35. For information about PIMCO, see: http://www.pimco.com/TopNav/Home/Default.htm.
36. McCulley (2007).
37. Bair (2009). Also see: Geitner (2008). SIVs are limited purpose companies that generally borrow short-term funds and invest in long-term assets such as mortgages and CDOs.
38. Board of Governors of the Federal Reserve System, H.8, Assets and Liabilities of Commercial Banks in the United States, various dates.
39. The first attempt at securitization was in 1870, and it was tried six times between 1870 and 1940. See Bernanke (2008a) n. 5.
40. 'Delinquencies and Foreclosures Continue to Climb in Latest MBA National Delinquency Survey', Mortgage Bankers Association, Press Release, May 28, 2009.
41. *BIS Quarterly Review* (2007, 2009).
42. Board of Governors of the Federal Reserve System (2008b).
43. Fisher (2008).
44. 12 U.S.C. 1831f(g)(1)(A); 12 C.F.R. 337.6(a)(2); FDIC Advisory Opinion (1994).
45. Office of the Comptroller of the Currency (2009). The Guidance can be found in the Federal Register/Vol. 74. No. 127, Monday, July 6, 2009, p. 32035.
46. Board of Governors of the Federal Reserve System (2008a).
47. 'Hedge Funds, Leverage, and the Lessons of Long-Term Capital Management', Report of the President's Working Group on Financial Markets, April, 1999, p. 23.
48. Based on the equity capital ratio of 10.15 percent for 'all FDIC insured institutions', First Quarter, 2009. The equity capital ratio is the 'bank's' equity capital, exclusive of the allowance for loan and lease losses, divided by the bank's total assets. FDIC Quarterly Banking Profile, (2009a). The term 'bank', as used here, includes all FDIC insured institutions – about 7,000 commercial banks and 1,200 savings institutions. The equity capital ratio for 'commercial banks' was 10.17 percent as reported in FDIC Quarterly Banking Profile (2009b).
49. US Census Bureau (2009, Table 729).
50. Federal Reserve Bank of Richmond (2009a).
51. Federal Reserve Bank of Richmond (2009b).
52. Simon and Mollenkamp (2009).
53. US Department of Treasury (2009, Table 1).
54. FDIC Quarterly Banking Profile (2009a).
55. Colonial BancGroup (2008, p. 1). The number of branches was 346 in August 2009.

56. Ibid., p. 51.
57. Colonial Bank (2009a, 2009b). See also: Burnett (2009).
58. Colonial Bank (2009b).
59. Colonial Bank (2009c).
60. FDIC Press Release (2009).
61. National Information Center, Top 50 BHCs, available at: http://www.ffiec.gov/nicpub-web/nicweb/Top50Form.aspx.
62. Founders Bank, Worth, IL ($966 million in assets; First National Bank of Danville, Danville, IL ($165 million); Rock River Bank, Oregon, IL ($77 million); John Warner Bank, Clinton, IL ($71 million); Elizabeth State Bank, Elizabeth, IL ($59 million); First State Bank of Winchester, Winchester, IL ($38 million). See Enrich and Paletta (2009).
63. NBER (2008).
64. For additional information, see: Gup (1998, 1999).
65. Section 511 of Public Law No. 111–24.
66. Gup (1999).

REFERENCES

Armistead, Louise (2009), 'RBS faces £500m loss on Cattles', Telegraph.co.uk, March 21, available at: http://www.telegraph.co.uk/finance/newsbysector/banks andfinance/5029194/RBS-faces-500m-loss-on-Cattles.html.

Bair, Sheila (2009), FDIC Chairman, Remarks at the 45th Annual Bank Structure and Competition Conference, Federal Reserve Bank of Chicago, May 7.

Bank of America (2009), 'International presence', *Investor Fact Book: Full Year 2008*, p. 7.

Bech, Morton L. and Tara Rice (2009), 'Profits and balance sheet developments at US commercial banks in 2008', *Federal Reserve Bulletin*, June, A57–97.

Bennhold, Katrin (2008), 'Sovereign wealth funds seek balance against Western regulation', *The New York Times*, January 24, available at: http://www.nytimes.com/2008/01/23/business/worldbusiness/23iht-fund.4.9447868.html?pagewanted=1

Bernanke, Ben (2008a), 'The mortgage meltdown, the economy and public policy', Speech at the University of California, Berueley/UCLA Symposium, October 31.

Bernanke, Ben (2008b), 'The future of mortgage finance in the United States', Speech at the University of California, Berkeley, CA, October 31.

Bertaut, Carol C., William L. Griever and Ralph W. Tyrone (2006), 'Understanding US cross-border securities data', *Federal Reserve Bulletin*, May, A59–75.

BIS Quarterly Review (2007), Table 19: Amounts outstanding of over-the-counter (OTC) derivatives, June, A 103.

BIS Quarterly Review (2009), Table 19: Amounts outstanding of over-the-counter (OTC) derivatives, June, A 103.

Board of Governors of the Federal Reserve System (2008a), Report Pursuant to Section 129 of the Emergency Economic Stabilization Act of 2008: Bridge Loan to the Bear Stearns Companies Inc. through JPMorgan Chase Bank, N.A., March 14, available at: http://www.federalreserve.gov/monetarypolicy/files/129bearstearnsbridgeloan.pdf.

Board of Governors of the Federal Reserve System (2008b), Federal Reserve Press

Release, September 16, (Re AIG), available at: http://www.federalreserve.gov/newsevents/press/other/20080916a.htm.

Burnett, Richard (2009), 'US Treasury Agents Raid Colonial Bank's Orlando Headquarters', Orlando Stentinel.com, August 3, available at: http://www.orlandosentinel.com/news/local/breakingnews/orl-bk-bank-orlando-080309,0,3976052.story.

Cecchetti, Stephen G. (2009), 'Crises and responses: the Federal Reserve in the early stages of the financial crises', *Journal of Economic Perspectives*, Vol. 23, No. 1, Winter, 51–75.

Citi Annual Report (2008), 'Dear Fellow Shareholders', available at: http://www.citigroup.com/citi/corporategovernance/ar.htm.

Colonial BancGroup (2008), 2008 Annual Report.

Colonial Bank (2009a), 'Colonial BancGroup Signs Definitive Agreement With Investors Led by Taylor, Bean & Whitaker for a $300 Million Investment', Press Release, March 31.

Colonial Bancgroup (2009b), 'Colonial BancGroup Signs Order With Regulators', Press Release, July 27.

Colonial Bank (2009c), 'Colonial BancGroup Reports Second Quarter 2009 Results', July 31.

Demyanyk, Yuliya (2009), 'Ten Myths about Subprime Mortgages', Economic Commentary, Federal Reserve Bank of Cleveland, May.

Ellis, David and Grace Wong (2007), 'Sovereign wealth funds strike again: Morgan Stanley becomes the latest financial firm to score an investment from the new power players in global finance', CNNMoney.com, December 19, available at: http://money.cnn.com/2007/12/19/markets/sovereign_funds/index.htm.

Enrich, David and Damian Paletta (2009), 'Hybrid securities doomed six banks', *Wall Street Journal*, July 7, C1.

FDIC (1995), *Statistics on Banking, Historical 1934–1994*, Vol. 1.

FDIC (1997), *History of the Eighties, Lessons for the Future*, Volume 1.

FDIC (2009), *Statistics at a Glance, Historical Trends as of March 31*.

FDIC Advisory Opinion (1994), Brokered Deposits: Are Funds Deposited in a Special Reserve Bank Account for the Exclusive Benefit of Customers Brokered Deposits Under Sections 29 and 29A of the FDI Act, Valerie J. Best, Counsel, FDIC–94–39, August 17.

FDIC Press Release (2009), 'BB&T, Winston-Salem, North Carolina, Assumes All of the Deposits of Colonial Bank', Montgomery, AL, August 14.

FDIC Quarterly Banking Profile (2009a), Table III-A, All FDIC Insured Institutions, First Quarter.

FDIC Quarterly Banking Profile (2009b), Commercial Bank Performance, Table III-A, FDIC Insured Commercial Banks, First Quarter.

Federal National Mortgage Association (2009), SEC Form 10-Q, March 31.

Federal Reserve Bank of Richmond (2009a), US Residential Mortgage Delinquency Rates seasonally adjusted, 1998Q1–2009Q1, available at: http://www.richmondfed.org/banking/markets_trends_and_statistics/trends/pdf/delinquency_and_foreclosure_rates.pdf.

Federal Reserve Bank of Richmond (2009b), US Residential Mortgage Foreclosure Rates, seasonally adjusted, 1998Q1–2009Q1, available at: http://www.richmondfed.org/banking/markets_trends_and_statistics/trends/pdf/delinquency_and_foreclosure_rates.pdf.

Fisher, Richard W. (2008), President, Federal Reserve Bank of Dallas, 'The

Egocentricity of the Present', Remarks before a Federal Reserve Bank of Dallas Community Forum San Antonio, TX, April 9.

Geitner, Timothy F. (2008), President and Chief Executive Officer, Federal Reserve Bank of New York, 'Reducing Systemic Risk in a Dynamic Financial System', Remarks at the Economic Club of New York, New York City, June 8 .

Getter, Darryl, E., Mark Jickling, Marc Labonte and Edward V. Murphy (2007), 'Financial Crises? The Liquidity Crunch of August 2007', CRS Report for Congress, RL34182.

Global Finance (2008), 'The World's Biggest Banks', October, p. 111.

Gup, Benton E. (1998), *Bank Failures in the Major Trading Countries of the World: Causes and Remedies*, Westport, CT: Quorum Books.

Gup, Benton E. (1999), *International Banking Crises: Large Scale Failures, Massive Government Interventions*, Westport, CT: Quorum Books.

McCulley, Paul (2007), Global Central Bank Focus: 'Teton Reflections', September 5, available at: http://www.pimco.com/LeftNav/Featured+Market+Commentary/FF/2007/GCBF+August-+September+2007.htm.

Muñoz, Sara Schaefer and Carrick Mollenkamp (2009), 'HSBC faces round two of subprime punishment', *The Wall Street Journal*, June 5, C1, C12.

myFICO (2009), Credit Education Center/Mortgage Crises Resource Center, 'Background information about the current mortgage crisis', available at: http://www.myfico.com/CreditEducation/Articles/Mortgage-Crisis/History.aspx (accessed July 28, 2009).

National Bureau of Economic Research (NBER) (2008), 'Business cycle expansion and contractions', available at: http://www.nber.org/cycles/.

Office of the Comptroller of the Currency (2009), 'Request for Comment on Proposed Interagency Liquidity Guidance', *OCC Bulletin*, 2009–21.

Simon, Ruth and Carrick Mollenkamp (2009), 'Mortgage servicers are pushed to modify more loans', *The Wall Street Journal*, July 29, A6.

US Census Bureau (1995), *Statistical Abstract of the United States: 1995*, http://www.census.gov/prod/www/abs/statab.html.

US Census Bureau (2004), *Statistical Abstract of the United States: 2003*, No. HS-1. Population: 1900 to 2002, Con., available at: http://www.census.gov/statab/hist/HS-01.pdf (accessed June 24, 2009).

US Census Bureau (2009), *Statistical Abstract of the United States: 2009*, http://www.census.gov/prod/www/abs/statab.html.

US Census Bureau News (2007), '50 Fastest-Growing Metro Areas Concentrated in West and South', Press Release CB07–51, April 5.

US Department of Labor, US Bureau of Labor Statistics (2008), *Women in the Labor Force: A Databook*, Table 2, Employment Status of the Civilian Noninstitutional Population 16 and Over by Sex, 1970–2007 Annual Averages.

US Department of Treasury (2009), 'Report on Foreign Holdings of US Securities at End-June 2008', April 30.

Winnett, Robert (2009), 'RBS Traders Hid Toxic Debt', Telegraph.co.uk, March 20, available at: http://www.telegraph.co.uk/finance/financetopics/recession/5025115/RBS-traders-hid-toxic-debt.html.

2. Spillover effects from the US financial crisis: some time-series evidence from national stock returns

Apanard Penny Angkinand, James R. Barth and Hyeongwoo Kim*

1 INTRODUCTION

The collapse of US housing prices and the ensuing mortgage market meltdown that began during the summer of 2007 triggered a global financial crisis. Unlike the financial crises that struck Southeast Asian countries in the summer of 1997, the more recent crisis initially started in one of the most advanced countries in the world, namely the United States. As a result of this crisis, there is widespread interest in understanding the extent to which the increasing interdependencies in trade and financial linkages among countries in recent years contributed to spillover effects from the United States to other countries.

There is ample factual evidence that national markets have become more interconnected with one another with respect to cross-border trade and capital flows during the past few decades (for example, see Forbes and Chinn, 2004). It seems reasonable to assume that these cross-border market linkages have increased the likelihood of shocks in an economically and financially important country to be transmitted internationally. This would particularly be the case in a country like the United States. One would expect sizable spillovers from the recent and severe US financial crisis to other countries given the overall importance of the US for the world's economy and financial markets. There is, however, as yet no or limited empirical evidence supporting such a contention in the current crisis. But there are studies involving earlier time periods, which include some disruptive episodes. For example, in an examination of German and US stock markets during 1980–2002, Bonfiglioli and Favero (2005) do not find any evidence of a co-movement or interdependence in stock market returns between these two economies in the long run. However, they do find that returns in these two markets tend to move together during periods of turmoil. Also, in a more comprehensive study, Bekaert et al. (2005) examine the degree of regional and global integration using stock market returns in 22 countries during 1980–98. They find that the degree of integration of stock returns in these countries is not as great as was generally thought at the time.

The most recent financial crisis in the United States, the worst since the Great Depression, provides a good opportunity to reassess the degree to which any interdependencies among stock market returns that existed in different countries may have changed over time, and especially prior to, during, and after various events characterizing the crisis. Our reassessment is based on an examination of the degree of co-movement between national stock market returns in 17, and in some cases 14, advanced economies and the US from January 1973 to February 2009.

To assess the degree of co-movement, one might simply proceed by producing various scatter plots of stock returns for each of the countries and the US for each decade, some of which are shown in Figure 2.1. Based on this approach, there appears to be evidence of higher positive correlations and thus increased interdependence over time, especially during the decade of the 2000s. No strong conclusions can be reached, however, until the evidence provided by these plots is confirmed with more formal time-series techniques to determine whether there has indeed been a significant increase in the co-movement of stock market returns across national borders. Such techniques are also appropriate to assess whether there have been significant spillover effects from the US to other developed countries. Pursuing this more rigorous approach in turn may help provide information about the reasons why the current crisis has been a truly global one and therefore may eventually last longer than would have been the case without an increased interdependence among countries. In this regard, we carefully examine the pre- and post-turmoil periods using the emergence of the US financial crisis in August 2007 and the bankruptcy of Lehman Brothers in September 2008 as dating or cut-off points for detecting spillover effects from the US to other parts of the world.

Although there have been many previous empirical studies analyzing the degree of co-movement in stock market returns across countries, the methodologies employed in those most closely related to our study have some limitations, as will be discussed below. We attempt to address these limitations by comparing the results from both a single-equation and a system approach in our examination of national stock market return co-movements. In the single-equation approach, we provide results for both ordinary least squares (OLS) and generalized method of moments (GMM) estimations. We find that the results from these two methods yield somewhat different results, with those from the OLS estimation being less

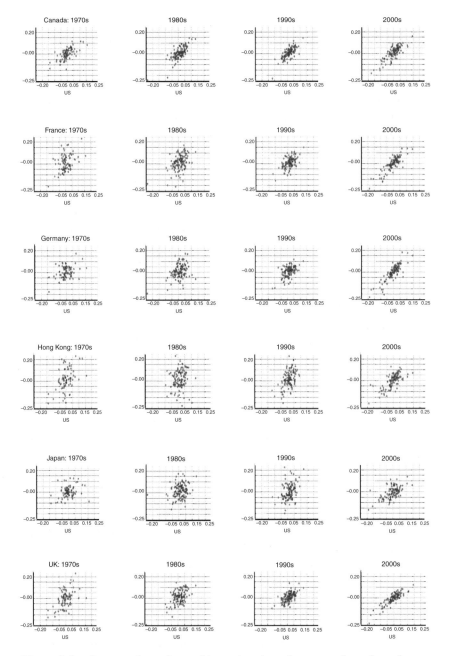

*Figure 2.1   Scatter plots of monthly national stock returns for selected
            countries and US stock returns by decade*

reliable. In the system approach, we use a structural vector autoregressive process (SVAR) to capture the contemporaneous and dynamic responses of stock returns in other countries to a shock in US stock returns. This methodology is superior to the reduced-form VAR employed by Forbes and Rigobon (2002) because it allows one to identify structural idiosyncratic shocks given appropriate identifying assumptions.

Based upon our empirical results, we find evidence of varying degrees of interdependence in stock market returns between the various countries in our sample and the US over time. In general, however, the degree of stock market interdependence between many of the advanced economies in our sample and the US remained relatively low during the 1970s and 1980s but then increased during the 1990s. In addition, the impulse-response analysis shows that both the short- and the long-run responses or spillover effects of many of these advanced countries' national stock returns to a shock in US stock returns are significant and largest during the 2000s. Although there is no complete uniformity in results for each and every country over time, there nonetheless has been a change in the degree of interdependence between the different countries and the US over time.

Focusing more specifically on the period of the recent crisis, we expect that foreign stock returns in those countries with the highest degrees of interdependencies will have the strongest spillover effects to movements in US stock returns after both the emergence of the US financial crisis in the summer of 2007 and the failure of Lehman Brothers in September 2008. We find that for all of the 17 advanced economies in our sample there is a greater degree of their stock market return co-movements with US stock market returns after the emerging crisis in August 2007. In the case of Japan, however, even though its stock market returns became more interdependent with US market returns during the 2000s, as compared to the other advanced countries, Japanese returns display the least degree of co-movement and smallest response to short- and long-run stock return shocks originating in the US. Furthermore, the short-run impulse responses or spillover effects of the different national stock returns to a shock in US returns after the bankruptcy of Lehman Brothers are greater in all countries in our sample, except Japan and Switzerland.

The next section presents several stylized facts to demonstrate the increasing interconnectedness between the advanced countries in our sample and the US. It also provides a brief review of related literature regarding the co-movement of stock market returns among countries. Section 3 presents our empirical model and discusses the estimation techniques employed, while Section 4 describes the data and presents the empirical results. Some concluding remarks are reported in the last section.

2   GROWING INTERDEPENDENCIES BETWEEN ADVANCED ECONOMIES AND THE UNITED STATES

What makes the current global crisis different from previous financial crises is not only its severity but that the severity is in large part due to the United States. The reason is that, as Table 2.1 shows, US GDP is slightly more than one-fifth of the world total and US stock market capitalization is about one-third of world market capitalization. The US is also the largest importer in the world (Table 2.1). This means that a decline in US GDP and US stock market capitalization can adversely affect other countries through various trade and financial linkages. Similar data for the other 17 countries in our sample are presented for comparative purposes.

To elaborate on the potential channels through which US shocks may

Table 2.1   Selected information on the role of sample countries in the world economy, 2008 (percent of world total)

	Stock market capitalization	GDP (PPP* basis)	Exports	Imports
Australia	2.0	1.1	0.9	1.1
Austria	0.3	0.5	0.9	1.0
Belgium	0.5	0.6	2.4	2.4
Canada	3.1	1.9	2.3	2.3
Denmark	0.4	0.3	0.6	0.6
France	4.6	3.1	3.1	3.7
Germany	3.4	4.2	7.4	6.2
Hong Kong	4.1	0.4	1.8	2.0
Italy	1.7	2.6	2.7	2.9
Japan	10.2	6.4	4.0	3.9
Netherlands	0.6	1.0	3.2	3.0
Norway	0.4	0.4	0.9	0.5
Singapore	0.8	0.3	1.7	1.7
Spain	2.0	2.0	1.4	2.1
Sweden	0.8	0.5	0.9	0.9
Switzerland	2.7	0.5	1.0	1.2
UK	6.2	3.2	2.3	3.3
USA	33.0	20.7	6.6	11.2
Total	76.9	49.7	44.3	49.8

Note: GDP, Exports and Imports are annual figures; Stock market capitalization is the year-end figure.* PPP = purchasing power party.

Source: Bloomberg, World Economic Outlook, and Direction of Trade Statistics.

have spread to other economies, Tables 2.2 and 2.3 provide a few stylized facts regarding trade and capital flow linkages between the US and the other advanced economies in our sample. This type of data is important because the spread of a financial crisis globally may occur or worsen because an adverse shock in one large country can be transmitted internationally through various channels involving import/export markets and capital markets as well as through changes in exchange rates and commodity prices (see, for example, Hernández and Valdés, 2001; Imbs, 2004; Ehrmann et al., 2005; Bayoumi and Swiston, 2009). Of course, the magnitude of the effect of a shock will depend to a large degree on the strength of linkages between countries.

Pursuing this line of reasoning, Table 2.2 shows that trade linkages

Table 2.2   *Trade linkages of sample countries with the US by decade*

Country	Total trade with US (share of a country's total trade)			Exports to US (share of a country's total exports)			Imports from US (share of a country's total imports)		
	1980–89	1990–99	2000–08	1980–89	1990–99	2000–08	1980–89	1990–99	2000–08
Australia	16.7	15.9	12.0	10.8	8.4	7.8	22.0	22.6	15.6
Austria	3.5	3.9	3.9	3.4	3.4	5.2	3.5	4.4	2.7
Belgium	na	6.3	6.1	na	5.1	6.2	na	7.6	6.0
Canada	68.4	73.4	71.6	69.7	81.3	84.1	67.0	65.6	58.7
Denmark	6.6	5.0	4.9	7.0	4.8	6.1	6.2	5.2	3.5
France	7.1	7.4	6.3	6.4	6.5	7.1	7.7	8.3	5.6
Germany	7.7	7.6	7.9	8.2	7.9	9.0	7.1	7.3	6.5
Hong Kong	19.1	15.0	11.5	28.8	22.8	17.8	9.8	7.5	5.5
Italy	7.4	6.5	6.1	8.8	7.7	8.3	6.0	5.1	3.9
Japan	27.1	26.5	19.9	32.3	29.4	24.5	20.3	22.7	14.6
Netherlands	6.3	6.3	6.2	4.1	4.0	4.3	8.4	8.8	8.4
Norway	6.3	6.9	6.6	4.8	6.5	7.2	8.0	7.5	5.6
Singapore	16.7	17.9	12.7	19.1	19.5	12.1	14.7	16.4	13.3
Spain	9.8	5.8	3.7	7.8	4.7	4.3	11.1	6.7	3.3
Sweden	9.3	8.2	7.3	10.0	8.7	9.9	8.5	7.6	4.2
Switzerland	7.6	8.2	8.9	8.8	9.5	11.0	6.5	6.9	6.8
UK	12.2	12.4	12.4	13.3	12.6	15.0	11.2	12.3	10.4
Average	14.5	13.7	12.2	15.2	14.3	14.1	13.6	13.1	10.3

Note: Total trade is imports plus exports.

Source: Direction of Trade Statistics, International Monetary Fund.

Table 2.3   Allocation of portfolio investment for sample countries and the United States

Country	Portfolio investment in US (share of a country's total portfolio investment abroad)		Portfolio investment of US (share of a country's total foreign portfolio investment)	
	2001	2007	2001	2007
Australia	56.0	44.6	32.5	32.3
Austria	13.4	7.9	3.7	7.3
Belgium	10.5	7.3	8.2	9.5
Canada	58.5	50.1	66.2	68.4
Denmark	24.6	18.8	16.2	19.8
France	16.4	9.1	18.5	18.6
Germany	13.7	10.8	11.5	13.2
Hong Kong	19.1	9.0	33.1	35.4
Italy	13.4	9.8	8.3	7.9
Japan	38.0	32.2	36.5	40.9
Netherlands	29.3	25.7	21.1	13.7
Norway	26.6	20.3	28.8	25.3
Singapore	17.1	12.4	45.0	37.8
Spain	9.8	7.3	14.0	10.7
Sweden	35.1	21.1	21.1	23.2
Switzerland	23.7	12.8	35.1	43.3
UK	23.7	26.1	39.8	31.5
Average	25.2	19.1	25.9	25.8

Source: The Coordinated Portfolio Investment Survey, International Monetary Fund.

between the US and our other advanced economies have changed over time. As may be seen, on average both the shares of their total exports and imports to the US have decreased slightly over time. According to the International Monetary Fund (IMF, 2007), the general and slight decrease in the importance of trade among many countries with the US is due to rapid growth in intraregional trade. In addition, the US now trades more with emerging market economies and other developing countries, and to a lesser extent with Japan and the euro area countries.

Table 2.3 provides some limited information on cross-border financial flows between our 17 countries and the US. These data show the degree to which each of our sample countries has portfolio investment in the US as well as the importance of US portfolio investment for each of these countries. These data are somewhat similar in pattern to the trade data discussed earlier insofar as there has been a slight decrease in such financial flows from 2001 to 2007 (earlier bilateral portfolio investments on a yearly basis are not available).

Despite the slight decline in the trade and financial linkages, the co-movement of stock returns between our other sample economies and the US appear to have been increasing substantially since the 1970s (see Figure 2.1).[1] This pattern suggests that stock market linkages may be an appropriate channel to focus on in examining the transmission of shocks associated with the collapse of the US mortgage and credit markets and corresponding spillover effects to other countries around the world.[2] The main reason is that stock prices reflect to a large degree future economic growth in countries and therefore disruptions in credit markets can adversely affect trade, financial flows and more broadly economic growth and employment. These developments, in turn, can be contemporaneously incorporated in stock prices. Indeed, this has been the case with the 2007–08 global crises, with world trade having declined, and recessions have occurred in many countries; stock prices and returns have also declined from their highs in earlier years. We therefore focus our study on stock market returns as a broad measure to assess interdependencies among the US and other countries with well-established stock markets.

There have been many empirical studies testing the extent to which there are co-movements in asset prices across countries. These tests have been utilized to examine stock market interdependence, financial market integration, the transmission of shocks across national borders, and financial contagion. An influential study by King and Wadhwani (1990), for example, examines whether there has been a change in correlation coefficients between Japan, UK, and US stock returns before and after the stock market crash of 1987. They find a significant increase in the coefficients after the crash, and argued that stock market returns fell jointly together after the crash because the private information set contains both idiosyncratic and systematic components. Bertero and Mayer (1990) and Lee and Kim (1993), as other examples, adopt a similar approach to a border set of countries and find further evidence that correlation coefficients for stock returns between the US and the other countries increased significantly after the 1987 crash. The results of the Bertero and Mayer study are based upon both daily and monthly stock returns for a sample of 23 industrialized and developing countries, while those of the Lee and Kim study are based upon weekly returns for 12 major countries.

Forbes and Rigobon (2002), in an important study, improve on testing for stock return co-movements based on correlation coefficients and consider the Mexican crisis in 1994 to 1995, the Asian crisis in 1997, and the US stock market crash in 1987. They argue that simple correlations are biased due to the presence of heteroskedasticity in market returns. During a crisis period, market volatility increases substantially and thereby renders invalid the assumption of a constant variance. Without a correction for the bias introduced by a non-constant variance the magnitude of cross-market correlations will be overstated, thereby potentially leading to false conclusions about the existence of contagion across countries. They therefore test for co-movements in stock returns in different countries by calculating correlation coefficients from a reduced-form VAR model, and then make adjustments for any bias that arises in the least squares estimation of a single equation. They find virtually no evidence of contagion during the crises they examine, and conclude that a greater degree of stock market return co-movements during the crisis periods simply reflects a continuation of the trend in market interdependence that had existed in the stable periods prior to the crises. Their methodology, however, has some limitations. In particular, their bias correction method assumes that the true beta coefficients in their empirical model are constant. Put differently, they assume that the degree of interdependence across countries does not change over time. If this assumption is invalid, their estimation method is inappropriate. In addition, their reduced-form VAR model does not isolate idiosyncratic shocks.

While some of the earlier techniques used in testing for stock market return interdependence and contagion among countries have been improved upon in several more recent studies, the evidence regarding the existence of contagion remains mixed. For instance, Candelon et al. (2005) argue that they provide a stronger measure of co-movements based on the notion of common cycles. Similar to the findings of Forbes and Rigobon (2002), they find evidence that a high degree of stock market co-movement exists across all time periods, pre- and post-crises, and thus no evidence of contagion in the case of the Asian crisis and weak evidence of contagion in the case of the Mexican crisis. In contrast, Bekaert et al. (2005) and Corsetti et al. (2005) find evidence of contagion in the case of the Asian crisis. The difference in findings is due to the last two studies distinguishing between the idiosyncratic and systematic components of stock market returns. In addition, Corsetti et al. argue that the results of Forbes and Rigobon are highly dependent on the specification of the idiosyncratic component.

Based on these studies, among others, it becomes clear that financial integration, co-movements or interdependence and contagion are distinctly used terms. However, the co-movement or interdependence of stock market returns is a necessary, if not a sufficient condition, for the occurrence of contagion. In the next sections, we implement a formal empirical investigation to examine the interdependence between 17 national stock market returns and US stock market returns, focusing most importantly on the two identifying sub-periods of the US crisis. In the latter case, we also examine whether there are stronger spillover effects from the US to the other countries in the post-crisis periods.

3 EMPIRICAL MODEL

Univariate Approach

Let p_t^i denote the log of the stock price index for country i and $r_t^i (= p_t^i - p_{t-1}^i)$ represent the continuously compounded stock return at time t. To study the contemporaneous co-movement of r_t^i and US stock returns, r_t^{US}, one may employ the following regression equation:

$$r_t^i = \alpha^i + \beta^i r_t^{US} + \varepsilon_t^i, \tag{2.1}$$

where ε_t^i is an idiosyncratic shock in country i. If r_t^{US} is orthogonal to ε_t^i, one can estimate β^i consistently by the OLS estimator.[3]

When there are common factors that govern the movements in both r_t^i and r_t^{US}, however, the orthogonality assumption is unlikely to hold and alternative estimators, such as the GMM estimator, should be considered. In the presence of serial correlation and/or conditional heteroskedasticity of ε_t^i, the standard error needs to be corrected appropriately.[4]

System Approach

When one is interested in examining the dynamic effects of a structural shock in US stock returns that occurs on the stock returns in other countries, it is convenient to use the following SVAR model:

$$A_0 y_t = A_1 y_{t-1} + A_2 y_{t-2} + \ldots + A_p y_{t-p} + u_t, \tag{2.2}$$

where $y_t = [r_t^{US} r_t^i]'$ is a vector of covariance stationary stock returns and $u_t = [u_t^{US} u_t^i]'$ is a vector of orthogonal structural shocks with unit variances, that is, $E u_t u_t' = I$.

The corresponding reduced-form VAR model is:

$$y_t = B_1 y_{t-1} + B_2 y_{t-2} + \ldots + B_p y_{t-p} + \varepsilon_t, \tag{2.3}$$

where:

$$B_i = A_0^{-1} A_i, i = 1, 2, \ldots, p \text{ and } \varepsilon_i = A_0^{-1} u_t, E \varepsilon_t \varepsilon_t' = \Sigma,$$

where Σ is the variance–covariance matrix. The VAR model (2.3) can be represented by the following moving average representation:

$$y_t = D(L)\varepsilon_t = D(L)Cu_t, \qquad (2.4)$$

where $D(L) = B(L)^{-1} = (I - B_1 - \ldots - B_p)^{-1}$ and $C = A_0^{-1}$ is the contemporaneous or short-run response matrix. We employ Sims's (1980) method to just-identify the system of equations (2.4) by assuming that C is a lower-triangular matrix, that is, u_t^i does not affect r_t^{US} contemporaneously.[5] Put differently,

$$\Sigma = PP' = CC',$$

where P is the Choleski decomposition factor. Note that the short-run response (ψ_S) of the level variable p_t^i to u_t^{US} is directly obtained from C, whereas the long-run response (ψ_L) can be obtained by $D(L)C = (\Sigma_{j=0}^{\infty} D_j)C$.

The univariate approach is used to test for the degree of interdependence and co-movement, whereas the system approach is used to assess the magnitude of any spillover effects that might exist.

4   EMPIRICAL RESULTS

In examining the interdependence of stock market returns between various countries and the US as well as the potential spillover effects during the recent crisis from the US to the other countries, we use weekly and monthly national stock market returns (obtained from Thomson Datastream) for the 18 advanced economies in our sample, from January 1973 to February 2009. All the countries have well-developed stock markets, some with large market capitalizations such as France, Germany, Japan, the UK and the US and some with small market capitalizations (Table 2.1). These countries also represent different regions of the world. To assess whether there have been any broad changes in the degree of interdependence over time, we estimate various models for the entire sample period as well as different sub-periods (that is, each decade and pre- and post-crisis identifying events).[6]

Tables 2.4–7 report the results of our assessment of whether there have been changes in the degree of interdependence of monthly national stock market returns over time between the 14 sample countries and the US using both single-equation and system approaches.[7] In Tables 2.8–11, we report similar results but for changes in the co-movements of weekly national stock market returns during the most recent decade, focusing on the pre- and post-periods associated with the US financial crisis. We examine two post-crisis periods: the first period is the emergence of the subprime mortgage market meltdown taken to be the first week of August 2007 (Barth et al., 2009b); we also consider the third week of September 2008 as an alternative start date when Lehman Brothers filed for bankruptcy. In both cases, the pre-turmoil period starts the first week of 2000 and the post-period begins the same week as the occurrence of the two events.

Based on the results reported in Tables 2.4–7, we find robust evidence of strong co-movement in stock market returns between each and every one of the sample countries and the US in the decade of the 2000s. The beta coefficients of national stock returns for each country with respect to those for the US obtained from both the OLS and GMM estimations in this period are significantly different from zero at the 1 percent significance level in all cases (Tables 2.4 and 2.6). The evidence of stock market return interdependence during the earlier decades of the 1970s through the 1990s is mixed, depending on which estimation technique is employed. The coefficients from the OLS estimation (Table 2.4) are significant in nearly all cases and do not vary much over time, whereas the coefficients from the GMM estimation are generally insignificant, particularly for the 1970s and 1980s (Table 2.6). However, the GMM coefficients do become significant in many countries in the 1990s, and significant in all sample countries in the 2000s. The results for the OLS estimation suggest that stock markets have always been interdependent since the early 1970s, which contradicts a general belief that the extent of market linkages has been increasing over time. We believe that the GMM estimates, which support this general belief, are more reliable for several reasons. First, the GMM estimates are more consistent with the scatter plots of monthly stock market returns in Figure 2.1, which exhibit weak correlations between the market returns in the earlier decades. Second, the OLS estimator is not even unbiased and is inconsistent when the exogeneity assumption is violated. Our informal test shows that this is indeed the case.[8] Third, the *J*-specification test statistics for the overidentifying restrictions proposed by Hansen (1982) indicate that the model specification from the GMM estimations reported in Tables 2.5–6 is good.

In sum, we find an increasing degree of stock market return interdependence between other advanced economies and the US over time. For many of these countries, the increase in interdependence became particularly evident during and after the 1990s. An interesting result based on the GMM estimation in Tables 2.5–6 is that the change over time in stock market return interdependence for the individual countries is reasonably

Table 2.4 Bivariate OLS estimation results for each sample country and the United States using monthly stock returns

$$r_t^i = \alpha^i + \beta^i r_t^{US} + \varepsilon_t^i$$

Country	Full	1970s	1980s	1990s	2000s
Australia	0.912 (0.062)*	0.847 (0.156)*	1.011 (0.155)*	0.755 (0.111)*	1.013 (0.071)*
Austria	0.523 (0.062)*	0.236 (0.084)*	0.241 (0.144)	0.489 (0.125)*	0.988 (0.091)*
Belgium	0.730 (0.050)*	0.620 (0.098)*	0.614 (0.122)*	0.569 (0.090)*	1.001 (0.082)*
Canada	0.907 (0.038)*	0.691 (0.083)*	0.947 (0.072)*	0.975 (0.078)*	1.034 (0.066)*
Denmark	0.667 (0.052)*	0.475 (0.126)*	0.574 (0.113)*	0.504 (0.103)*	0.971 (0.074)*
France	0.848 (0.057)*	0.788 (0.153)*	0.727 (0.137)*	0.750 (0.104)*	1.061 (0.062)*
Germany	0.725 (0.051)*	0.387 (0.109)*	0.526 (0.119)*	0.668 (0.095)*	1.155 (0.067)*
Hong Kong	0.948 (0.094)*	1.012 (0.285)*	0.910 (0.217)*	1.184 (0.180)*	0.834 (0.082)*
Italy	0.678 (0.071)*	0.433 (0.174)*	0.445 (0.158)*	0.715 (0.161)*	0.991 (0.076)*
Japan	0.480 (0.062)*	0.306 (0.110)*	0.313 (0.123)*	0.680 (0.182)*	0.604 (0.081)*
Netherlands	0.855 (0.042)*	0.711 (0.093)*	0.696 (0.083)*	0.688 (0.078)*	1.162 (0.072)*
Singapore	1.052 (0.072)*	1.288 (0.224)*	1.050 (0.142)*	1.046 (0.130)*	0.930 (0.084)*
Switzerland	0.683 (0.044)*	0.562 (0.105)*	0.608 (0.098)*	0.710 (0.097)*	0.821 (0.057)*
UK	0.868 (0.049)*	1.041 (0.162)*	0.800 (0.103)*	0.715 (0.083)*	0.892 (0.046)*

Notes: (i) The sample period is January 1973 to February 2009. (ii) The β^i estimates are reported and standard errors are in parentheses. (iii) Standard errors are adjusted using the quadratic spectral kernel with automatic bandwidth selection method. (iv) * indicates a 5% significance level.

*Table 2.5   GMM estimation results: full time period using monthly stock
returns for each sample country and the United States*

$$r_t^i = \alpha^i + \beta^i r_t^{US} + \varepsilon_t^i, z_t^i = [r_{t-1}^i \ldots r_{t-p}^i \ldots r_{t-1}^{US} \ldots r_{t-p}^{US}]'$$

Country	$\beta_{GMM}^i(se)$	$J(pv)$
Australia	1.814 (0.858)*	2.379 (0.936)
Austria	1.823 (0.871)*	5.977 (0.542)
Belgium	1.538 (0.511)*	3.915 (0.790)
Canada	1.432 (0.455)*	5.236 (0.631)
Denmark	0.961 (0.422)*	7.373 (0.391)
France	1.704 (0.583)*	4.738 (0.692)
Germany	0.929 (0.419)*	8.475 (0.293)
Hong Kong	1.384 (0.557)*	5.291 (0.625)
Italy	1.282 (0.422)*	9.135 (0.243)
Japan	1.230 (0.634)	5.265 (0.628)
Netherlands	0.986 (0.397)*	4.367 (0.737)
Singapore	1.489 (0.737)*	3.569 (0.828)
Switzerland	1.130 (0.352)*	2.735 (0.908)
UK	1.659 (0.588)*	4.128 (0.765)

Notes: (i) The sample period is January 1973 to February 2009. (ii) The β^i estimates are obtained by the 5-step iterative GMM estimator. (iii) The quadratic spectral kernel with automatic bandwidth selection method is used to adjust standard errors. (iv) The set of instruments includes 4 lags of national stock returns and the US stock returns. (v) J refers to the overidentifying restrictions test statistic by Hansen (1982) and pv denotes associated p-values. (vi) * indicates a 5% significance level.

uniform. In particular, the increased co-movement of stock market returns with the US in the 2000s compared to the 1990s is clearly observed for the smaller advanced economies as measured by GDP and market capitalization (Table 2.1). Specifically, the coefficients in the 2000s become somewhat larger and statistically significant for Australia, Austria, Belgium, Denmark, Italy, the Netherlands, and Switzerland.

For the larger advanced economies, Canada and Japan both clearly share a similar pattern in that there is greater stock market return interdependence in the 2000s relative to the 1990s. In the case of France, Germany, and the UK, they do not display a similar increase in interdependence over the period based on their slightly smaller coefficients. However, when taking into account the much smaller standard errors associated with these coefficients indicating sharper estimates, one may conclude that for these countries there has been an increase in interdependence. The last three countries also have relatively high degrees of interdependence

Table 2.6   GMM estimation results: sub-periods using monthly stock returns for each sample country and the United States

$$r_t^i = \alpha^i + \beta^i r_t^{US} + \varepsilon_t^i, z_t^i = [r_{t-1}^i \ldots r_{t-p}^i r_{t-1}^{US} \ldots r_{t-p}^{US}]'$$

Country	1970s		1980s	
	$\beta_{GMM}^i(se)$	$J(pv)$	$\beta_{GMM}^i(se)$	$J(pv)$
Australia	0.864 (0.473)	15.63 (0.029)	1.033 (0.864)	3.801 (0.802)
Austria	−0.342 (0.439)	2.213 (0.947)	0.496 (0.391)	9.887 (0.195)
Belgium	1.357 (0.345)*	6.550 (0.477)	1.955 (1.120)	1.573 (0.980)
Canada	0.669 (0.333)*	4.680 (0.699)	0.574 (0.252)*	5.853 (0.557)
Denmark	0.627 (0.435)	6.803 (0.450)	0.378 (0.469)	6.053 (0.534)
France	2.181 (0.716)*	4.544 (0.715)	0.916 (0.736)	5.047 (0.654)
Germany	−0.806 (0.456)	6.023 (0.537)	−0.030 (0.582)	7.193 (0.409)
Hong Kong	−0.206 (1.283)	8.116 (0.322)	1.484 (0.781)	3.492 (0.836)
Italy	−1.188 (0.929)	5.333 (0.619)	0.399 (0.482)	9.520 (0.217)
Japan	0.010 (0.317)	4.767 (0.688)	0.324 (0.633)	7.855 (0.346)
Netherlands	0.561 (0.328)	5.317 (0.621)	0.411 (0.425)	4.976 (0.663)
Singapore	−0.274 (1.063)	3.304 (0.856)	1.124 (0.467)*	7.001 (0.429)
Switzerland	0.156 (0.297)	7.116 (0.417)	0.983 (0.358)*	6.558 (0.476)
UK	3.050 (0.858)*	3.465 (0.839)	0.670 (0.544)	3.341 (0.852)

Country	1990s		2000s	
	$\beta_{GMM}^i(se)$	$J(pv)$	$\beta_{GMM}^i(se)$	$J(pv)$
Australia	0.958 (0.363)*	3.856 (0.796)	1.118 (0.231)*	11.66 (0.112)
Austria	0.649 (0.497)	6.457 (0.488)	0.757 (0.257)*	4.607 (0.708)
Belgium	0.297 (0.410)	3.024 (0.883)	0.545 (0.194)*	7.030 (0.426)
Canada	0.836 (0.279)*	7.187 (0.410)	1.248 (0.220)*	12.95 (0.073)
Denmark	0.866 (0.457)	1.598 (0.979)	1.234 (0.268)*	6.978 (0.431)
France	1.346 (0.363)*	7.879 (0.343)	1.073 (0.121)*	9.527 (0.217)
Germany	1.075 (0.366)*	5.822 (0.561)	1.053 (0.124)*	7.677 (0.362)
Hong Kong	2.414 (1.217)*	7.278 (0.400)	0.934 (0.231)*	4.624 (0.706)
Italy	0.429 (0.488)	10.44 (0.165)	1.317 (0.160)*	6.332 (0.502)
Japan	0.467 (0.767)	6.715 (0.459)	1.231 (0.382)*	7.446 (0.384)
Netherlands	0.905 (0.281)*	7.402 (0.388)	1.096 (0.179)*	8.355 (0.302)
Singapore	0.983 (0.410)*	6.198 (0.517)	0.981 (0.266)*	11.29 (0.126)
Switzerland	0.648 (0.392)	4.597 (0.709)	1.121 (0.157)*	7.933 (0.339)
UK	1.108 (0.290)*	1.557 (0.980)	0.877 (0.149)*	12.51 (0.085)

Notes: (i) The sample period is January 1973 to February 2009. (ii) The β^i estimates are obtained by the 5-step iterative GMM estimator. (iii) The quadratic spectral kernel with automatic bandwidth selection method is used to adjust standard errors. (iv) The set of instruments includes 4 lags of national stock returns and US stock returns. (v) J refers to the overidentifying restrictions test statistic by Hansen (1982) and pv denotes associated p-values. (vi) * indicates a 5% significance level.

as compared to the other countries during the 1990s. Hong Kong and Singapore share a similar pattern to these three larger countries. In sum, even though for a limited number of countries there were high degrees of interdependence in the earlier decades, it seems obvious that stronger degrees of interdependence in the 2000s were virtually everywhere in terms of either larger coefficients or smaller standard errors.

Our results on interdependence are not fully consistent with those reported by Bekaert et al. (2009) and Morona and Beltratti (2008), who find that the co-movement of stock market returns has increased only among selected countries, not all. Specifically, while they find increased stock return co-movement between European countries and the US over time, their results also indicate that US stock market returns are less interdependent with Asian stock market returns. Bekaert et al. base their results on aggregate portfolio returns for 23 countries during 1980 to 2005, while Morona and Beltratti focus on four major markets, Germany, Japan, the UK and the US, over the period from 1973 to 2004. These findings, in contrast to ours in some cases, suggest that investors may still benefit from portfolio diversification when diversifying across a geographically diverse group of countries. The differences in some of the findings may be due to a greater degree of interdependence among countries that occurred during the recent crisis, something that the other two studies could not have taken into account given when they were completed.

Turning to the issue of spillover effects, we can now compare the response of national stock returns for other countries to a US return shock for the 2000s relative to that in earlier decades. Both the short- and long-run responses in all markets to such a shock are substantially larger and significant at least at the 10 percent level in the 2000s. The long-run responses, however, are less significant and much smaller in earlier decades (Table 2.7). To elaborate, a 1 percent negative shock originating from the US occurring in the 2000s leads to a drop in German stock returns by 1.2 per cent in the short run. The initial negative shock that affects German stock returns continues, yielding a 1.8 percent decline in the long run. In the 1990s, in contrast, the response of German stock returns is 0.7 percent in the short run, and an even smaller 0.5 percent in the long run (Figure 2.2 and Table 2.7).

Given the evidence presented above of a higher degree of stock market return interdependence between our sample countries and the US in the 2000s, we now investigate specifically whether there has been a change in the pre- and post-US financial crisis degree of interdependence using weekly data. If there has been an increase in interdependence, this would plausibly be an indication that the US crisis spilled over substantially more to other advanced economies. In addition to examining interdependence,

Table 2.7 *National stock return responses to a 1% US stock return shock: monthly returns*

$$y_t = D(L)\varepsilon_t = D(L)Cu_t$$

$$y_t = [r_t^{US} r_t]',\ \varepsilon_t = [\varepsilon_t^{US}\varepsilon_i]',\ u_t = [u_t^{US} u_t]'$$

$$Eu_t u_t' = I,\ E\varepsilon_t\varepsilon_t' = \Sigma = CC'$$

Country	1970s				1980s			
	ψ_S	90% C.I.	ψ_L	90% C.I.	ψ_S	90% C.I.	ψ_L	90% C.I.
Australia	0.874	[0.578,1.175]	1.066	[0.379,2.079]	0.921	[0.306,1.382]	1.136	[0.385,1.852]
Austria	0.278	[0.117,0.429]	0.111	[-0.330,0.549]	0.219	[-0.058,0.442]	0.910	[-0.183,2.104]
Belgium	0.632	[0.466,0.813]	0.391	[-0.145,0.984]	0.501	[0.205,0.705]	0.255	[-0.496,0.893]
Canada	0.690	[0.561,0.841]	0.755	[0.369,1.320]	0.931	[0.780,1.048]	0.994	[0.599,1.481]
Denmark	0.444	[0.170,0.752]	0.434	[-0.305,1.241]	0.563	[0.384,0.813]	0.403	[-0.182,1.073]
France	0.824	[0.523,1.106]	0.897	[0.030,1.847]	0.660	[0.479,0.843]	0.916	[0.206,1.816]
Germany	0.432	[0.208,0.659]	0.261	[-0.193,0.798]	0.499	[0.194,0.712]	0.595	[-0.149,1.327]
Hong Kong	1.094	[0.741,1.407]	2.396	[1.479,3.792]	0.867	[-0.027,1.530]	0.883	[-0.126,1.708]
Italy	0.513	[0.270,0.749]	0.340	[-0.231,0.966]	0.364	[0.086,0.588]	0.952	[0.008,2.018]
Japan	0.345	[0.104,0.603]	0.506	[-0.104,1.216]	0.289	[0.070,0.575]	0.753	[0.275,1.383]
Netherlands	0.751	[0.491,1.027]	0.768	[0.277,1.407]	0.661	[0.493,0.780]	0.697	[0.329,1.110]
Singapore	1.360	[0.954,1.795]	1.786	[0.865,3.199]	1.013	[0.496,1.346]	1.170	[0.350,1.891]
Switzerland	0.576	[0.366,0.810]	0.599	[0.127,1.236]	0.536	[0.314,0.683]	0.642	[0.005,1.230]
UK	0.930	[0.639,1.278]	1.489	[0.573,2.821]	0.780	[0.541,0.932]	0.776	[0.334,1.220]

Country	1990s				2000s			
	ψ_S	90% C.I.	ψ_L	90% C.I.	ψ_S	90% C.I.	ψ_L	90% C.I.
Australia	0.750	[0.553,0.925]	0.623	[0.305,0.969]	1.018	[0.853,1.173]	1.596	[0.921,2.539]
Austria	0.541	[0.208,0.805]	0.530	[0.199,0.844]	0.913	[0.675,1.149]	1.765	[0.754,3.219]
Belgium	0.602	[0.397,0.758]	0.405	[-0.034,0.802]	0.985	[0.763,1.203]	1.790	[0.939,3.124]
Canada	0.969	[0.761,1.160]	0.833	[0.546,1.158]	1.045	[0.909,1.180]	1.705	[1.010,2.727]
Denmark	0.519	[0.320,0.683]	0.388	[0.004,0.779]	0.966	[0.808,1.145]	1.779	[1.067,2.878]
France	0.716	[0.514,0.878]	0.597	[0.284,0.895]	1.106	[0.981,1.231]	1.749	[1.131,2.769]
Germany	0.686	[0.473,0.863]	0.498	[0.149,0.823]	1.211	[1.074,1.355]	1.835	[1.195,2.828]
Hong Kong	1.166	[0.896,1.446]	0.445	[-0.255,1.113]	0.829	[0.645,1.030]	1.479	[0.818,2.452]
Italy	0.847	[0.543,1.106]	0.994	[0.420,1.607]	1.006	[0.860,1.152]	1.783	[1.030,2.926]
Japan	0.701	[0.392,1.012]	-0.008	[-0.799,0.677]	0.545	[0.374,0.701]	1.335	[0.719,2.266]
Netherlands	0.676	[0.542,0.791]	0.496	[0.281,0.716]	1.178	[0.991,1.385]	1.978	[1.200,3.188]
Singapore	1.116	[0.858,1.379]	0.418	[-0.419,1.182]	0.963	[0.791,1.137]	1.816	[1.077,2.970]
Switzerland	0.756	[0.512,0.949]	0.537	[0.190,0.860]	0.765	[0.644,0.876]	1.238	[0.849,1.822]
UK	0.717	[0.595,0.832]	0.533	[0.323,0.769]	0.901	[0.804,1.001]	1.604	[0.981,2.581]

Notes: (i) Observations span from January 1973 to February 2009. (ii) The response functions are obtained from the bivariate SVAR estimations with an identifying assumption that the national stock return shocks do not contemporaneously affect US stock returns. (iii) The number of lags was set at 4 by the Akaike Information Criteria. (iv) ψ_S denotes contemporaneous responses of the national stock returns to a 1% US stock return shock, measured by the Choleski decomposition factor (*C*). (v) ψ_L denotes long-run responses of the national stock returns to a 1% US stock return shock, measured by *D(L)C*. (vi) The 90% confidence intervals (C.I.) were obtained by taking 5% and 95% percentiles from 10,000 nonparametric bootstrap simulations for each country.

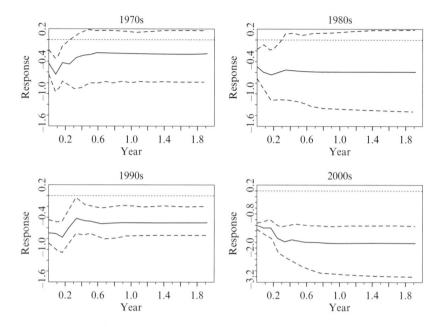

Note: 90% confidence bands were obtained by taking 5% and 95% percentiles from 10,000
nonparametric bootstrap simulations.

Figure 2.2   *Responses of German stock returns to a −1% structural US
             return shock*

we estimated the spillover effects from a shock to US stock market returns
to our other sample countries. The interdependence results are based
on the univariate approach using the GMM estimators and reported in
Tables 2.8 and 2.10. The spillover effects are based on the system approach
using the coefficients of impulse responses from a VAR model and are
reported in Tables 2.9 and 2.11. Tables 2.8 and 2.9 refer to the first way
used to identify the pre- and post-crisis periods (emerging crisis), while
Tables 2.10 and 2.11 refer to the second way (Lehman Brothers failure),
as discussed earlier.

The results in Table 2.8 show that the coefficients for the co-movement
of stock returns during the post-emerging crisis period increase substantially for all but two countries compared to the pre-emerging crisis period
in terms of both magnitude and significance. The exceptions are the results
for Germany and Japan, with Germany becoming somewhat less interdependent with the US and the co-movement between stock returns in Japan
and the US becoming significantly negative. As Table 2.10 shows, the

Table 2.8 Estimation results: emerging US crisis episode

$$r_t^i = \alpha^i + \beta^i r_t^{US} + \varepsilon_t^i, \quad z_t^i = [r_{t-1}^i \ldots r_{t-p}^i r_{t-1}^{US} \ldots r_{t-p}^{US}]'$$

Country	Pre-episode		Post-episode	
	$\beta^i_{GMM}(se)$	$J(pv)$	$\beta^i_{GMM}(se)$	$J(pv)$
Australia	−0.670 (0.461)	5.999 (0.540)	1.228 (0.228)*	5.572 (0.591)
Austria	0.117 (0.299)	17.22 (0.016)	0.146 (0.432)	5.160 (0.640)
Belgium	0.615 (0.305)*	8.913 (0.259)	0.875 (0.231)*	13.00 (0.072)
Canada	0.919 (0.245)*	7.753 (0.355)	1.324 (0.188)*	7.252 (0.403)
Denmark	−0.120 (0.248)	6.183 (0.519)	1.300 (0.256)*	6.973 (0.432)
France	0.672 (0.148)*	8.661 (0.278)	1.210 (0.225)*	9.747 (0.203)
Germany	0.905 (0.220)*	7.220 (0.406)	0.575 (0.211)*	8.271 (0.309)
Hong Kong	−0.346 (0.507)	9.274 (0.234)	0.529 (0.271)	4.230 (0.753)
Italy	0.681 (0.239)*	5.580 (0.590)	1.059 (0.200)*	10.48 (0.163)
Japan	−0.082 (0.385)	14.13 (0.049)	−1.005 (0.410)*	4.084 (0.770)
Netherlands	0.357 (0.245)	8.326 (0.305)	0.681 (0.229)*	10.98 (0.139)
Norway	−0.291 (0.503)	7.946 (0.337)	1.550 (0.395)*	8.680 (0.276)
Singapore	−0.471 (0.508)	7.116 (0.417)	0.388 (0.381)	4.950 (0.666)
Spain	0.612 (0.228)*	6.869 (0.443)	1.371 (0.221)*	8.778 (0.269)
Sweden	−0.052 (0.435)	3.796 (0.803)	0.995 (0.180)*	8.223 (0.313)
Switzerland	0.286 (0.308)	12.04 (0.099)	0.496 (0.205)*	6.442 (0.489)
UK	0.126 (0.217)	6.882 (0.441)	1.609 (0.227)*	6.586 (0.473)

Notes: (i) The sample periods of pre- and post-episode are the first week of 2000 to the last week of July 2007 and the first week of August 2007 to the last week of February 2009, respectively. (ii) Standard errors (*se*) are adjusted by the quadratic spectral kernel with automatic bandwidth selection method. (iii) The set of instruments includes 4 lags of national stock returns and US stock returns. (iv) *J* refers to the overidentifying restrictions test statistic by Hansen (1982) and *pv* denotes associated *p*-values. (v) * indicates a 5% significance level.

Table 2.9 National stock return responses to a 1% US stock return shock: emerging US crisis episode

$$y_t = D(L)\varepsilon_t = D(L)Cu_t$$

$$y_t = [r_t^{US}, y_t^i]', \quad \varepsilon_t = [\varepsilon_t^{US}, \varepsilon_t^i]', \quad u_t = [u_t^{US}, u_t^i]'$$

$$Eu_t u_t' = I, \quad E\varepsilon_t \varepsilon_t' = \Sigma = CC'$$

Country	Pre-episode				Post-episode			
	ψ_S	90% C.I.	ψ_L	90% C.I.	ψ_S	90% C.I.	ψ_L	90% C.I.
Australia	0.542	[0.447,0.641]	0.665	[0.519,0.831]	1.235	[0.964,1.513]	1.493	[0.958,2.392]
Austria	0.221	[0.128,0.323]	0.477	[0.298,0.683]	1.181	[0.865,1.439]	2.041	[1.076,3.645]
Belgium	0.555	[0.455,0.659]	0.648	[0.474,0.840]	1.250	[1.021,1.442]	2.039	[1.108,3.638]
Canada	0.749	[0.676,0.829]	0.763	[0.607,0.951]	1.135	[0.855,1.407]	1.400	[0.927,2.198]
Denmark	0.478	[0.380,0.581]	0.673	[0.499,0.875]	1.132	[0.864,1.386]	1.591	[0.912,2.694]
France	0.861	[0.774,0.953]	0.772	[0.588,0.988]	1.023	[0.844,1.191]	1.133	[0.669,1.869]
Germany	0.859	[0.764,0.959]	0.853	[0.646,1.100]	1.017	[0.839,1.191]	1.130	[0.661,1.890]
Hong Kong	0.771	[0.664,0.884]	0.760	[0.564,0.987]	1.190	[0.860,1.466]	1.398	[0.772,2.335]
Italy	0.670	[0.570,0.777]	0.565	[0.357,0.794]	0.974	[0.778,1.152]	1.219	[0.736,2.029]
Japan	0.526	[0.403,0.661]	0.557	[0.368,0.764]	0.533	[0.379,0.727]	0.705	[0.370,1.230]
Netherlands	0.816	[0.728,0.911]	0.791	[0.630,0.992]	1.187	[0.984,1.362]	1.829	[0.918,3.354]

Norway	0.602	[0.494,0.717]	0.830	[0.612,1.080]	1.399	[1.072,1.725]	2.150	[1.180,3.750]
Singapore	0.600	[0.503,0.705]	0.727	[0.563,0.923]	0.990	[0.748,1.199]	1.414	[0.816,2.348]
Spain	0.674	[0.582,0.774]	0.655	[0.479,0.865]	1.017	[0.764,1.235]	1.177	[0.542,2.076]
Sweden	1.057	[0.947,1.169]	1.105	[0.868,1.371]	1.413	[1.187,1.603]	1.437	[0.855,2.391]
Switzerland	0.655	[0.575,0.733]	0.715	[0.569,0.892]	0.712	[0.581,0.842]	0.816	[0.464,1.355]
UK	0.713	[0.635,0.797]	0.587	[0.450,0.751]	1.049	[0.852,1.222]	1.276	[0.779,2.080]

Notes: (i) The sample periods of pre- and post-episode are the first week of July 2007 and the first week of August 2007 to the last week of February 2009, respectively. (ii) The response functions are obtained from the bivariate SVAR estimations with an identifying assumption that the national stock return shocks do not contemporaneously affect US stock returns. (iii) The number of lags was set at 4. (iv) ψ_S denotes contemporaneous responses of the national stock return index to a 1% US stock index shock, measured by the Choleski decomposition factor (C). (v) ψ_L denotes long-run responses of the national stock returns to a 1% US stock return shock, measured by $D(L)C$. (vi) The 90% confidence intervals (C.I.) were obtained by taking 5% and 95% percentiles from 10,000 nonparametric bootstrap simulations for each country.

Table 2.10   Estimation results: Lehman Brothers' episode

$$r_t^i = \alpha^i + \beta^i r_t^{US} + \varepsilon_t^i, z_t^i = [r_{t-1}^i \ldots r_{t-p}^i, r_{t-1}^{US} \ldots r_{t-p}^{US}]'$$

Country	Pre-episode		Post-episode	
	$\beta_{GMM}^i(se)$	$J(pv)$	$\beta_{GMM}^i(se)$	$J(pv)$
Australia	−0.259 (0.369)	11.23 (0.129)	0.542 (0.302)	5.469 (0.603)
Austria	0.331 (0.297)	16.59 (0.020)	−0.026 (0.528)	4.534 (0.717)
Belgium	0.679 (0.272)*	8.869 (0.262)	1.217 (0.180)*	7.289 (0.399)
Canada	0.774 (0.268)*	11.80 (0.107)	1.028 (0.216)*	6.610 (0.471)
Denmark	−0.182 (0.289)	8.581 (0.284)	0.219 (0.476)	6.376 (0.497)
France	0.650 (0.136)*	11.00 (0.139)	−0.055 (0.639)	3.805 (0.802)
Germany	0.942 (0.217)*	6.878 (0.442)	0.797 (0.198)*	7.311 (0.397)
Hong Kong	−0.001 (0.368)	14.61 (0.041)	0.113 (0.192)	3.804 (0.802)
Italy	0.817 (0.243)*	5.346 (0.618)	0.771 (0.399)	6.644 (0.467)
Japan	−0.112 (0.359)	14.65 (0.041)	−0.864 (0.514)	6.028 (0.536)
Netherlands	0.385 (0.207)	8.979 (0.254)	0.862 (0.269)*	8.486 (0.292)
Norway	−0.122 (0.465)	12.74 (0.079)	−0.073 (0.689)	5.735 (0.571)
Singapore	−0.363 (0.420)	7.069 (0.422)	1.053 (0.217)*	6.748 (0.456)
Spain	0.770 (0.192)*	4.821 (0.682)	0.437 (0.429)	3.772 (0.806)
Sweden	0.165 (0.332)	8.551 (0.287)	0.602 (0.268)*	4.393 (0.734)
Switzerland	0.268 (0.237)	13.62 (0.058)	0.615 (0.158)*	4.155 (0.762)
UK	0.215 (0.211)	10.35 (0.170)	1.355 (0.224)*	6.618 (0.470)

Notes: (i) The sample periods of pre- and post-episode are the first week of 2000 to the second week of September 2008 and the third week of September 2008 to the last week of February 2009, respectively. (ii) Standard errors (*se*) are adjusted by the quadratic spectral kernel with automatic bandwidth selection method. (iii) The set of instruments includes 4 lags of national stock returns and US stock returns. (iv) *J* refers to the overidentifying restrictions test statistic by Hansen (1982) and *pv* denotes associated *p*-values. (v) * indicates a 5% significance level.

evidence for increased stock market return interdependence after Lehman Brothers filed for bankruptcy on September 14, 2008 compared to the pre-bankruptcy period is very weak. Indeed, only in the case of Singapore and the UK is there evidence of significantly greater interdependence. It should be noted in this regard, however, that there are relatively few observations following the collapse of Lehman Brothers (our observations end in February 2009). In addition, the pre-episode period of the Lehman Brothers bankruptcy includes the period from August 2007 to September 2008 during which we found a substantial increase in national stock market return co-movement.

The results from the impulse response analysis confirm that there are spillover effects from US stock market returns to the stock market returns of the other advanced countries when the financial crisis emerged in the US (Table 2.9). For example, a 1 percent drop in US stock returns is associated with a 1.05 percent short-run decline and a 1.28 percent long-run decline in UK stock returns. Before the crisis emerged, the magnitude of the spillover effect from a US shock is smaller; a 1 percent drop in US stock returns is associated with a 0.71 percent contemporaneous decline in UK stock market returns and to a somewhat smaller 0.59 percent decline in the long run. A similar pattern holds for the other countries.

Following the collapse of Lehman Brothers, although the GMM estimations do not indicate a pattern of large increases in the co-movement of stock returns for the 17 sample countries and the US (Table 2.9), the impulse response analysis in Table 2.11 indicates almost always larger spillover effects than in the pre-crisis period. In particular, the magnitude of both short- and long-run national stock return responses to a shock in US stock returns is larger after the failure of Lehman Brothers in all sample countries, except Japan. In addition, the contemporaneous responses in countries to a US shock are also higher during the post-Lehman Brothers' failure than the post-emerging crisis period, except in the cases of Japan and Switzerland. These results suggest that the bankruptcy of Lehman Brothers contributed the most to spreading the crisis worldwide. Frank and Hesse (2009) and Dooley and Hutchison (2009) also find that the collapse of Lehman Brothers triggered the global financial crisis. Their sample, unlike ours, focuses mainly on emerging market economies, however.

5   CONCLUSION

Generally, we find an increase in interdependence between national stock market returns over time as well as spillover effects from a shock to US stock returns to other advanced countries. Furthermore, we also find that the results are reasonably uniform for countries, with respect to both interdependence and spillover effects. Most importantly, given the focus of our chapter, we find that spillover effects from the US to other industrial countries were greatest after the emergence of the US subprime mortgage market meltdown in the summer of 2007, especially after the collapse of Lehman Brothers.

Our results, as well as those of others, raise the issue of the underlying reason why the degree of stock return interdependence among the countries with the US increased and the spillover effects became greater after as compared to before the US financial crisis. Some possible explanations for

Table 2.11 National stock return responses to a 1% US stock return shock: Lehman Brothers' episode

$$y_t = D(L)\varepsilon_t = D(L)Cu_t$$

$$y_t = [r_t^{US}, r_t^i]', \varepsilon_t = [\varepsilon_t^{US}, \varepsilon_t^i]', u_t = [u_t^{US}, u_t^i]'$$

$$Eu_t u_t' = I, E\varepsilon_t \varepsilon_t' = \Sigma = CC'$$

Country	Pre-episode				Post-episode			
	ψ_S	90% C.I.	ψ_L	90% C.I.	ψ_S	90% C.I.	ψ_L	90% C.I.
Australia	0.625	[0.529,0.727]	0.739	[0.581,0.917]	1.328	[0.791,1.904]	1.372	[0.587,5.268]
Austria	0.314	[0.220,0.419]	0.585	[0.404,0.792]	1.460	[0.874,1.818]	1.956	[0.517,7.730]
Belgium	0.624	[0.523,0.732]	0.701	[0.521,0.906]	1.363	[0.818,1.933]	3.992	[−20.90,31.42]
Canada	0.768	[0.689,0.853]	0.820	[0.669,0.997]	1.236	[0.812,1.956]	1.328	[0.528,4.460]
Denmark	0.542	[0.444,0.643]	0.707	[0.545,0.895]	1.415	[1.087,1.726]	1.768	[0.589,6.835]
France	0.866	[0.782,0.958]	0.792	[0.616,0.998]	1.150	[0.853,1.514]	1.006	[0.111,3.616]
Germany	0.856	[0.766,0.955]	0.844	[0.652,1.072]	1.176	[0.902,1.534]	1.009	[0.235,3.722]
Hong Kong	0.807	[0.701,0.918]	0.817	[0.622,1.038]	1.400	[0.832,1.877]	1.262	[0.102,4.513]
Italy	0.682	[0.586,0.781]	0.611	[0.422,0.821]	1.164	[0.849,1.549]	1.192	[0.230,4.548]
Japan	0.546	[0.437,0.665]	0.579	[0.414,0.767]	0.522	[0.122,1.160]	0.562	[−0.492,2.575]
Netherlands	0.848	[0.757,0.945]	0.843	[0.680,1.040]	1.385	[0.938,1.701]	1.836	[−0.399,7.533]

Norway	0.654	[0.536,0.782]	0.938	[0.718,1.191]	1.599	[1.133,2.156]	1.891	[0.030,8.064]
Singapore	0.646	[0.553,0.743]	0.760	[0.595,0.948]	1.086	[0.694,1.396]	1.399	[0.565,5.398]
Spain	0.689	[0.598,0.789]	0.669	[0.487,0.882]	1.241	[0.884,1.669]	1.251	[−0.230,4.521]
Sweden	1.066	[0.962,1.175]	1.086	[0.870,1.343]	1.623	[1.279,1.920]	1.523	[0.372,6.568]
Switzerland	0.660	[0.581,0.738]	0.685	[0.550,0.841]	0.685	[0.380,1.036]	0.883	[0.106,3.711]
UK	0.739	[0.662,0.819]	0.627	[0.494,0.778]	1.178	[0.860,1.532]	1.077	[0.260,3.800]

Notes: (i) The sample periods of pre- and post-episode are the first week of 2000 to the second week of September 2008 and the third week of September 2008 to the last week of February 2009, respectively. (ii) The response functions are obtained from the bivariate SVAR estimations with an identifying assumption that the national stock return shocks do not contemporaneously affect US stock returns. (iii) The number of lags was set at 4. (iv) ψ_S denotes contemporaneous responses of the national stock returns to a 1% US stock return shock, measured by the Choleski decomposition factor (C). (v) ψ_L denotes long-run responses of the national stock returns to a 1% U.S. stock return shock, measured by $D(L)C$. (vi) The 90% confidence intervals (C.I.) were obtained by taking 5% and 95% percentiles from 10,000 nonparametric bootstrap simulations for each country.

the changing pattern and magnitude in the co-movement of national stock market returns are as follows. First, the current global crisis was triggered in the US, which has the largest economy and the biggest financial markets in the world. In estimating and comparing the output spillover effects of shocks from the US, the euro area, and Japan, to other parts of the world, Bayoumi and Swiston (2008) find that the largest spillovers originated in the US. They also find that financial linkages are the most important channel in transmitting shocks between the countries. Second, countries are now affected to a greater extent by global shocks than before, and to a lesser extent by country-specific shocks. As Forbes and Chinn (2004) argue, country-specific factors have become less important in explaining a country's stock market returns, while increasing bilateral trade and financial linkages have become more important factors. Eichengreen et al. (2009) also show that the ability of a relatively small number of common factors to explain the variation in the riskiness (measured by credit default swap premiums) of financial institutions in different countries rose to an exceptionally high level after the emergence of the US financial crisis. Third, the concern over counterparty risk reached a record high during the tumultuous period. This contributed to a liquidity freeze, credit crunch and flight to safety insofar as heightened uncertainty and loss of confidence undermined the proper functioning of the global financial system (Barth et al., 2009a).

The bottom line is that much more work remains to be done to better assess the basic factors that can explain the degree to which a change in interdependence among countries and a change in the magnitude of spillover effects from one country to others contributed to the severity and global nature of the recent crisis. This is essential to better assist policy makers in promoting greater regulatory responsibility for mitigating, if not eliminating, the likelihood of another systemic financial crisis.

NOTES

*   The authors are grateful for helpful comments from Levan Efremidze, Thomas D. Willett and Jingging Xu.
1. The scatter plots are quite similar for the other countries in our sample.
2. The channels through which a crisis spreads are different for different crisis episodes. Hernández and Valdés (2001), for example, find that the trade linkage is the important transmission channel during the Thailand and Brazilian crises, whereas financial competition is the only relevant channel in the case of the Russian crisis.
3. Conventional unit-root tests for the stock price indices imply that the stock indices are integrated of order one, indicating that stock returns are covariance stationary. This means the usual finite sample and large sample properties of the OLS estimator apply.

4. We use Andrews's (1991) quadratic spectral kernel with automatic bandwidth selection method.
5. This may be a quite restrictive assumption in the case that u_t^i is the structural shock to the UK stock market, for instance. However, our results were qualitatively similar with different orderings of the variables.
6. We focus on broad trends over time and do not focus on all the specific periods of crisis except for the recent US crisis, which is the main focus of our chapter.
7. Due to a lack of data, the results for stock market return interdependence between Norway, Spain and Sweden and the US are not reported.
8. We regressed r_t^{US} on a constant, r_t^i, and r_{t-1}^{US}. We obtained strong significantly positive coefficients on r_t^i for all countries, whereas the coefficients on r_{t-1}^{US} were mostly insignificant. Therefore, it seems that the exogeneity assumption clearly fails. All results are available upon request.

REFERENCES

Andrews, Donald W.K. (1991), 'Heteroskedasticity and autocorrelation consistent covariance matrix estimation', *Econometrica*, **59**(3), 817–58.

Barth, James R., Tong Li and Triphon Phumiwasana (2009a), 'The US financial crisis: credit crunch and yield spreads', in Robert Pringle and Nick Carver (eds), *RBS Reserve Management Trends*, London: Central Banking Publications, pp. 35–52.

Barth, James R., Tong Li, Wenling Lu, Triphon Phumiwasana and Glenn Yago (2009b), *The Rise and Fall of the US Mortgage and Credit Markets: A Comprehensive Analysis of the Meltdown*, New York: John Wiley.

Bayoumi, Tamim and Andrew Swiston (2009), 'Foreign entanglements: estimating the source and size of spillovers across industrial countries', *IMF Staff Papers*, **56**(2), 353–83, International Monetary Fund, Washington, DC.

Bekaert, Greet, Campbell R. Harvey and Angela Ng (2005), 'Market integration and contagion', *Journal of Business*, **78**(1), 39–69.

Bekaert, Greet, Robert J. Hodrick and Xiaoyan Zhang (2009), 'International stock return comovements', *Journal of Finance*, **64**(6), 2591–626.

Bertero, Elisabetta and Colin Mayer (1990), 'Structure and performance: global interdependence of stock markets around the crash of October 1987', *European Economic Review*, **34**, 1155–80.

Bonfiglioli, Alessandra and Carlo A. Favero (2005), 'Explaining co-movements between stock markets: the case of US and Germany', *Journal of International Money and Finance*, **24**, 1299–316.

Candelon, Bertrand, Alain Hecq and Willem F.C. Verschoor (2005), 'Measuring common cyclical features during financial turmoil: evidence of interdependence not contagion', *Journal of International Money and Finance*, **24**, 1317–34.

Corsetti, Giancarlo, Marcello Pericoli and Massimo Sbracia (2005), 'Some contagion, some interdependence: more pitfalls in tests of financial contagion', *Journal of International Money and Finance*, **24**, 1177–99.

Dooley, Michael and Michael Hutchison (2009), 'Transmission of the US subprime crisis to emerging markets: evidence on the decoupling–recoupling hypothesis', *Journal of International Money and Finance*, **28**(8), 1331–49.

Ehrmann, Michael, Marcel Fratzscher and Roberto Rigobon (2005), 'Stocks, bonds, money markets and exchange rates: measuring international financial transmission', NBER Working Paper 11166, National Bureau of Economic Research, Cambridge, MA.

Eichengreen, Barry, Ashoka Mody, Milan Nedeljkovic and Lucio Sarno (2009), 'How the subprime crisis went global: evidence from bank credit default swap spreads', NBER Working Paper 14904, National Bureau of Economic Research, Cambridge, MA.

Forbes, Kristin J. and Menzie D. Chinn (2004), 'A decomposition of global linkages in financial markets over time', *Review of Economics and Statistics*, **86**(3), 705–22.

Forbes, Kristin J. and Roberto Rigobon (2002), 'No contagion, only interdependence: measuring stock market comovements', *Journal of Finance*, **57**(5), 2223–61.

Frank, Nathaniel and Heiko Hesse (2009), 'Financial spillovers to emerging markets during the global financial crisis', Finance a úvěr-*Czech Journal of Economics and Finance*, **59**(6), 507–21.

Hansen, Lars P. (1982), 'Large sample properties of generalized method of moments estimators', *Econometrica*, **50**, 1029–54.

Hernández, Leonardo F. and Rodrigo O. Valdés (2001), 'What drives contagion trade, neighborhood, or financial links?', *International Review of Financial Analysis*, **10**, 203–18.

Imbs, Jean (2004), 'Trade, finance, specialization, and synchronization', *Review of Economics and Statistics*, **86**, 723–34.

International Monetary Fund (IMF) (2007), 'Spillovers and cycles in the global economy', *World Economic Outlook*, April, International Monetary Fund, Washington, DC.

King, Mervyn A. and Sushil Wadhwani (1990), 'Transmission of volatility between stock markets', *Review of Financial Studies*, **3**, 5–33.

Lee, Sang B. and Kwang J. Kim (1993), 'Does the October 1987 crash strengthen the comovement among national stock markets?', *Review of Financial Economics*, **3**, 89–102.

Morona, Claudio and Andrea Beltratti (2008), 'Comovements in international stock markets', *Journal of International Financial Markets, Institutions and Money*, **18**, 31–45.

Sims, Christopher A. (1980), 'Macroeconomics and reality', *Econometrica*, **48**, 1–47.

3. Canadian banks and the North American housing crisis

James A. Brox

1 INTRODUCTION

This chapter examines the recent performance of Canadian banks in light of the recent North American housing crisis. The extent of the spread of the housing crisis to the Canadian housing sector is analyzed, and the resulting impacts on the Canadian banks' balance sheets are studied using information from the Canadian financial flow matrix as published by Statistics Canada. The chapter shows that while there has indeed been some spillover from the United States into both the housing and banking sectors, these effects are much more modest than those in the US. Some policy issues with respect to tax and regulatory structure are discussed in conclusion.

The subprime housing crisis and the meltdown in the American banking sector has had an impact on Canadian banks and on the Canadian economy in general. However, as of mid-2009, no Canadian bank has failed, none has required a financial 'bailout', and all appear to be profitable. The Bank of Canada has injected liquidity into the economy to ease pressure on the banks, but there has been no major change in financial regulation as a result of the crisis in the US and elsewhere.

Recently the International Monetary Fund (IMF 2009, 16) reported: 'Canada's financial stability amid the turbulence bears testimony to effective supervision and regulation. Rigorous limits on leverage and targeted capital ratios well above Basel standards have helped to avoid vulnerabilities'. Reasons for this assessment are given as:

- *Stringent capital requirements:* Solvency standards apply to banks' consolidated commercial and securities operations. Tier 1 capital generally significantly exceeds the required 7 percent target (which in turn exceeds the Basel Accord minimum of 4 percent). The leverage ratio is limited to 5 percent of total capital.
- *Low risk tolerance and conservative balance sheet structures:* Banks have a profitable and stable domestic retail market, and (like their customers)

exhibit low risk tolerance. Banks had smaller exposures to 'toxic' structured assets and relied less on volatile wholesale funding than many international peers.

- *Conservative residential mortgage markets*: Only 5 percent of mortgages are nonprime and only 25 percent are securitized (compared with 25 percent and 60 percent, respectively, in the United States). Almost half of residential loans are guaranteed, while the remaining have a loan-to-value ratio (LTV) below 80 percent – mortgages with LTV above this threshold must be insured for the full loan amount (rather than the portion above 80 percent LTV, as in the United States). Also mortgage interest is non-deductible from taxes, encouraging borrowers to repay quickly. (IMF, 2009, 6)

Numerous studies of the financial situation have already appeared. Wheelock (2008) notes the parallel between the recent housing finance crisis in the US and that of the Great Depression. Wagster (2007) shows how the adoption of explicit deposit insurance expanded risk-shifting incentives for Canadian banks, resulting in reduced systematic risk in the stock market as a whole, even as it increased non-systematic risk in the banking sector. Van Roy (2008) studies the impact of the Basel Accord on the risk-weighted asset to capital ratios for banks in six G10 countries. The results show that only in the US did weakly capitalized banks which faced market pressure increase their capital ratios faster than the well-capitalized banks. Brox (2009) uses a financial flow model of the Canadian banking sector to study bank portfolio behaviour and to forecast further adjustments resulting from the crisis.

Mizen (2008) looks at changes in US regulation and supervision required to prevent future occurrences of financial panics like the one created by the credit crunch following the subprime mortgage defaults. Torrance (2008) examines how public infrastructure is being shifted from public good to private property. This 'financialization' of infrastructure is resulting in cities and regions being valued on a quarter-to-quarter basis, potentially destabilizing housing markets. Further, Baker et al. (2008) examine default risk and redemption laws allowing local political games to affect the risk of mortgage default.

The remainder of this chapter is organized as follows: Section 2 provides some general comments on the spread of the financial crisis from the US to Canada. Section 3 gives some rationale for the better performance of the Canadian housing sector. Differences between the banking sectors in the US and Canada are discussed in Section 4, and summary comments and policy conclusions are presented in the final section.

2   CANADA AND THE NORTH AMERICAN FINANCIAL CRISIS

While the American economy entered recession in mid-2007, the Canadian economy remained strong until the fourth quarter of 2008. In the US, the recession started in the financial and housing sectors and spread to the rest of the economy. In Canada the recession started with a collapse of exports mainly to the US and spread to the rest of the economy including the banking and housing sectors. This spread is understandable since Canada is a very open economy with over 40 percent of production being exported and with more than 80 percent of these exports going to the US in the pre-recession period. However, by 2008 the percentage of Canadian exports going to the US dropped to 75 percent, resulting in total exports accounting for only 35 percent of GDP. Figure 3.1 shows the importance of trade to the Canadian economy.

This reduction in export demand from the US had a major effect on production and employment in many sectors of the Canadian economy, notably on manufacturing and the resource sectors. The reduction in employment and income generated in these sectors spread to other sectors of domestic demand in a predictable manner. Therefore it is not surprising that the banking and housing sectors in Canada were also adversely affected. What is surprising is how little these sectors were affected.

Figure 3.2 reports the Canadian rate of unemployment. Unemployment

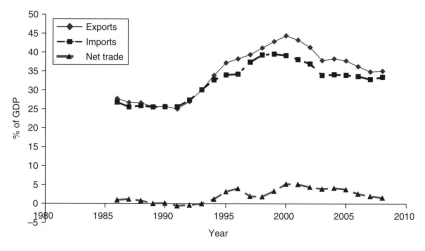

Source: Statistics Canada, data from CANSIM Table 379-0027.

Figure 3.1   Canadian international trade

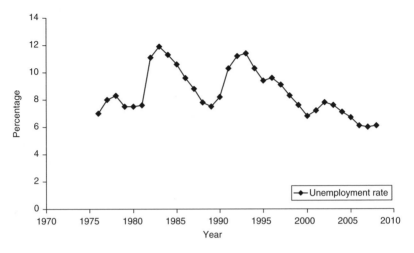

Source: Statistics Canada data from CANSIM Table 282-0087.

Figure 3.2 Canadian unemployment rate

in Canada had been dropping since the formation of the North American Free Trade Agreement (NAFTA), and the increased trade activity which followed. There was a slight upward movement apparent following the 2000 'dot com' bubble collapse, but during 2008 the current crisis had little impact. No doubt 2009 and 2010 will show a different story.

As the effects of the crisis began to spread to Canada, the government did take action. While there have been no direct bailouts in the financial sector, the federal government and the government of Ontario participated in the American-led bailout of the auto industry. As well, the Bank of Canada aided the financial system by setting interest rates near zero[1] and significantly increased liquidity in the system.

3 CANADIAN HOUSING MARKET

The Canadian housing sector has remained relatively stable throughout the current financial crisis. The American housing market, on the other hand, exhibited the classic sign of a bubble which inevitably burst. Figure 3.3 shows the average house prices for a single detached residence in both Canada and the US. Moreover, although the decline in Canadian housing prices was late in coming, the Canadian Real Estate Association (CREA) announced that 'national resale housing market activity returned to pre-recession levels in May 2009. The rebound in activity is being led by an

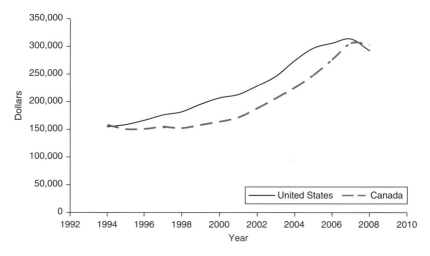

Sources: Canada: Canadian Mortgage and Housing Corporation; United States: US National Association of Realtors.

Figure 3.3 Average house prices

increase in transactions in some of the most expensive markets in the country' (Klump, 2009).

Mortgage lending in Canada has changed dramatically in the last 50 years. Prior to 1954, banks were not permitted to make mortgage loans. Thus most house purchases were financed by individuals or insurers (Harris and Ragonetti, 1998). The 1954 Bank Act amendments allowed banks to make mortgage loans insured under the National Housing Act, and the 1967 amendments allowed them to make conventional mortgage loans. The 1967 Bank Act also lifted the 6 percent interest rate cap on bank loans, which was binding at the time. The 1992 amendments attempted to make the mortgage market more competitive by giving banks greater access, but in fact had the opposite effect since banks were allowed to own trust companies and thus captured the majority of the market (Freedman, 1998). On the other hand, in the US, the depository institution share of residential mortgage loan holdings has declined from 75 percent to about 30 percent over the same 1970–2007 period.

Why has the Canadian mortgage market been more stable during the financial crisis of 2008–09 than that in the US? One reason is that Canadians have more equity in their homes than Americans do. Figure 3.4 shows the homeowners' equity in their homes as a percentage of the market value of the homes for both the US and Canada. Dunning (2008)

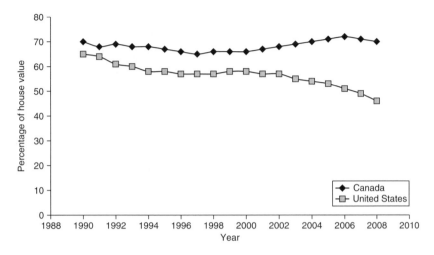

Sources: Canada: Statistics Canada; United States: Bureau of Economic Analysis (BEA).

Figure 3.4   Housing equity

notes that the decline in American home equity began in 2004, well before the current crisis, but the question remains, why? A major reason is the tax deductibility of home mortgage in the US. Americans have an incentive *not* to pay off their mortgages, while Canadians have the incentive to do the opposite.

Kiff (2009) analyzes mortgage affordability in the US and Canada. He finds that in most respects affordability is the same in both countries. What, therefore, explains the rapid collapse in the US and the stability in Canada? In addition to the reduced equity caused by mortgage deductibility, Kiff argues that mortgage securitization is not as pervasive in Canada as in the US (29 percent compared to about 60 percent). Since Canadian issuers retain mortgages on their books, there is more incentive to control risk than in the US where securitization eventually caused a breakdown in the incentive to control risk and the abandonment of credit quality (Klyuev, 2008).

Mortgage insurance also plays a big role. Unlike in the US where mortgage insurance covers only losses that exceed the loan-to-value ceiling, in Canada it covers the full amount of the loan. Also, in Canada the entire premium is paid upfront by the borrower, whereas in the US part is paid upfront by the lender and part paid monthly by the borrower. Hence, when the economy declines, American lenders foreclose and Canadian lenders do not.

4   THE CANADIAN BANKING SECTOR

The Canadian and American banking sectors are both relatively highly regulated. However the nature and purpose of the regulations have tended to be quite different. Canadian banks are highly concentrated, with the top six banks on the eve of the crisis accounting for more than 90 percent of bank assets. The American banking system, on the other hand, is much more competitive with more than 8,000 commercial banks.[2]

Canadian banks operate nationally and increasingly internationally. Historically American regulations were designed to limit banks to one state and in some cases to one branch. Recently the two systems have moved towards each other. The introduction of bank holding companies in the US has allowed interstate operations, and increasing internationalization of Canadian banks and the entry of foreign banks into Canada has meant that Canadian banks have faced more competition.

Canadian banks are regulated by the Bank of Canada and by the Office of the Superintendent of Financial Institutions (OSFI). While some regulations are legislated, the oligopolistic nature of the Canadian system allows for the effective use of 'moral suasion'. Effectively officials can say 'do as I say or you will be punished'. The risk of withdrawal of government deposits is an effective control mechanism.

Although the Canadian and American banking sectors historically have been very different, with the Canadian sector being more regulated and more concentrated than that in the US, the liberalization of trade in financial services contained in Chapter 14 of NAFTA suggests that the difference between the financial behaviour of American agents and those found in earlier studies of Canadian sectors may have lessened. Such changes in response to increased financial integration under NAFTA are analyzed by Trivoli and Graham (1998) and Salehizadeh (1998) for Mexico, and to some extent by Paraskevopoulos et al. (1996) and Serletis and Krause (1996) for Canada.

With respect to Canada under NAFTA, some have argued that Canada and the US form an optimal currency area and thus the adoption of a common currency and further integration of the financial systems would be beneficial (Courchene and Harris, 2000; Grubel, 2000; Michelis, 2004), while others (Carr and Floyd, 2002; Murray et al., 2003) argue that, in spite of exchange rate volatility, Canada is better served by a floating exchange rate and a certain degree of financial independence. Ewing et al. (1999) find that North American stock markets remained segmented following NAFTA.

Stocks of assets and liabilities of the Canadian banking sector are summarized in Table 3.1. The major liability shift over the period is a growth

Table 3.1   Canadian banks, portfolio composition (%)

	1961	1971	1981	1991	2001	2008
Assets						
Real assets	1.95	1.51	1.40	1.88	1.69	1.13
Money	7.86	5.28	3.40	2.21	0.08	0.00
Shorts	8.08	5.95	3.40	5.07	1.17	2.66
Foreign assets	0	13.78	7.94	6.78	5.27	7.95
Loans	49.26	52.27	62.10	43.70	26.70	28.40
Mortgages	6.62	23.10	6.94	25.70	28.30	22.50
Bonds	22.40	12.45	0.69	2.88	5.58	3.33
Longs	3.81	3.67	14.10	11.70	30.40	34.00
Liabilities						
Deposits	91.95	76.01	60.30	62.80	56.60	53.40
Foreign	0	17.62	24.50	14.54	10.30	9.70
Longs	8.05	6.36	15.20	22.46	33.10	36.90
(equity)	7.50	5.40	4.50	7.50	7.30	7.70

Source: Statistics Canada, data from CANSIM Table 378-0001.

in long-term liabilities and stocks in place of deposit liabilities. There have also been modest increases in foreign liabilities. Throughout, the ratio of total liabilities held in the form of equity has remained constant at approximately 7.5 percent. The asset portfolio appears relatively stable. However, the proportion of the portfolio in the form of reserve assets (deposits, short-term paper, and government bonds) has declined following the phase-out of reserve requirements, and holdings of long-term assets, mortgages, and foreign assets have increased. The increase in foreign asset holdings and mortgages has to some extent also been at the expense of conventional lending by the banks. This has reduced the risk exposure of the banks since Canadian mortgages tend to be relatively low risk as Canadians build up equity in their homes, partially because, as mentioned above, unlike in the US, mortgage payments are not tax deductible.

Figure 3.5 shows the movement in the share of bank assets among foreign currency assets, conventional lending, and residential mortgages. We note that after a brief foray into the international realm, foreign assets have generally been less than 10 percent of total bank assets. There also seems to be a direct substitution between conventional lending and residential mortgage lending. Mortgage lending appears to decline relatively in recessionary periods while other forms of bank lending take up the slack.

Laurence Klein (2003, 269) argues that work with the flow-of-funds (FF) accounts 'is more urgent, particularly in interpreting the international

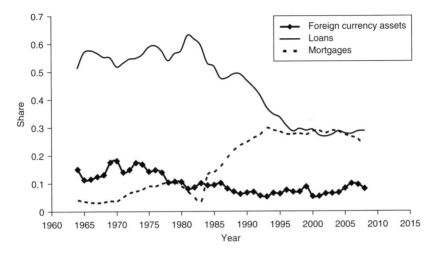

Source: Statistics Canada data from CANSIM Table 378-0001.

Figure 3.5 Proportions of Canadian bank assets

economy in the age of globalization'. Additionally, Klein states, 'I would go so far as to say that deep economic understanding of what has happened in the currency/financial crises of Latin America and East Asia (even the US S&L crisis) requires resorting to careful FF analysis' (p. 270). The same statement could be made with respect to analyzing of the current financial crisis. Therefore, Brox (2009) creates a model of the Canadian banking sector based on the financial-flow accounts of Canada and uses this model to make out-of-sample forecasts of the crisis period to show that the system has remained stable.

In the relatively short history of financial model building, many models have tended to abandon asset demand and supply in favour of a term-structure approach for determining interest rates, as do the US financial models of Tinbergen (1939), de Leeuw (1969), and Silber (1970). Others, following the Brainard and Tobin (1968) 'pitfalls' paper, impose the sources-equal-uses balance-sheet approach, as do the US financial flow models by Bosworth and Duesenberry (1973), Backus et al. (1980) and several UK models such as that in Green (1982). In Canada, a financial sector consisting of seven liquid asset demand equations has been part of the Bank of Canada's econometric model of the Canadian economy (1971). Hendershott (1977), in his US FF model, follows a quite different approach in estimating directly behavioural parameters of the asset demand and supply equations.

The model of Brox and Maclean (1986), for the Canadian non-financial corporate sector, is most heavily influenced by Hendershott's study. Brox and Cornwall (1989) estimate a 110 equation model for the entire Canadian financial-flow matrix. Brox (2009) updates the banking sector of this model to test for stability of the system and to incorporate recent developments. The resulting similarity of approach allows some comparison of US and Canadian financial behaviour.

To specify the model for any sector, we begin with the balance-sheet identity:

$$NW = RA + \Sigma_i F_i, \tag{3.1}$$

which states that net worth (NW) is equal to real assets (RA) plus the sum of financial assets and negatively signed liabilities (F). For the flows model, consistent with the published data, we take the first difference of equation (3.1), and subtract valuation changes from the assets where they accrue to obtain:

$$SAV = \Delta RA + \Sigma_i \Delta Fi. \tag{3.2}$$

The typical asset demand or supply equation for estimation is:

$$\Delta F_i + a_{i1}SAV + a_{i2}\Delta RA + \Sigma_i b_{ij}X_j. \tag{3.3}$$

where X_j represents portfolio shift variables, including interest rates and economic activity indicators. The balance-sheet identity (3.2) implies the following constraints:

$$\Sigma_i a_{i1} = 1; \ \Sigma_i a_{i2} = -1; \ \Sigma_i b_i = 0 \tag{3.4}$$

The Canadian financial-flow data, published quarterly by Statistics Canada, are, for the most part, consistent with other data in the System of National Accounts. Details of the data sources and the specification of and estimation of the model of the banking sector are found in Brox (2009).

Given the importance placed on mortgage lending to the stability of banking in this chapter, we reproduce the results for the mortgage equation here:

$$\Delta MOR = 0.038\Delta LM + 0.183\Delta LFOR - 1851.0 + 716.68S_1 + 987.54S_2$$

$$- 294.40S_3 + 0.62\Delta TFA_{-1} + 0.002\Delta GDP + 0.0009\Delta INFL$$

$$- 0.0019NAFTA + 0.0026\Delta RMT - 0.0005\Delta RPM. \tag{3.5}$$

These results indicate that initially Canadian banks invest approximately 4 percent of new domestic deposits in mortgages. Additionally 18 percent of new foreign funds raised are invested in mortgage holdings. Everything else constant, 60 percent of new assets are reallocated to mortgages in a lagged portfolio adjustment. As expected, mortgage holdings are positively related to changes in the mortgage rate, increases in general economic activity (GDP), and increases in the rate of inflation, and negatively related to general lending rates. Perhaps surprisingly, mortgage lending has been negatively affected by the changes in the financial system following the formation of NAFTA.

The out-of-sample forecasts for all nine equations in the model produced Theils's U-statistics less than unity (mortgages have a U-stat of 0.475), indicating that the model is performing exceedingly well. In addition, the bias component of the error never exceeds 7 percent. These forecasts confirm that the Canadian banking system has operated in a business-as-usual fashion during the financial crisis. Further details of the modelling and forecast results are presented in Brox (2009).

5   CONCLUSIONS

Until recently, Canadian banks have been criticized as being too small and too conservative. In the late 1990s and early 2000s a number of the larger banks attempted to merge to become more competitive. The government of the day refused the required permission for the mergers. However, a recent report by Bloomberg News (Pasternak and Alexander, 2009) puts four Canadian banks among North America's top 10, and in October 2008 the World Economic Forum ranked Canada as the soundest financial system (WEF, 2008). Indeed, former Prime Minister Jean Chrétien was recently quoted as saying that the high ranking of the largest Canadian banks shows that he made the right decision a decade ago when he prevented the banks from merging to become US-style banking giants.[3] In the same week Prime Minister Stephen Harper said on US television that Canada has achieved a balance in the regulation of its banks that will serve the country well once the global economy begins to recover.[4]

In the fourth quarter of 2008 all of the big six Canadian banks made profits,[5] although lower than those made the year earlier. None received a government bailout. In contrast, in the same period American banks lost more than $25 billion and more than 25 banks failed, more than the total number of domestic banks in Canada. Why have the Canadian banks outperformed their American counterparts? They have more capital reserves, partly because of their conservative business practices and partly because of the requirements of the OSFI. Again, because of the more conservative business practices of the Canadian banks, they have not been as exposed to the American subprime mortgage market or other high-risk derivative securities. The government's refusal to permit mergers, both domestically and with large multinational banks, has reinforced this conservative behaviour.

Why has Canada been alone in the Western world in its ability to withstand this crisis? The answer would appear to be because of the conservative lending practices of the Canadian banks and because of a better regulatory regime.

The housing mortgage market in Canada is also a factor. Lending has been more conservative, with those being unable to afford housing being denied mortgages. Additionally, the fact that mortgage interest costs are not tax deductible, while interest costs for many other investments are, causes Canadians to repay the mortgage debt that they take on.

NOTES

1. The bank rate was set at 0.25 percent in mid-2009.
2. For details on the development and differences between the Canadian and American banking systems see Mishkin and Serletis (2004).
3. Source: CTV news service, 'Banks rise in ranking amid credit crisis', available at: http://www.ctv.ca/servlet/ArtileNews/story/CTVNews/20090317 (accessed September 15, 2009).
4. Source: CBC News, 'Harper credits regulation for preventing bank bailouts', available at: http://www.cbc.ca/money/story/2009/03/29 (accessed September 15, 2009).
5. The total profits of the big six Canadian banks in the quarter ending January 31, 2009 was slightly more than Can $3 billion.

REFERENCES

Backus, D., Brainard, W.C., Smith, G. and Tobin, J. (1980), 'A model of US financial and nonfinancial behaviour', *Journal of Money, Credit and Banking*, **12**, 159–93.

Baker, M.J., Miceli, T.J., Thomas, J. and Sirmans, C.F. (2008), 'An economic theory of mortgage redemption laws', *Real Estate Economics*, **36** (1), 31–45.

Bosworth, B. and Duesenberry, J.S. (1973), 'A flow of funds model and its implications', *Issues in Federal Debt Management*, Federal Reserve Bank of Boston, 39–149.

Brainard, W.C. and Tobin, J. (1968), 'Pitfalls in financial model building', *American Economic Review*, **58**, 99–122.

Brox, J.A. (2009), 'Too small to fail: Canadian banks, regulation, and the North American financial crisis', *Journal of Economic Asymmetries*, **6** (2), 31–46.

Brox, J.A. and Cornwall, W.A. (1989), *A Model of the Canadian Financial Flow Matrix*, Ottawa: Statistics Canada.

Brox, J.A. and Maclean, W.A. (1986), 'The financial behaviour of Canadian private corporations and government enterprise: a flow of funds analysis', *Bulletin of Economic Research*, **38**, 49–66.

Carr, J.L. and Floyd, J.E. (2002), 'Real and monetary shocks to the Canadian dollar: do Canada and the United States form an optimal currency area?', *North American Journal of Economics and Finance*, **13**, 21–39.

Courchene, T.J. and Harris, R.G. (2000), 'North American monetary union: analytical principles and guidelines', *North American Journal of Economics and Finance*, **11** (1), 3–18.

deLeeuw, F. (1969), 'A condensed model of financial behaviour', in Duesenberry, J.S., Fromm, G., Klien, L.R., and Kuh, E. (eds), *The Brookings Model: Some Further Results*, Washington, DC: Brookings Institute, pp. 465–530.

Dunning, W. (2008), 'Risks are contained within the Canadian mortgage market', Canadian Association of Accredited Mortgage Professionals, October.

Ewing, B.T., Payne, J.E. and Sowell, C. (1999), 'NAFTA and North American stock market linkages: an empirical note', *North American Journal of Economics and Finance*, **10** (2), 443–51.

Freedman, C. (1998), 'The Canadian Banking System', Bank of Canada Technical Report No. 81, March.

Green, C.J. (1982), 'Monetary policy and the structure of interest rates in the United Kingdom', unpublished PhD dissertation, Yale University.

Grubel, H.G. (2000), 'The merit of Canada–US monetary union', *North American Journal of Economics and Finance*, **11** (1), 19–40.

Harris, R. and Ragonetti, D. (1998), 'Where credit is due: residential mortgage finance in Canada, 1901 to 1954', *Journal of Real Estate Finance and Economics*, **16** (2), 223–38.

Hendershott, P.H. (1977), *Understanding Capital Markets: Vol. 1: A Flow of Funds Model*, Lexington, MA: Lexington Books.

IMF Staff (2009), *IMF Country Report: Canada*, Washington, DC: International Monetary Fund, May.

Kiff, J. (2009), 'Canadian residential mortgage markets: boring but effective?', International Monetary Fund Working Paper 09–130, June.

Klein, L.R. (2003), 'Some potential linkages for input–output analysis with flow-of-funds', *Economic Systems Research*, **15** (3), 269–77.

Klump, G. (2009), 'National resale housing continues to rise in May', CREA News, available at: http://creanews.ca/2009/06/15/national-resale-housing-continues-to-rise-in-may/ (accessed September 15, 2009).

Klyuev, V. (2008), 'Show me the money: access to finance for small borrowers in Canada', International Monetary Fund Working Paper 08–22, January.

Michelis, L. (2004), 'Prospects of a monetary union in North America: an empirical investigation', in Michelis, L. and Lovewell, M. (eds), *Exchanges Rates, Economic Integration and the International Economy*, Toronto: Athenian Policy Forum Press, pp. 114–35.

Mishkin, F.S. and Serletis, A. (2004), *The Economics of Money, Banking, and Financial Markets*, Toronto: Addison-Wesley.

Mizen, P. (2008), 'The credit crunch of 2007–2008: a discussion of the background, market reactions, and policy responses', *Federal Reserve Bank of St. Louis Review*, **90** (5): 531–67.

Murray, J., Schembri, L. and St-Amant, P. (2003), 'Revisiting the case for flexible exchange rates', *North American Journal of Economics and Finance*, **14**, 207–40.

Paraskevopoulos, C.C., Paschakis, J. and Smithin, J. (1996), 'Financial integration between Canada and the US: an empirical analysis', in Paraskevopoulos, C.C., Grinspun, R. and Eaton, G.E. (eds), *Economic Integration in the Americas*, Cheltenham, UK and Brookfield, VT: Edward Elgar, pp. 9–20.

Pasternak, S.B. and Alexander, D. (2009), 'Canada's banks climb in rankings as US giants stumble', *Bloomberg News*, Monday, March 16.

Salehizadeh, M. (1998), 'Financial flows to Mexico: implications for foreign investors', *The International Trade Journal*, **12**, 23–48.

Serletis, A. and Krause, D. (1996), 'Empirical evidence on the long-run neutrality hypothesis using low-frequency international data', *Economics Letters*, **50** (3), 323–7.

Silber, W.L. (1970), *Portfolio Behaviour of Financial Institutions*, New York: Holt, Rhinehart & Winston.

Tinbergen, J. (1939), *Business Cycles in the United States of America, 1919–1932*, Geneva: League of Nations.

Torrance, M.I. (2008), 'Forcing global governance? Urban infrastructures as networked financial products', *International Journal of Urban and Regional Research*, **32** (1), 1–21.

Trivoli, G.W. and Graham, R.G. (1998), 'Strategic factors for trading and investing in Latin America by US businesses during the post-NAFTA era', *Atlantic Economic Journal* **26**, 129–36.

Van Roy, P. (2008), 'Capital requirements and bank behaviour in the early 1990s: cross-country evidence', *International Journal of Central Banking*, **4** (3), 29–60.

Wagster, J.D. (2007), 'Wealth and risk effects of adopting deposit insurance in Canada: evidence of risk shifting by banks and trust companies', *Journal of Money, Credit and Banking*, **39** (7), 1651–81.

Wheelock, D.C. (2008), 'The federal response to home mortgage distress: lessons from the Great Depression', *Federal Reserve Bank of St. Louis Review*, **90** (3), 133–48.

World Economic Forum (WEF) (2008), *The Financial Development Report 2008*, Geneva: World Economic Forum.

PART II

Europe

4. The German banking system and the financial crisis

Horst Gischer and Peter Reichling

1 INTRODUCTION

Although the blazing fire of the international financial crisis seems to be extinguished, its causes are still being analyzed. The attention of economic and political circles is still focused on the issue of who is responsible for the crisis. However, being rich in mutual allegations of careless risk handling, this debate has not resulted in an appropriate mechanism which would help to avoid similar financial market shocks in the future.

In contrast to the above-mentioned discussion, our contribution omits the question of responsibility. Instead, emphasis is placed on the consequences of the financial crisis for national and international markets. In the following, we attempt to contribute to the discussion about an appropriate and reasonable architecture of financial markets. For any debate of this kind, it is indispensable to consider the special features of national economies, which are known in the literature under the term 'corporate governance'.

This chapter focuses on the German banking system, which has been criticized as inefficient, non-productive and in need of consolidation.[1] However, the German banking system turned out to be especially insusceptible to exogenous shocks, such as the current crises. Therefore, our attention is primarily concentrated in the institutional agents in the German financial market.

A special focus is on the issue of the strategic direction of bank business models that concentrate on particular business areas and client segments. This differentiation is supplemented by a regional component, which is of fundamental importance for particular banking institutions in Germany.

2 INSTITUTIONAL FRAMEWORK

A striking feature of the German banking system is the coexistence of three rival groups of banking institutions, namely commercial banks (including

Table 4.1   Corporate governance characteristics of banking systems

Corporate governance system	Anglo-Saxon system	Continental European system
Business objective	Maximize shareholder value	Corporate interest (stakeholder value approach)
Investment projects	Marketable	Company specific
Time horizon	Short term	Long term
Protective mechanism	Flexible capital and labor markets	Codetermination and control rights

the so-called 'big banks'), savings banks, and mutual cooperative banks. While commercial and mutual cooperative banks are privately owned, saving banks are public property. All three groups are 'universal banks', which offer a wide range of financial services. Consequently, all banks are subject to identical supervisory regulations.

Table 4.1 shows that the corporate governance framework of German banks differs greatly from the Anglo-Saxon system.[2] Specifically, savings banks and mutual cooperative banks concentrate mainly on the needs of their clients, and they are not very involved in international capital market operations. They extend credit primarily to small- and medium-sized enterprises, and offer deposit services to retail banking customers.

Concentration on regional markets, which is one of the main characteristics of savings and mutual cooperative banks, requires a high ability to adapt to the economic conditions of the respective region. Especially in relatively sparsely populated areas with an agricultural focus and a poorly diversified industrial structure, savings and mutual cooperative banks are often the only accessible financial service providers. However, because of the below-average prosperity of such regions, only a limited profitable banking business is possible in these areas.

Figure 4.1 illustrates the different focuses of business segments of various German banking groups.[3] More than one-third of deposits in large commercial banks come from abroad. In contrast, foreign deposits account for less than 5 percent of all deposits in the case of savings and mutual cooperative banks. While savings and mutual cooperative banks grant loans mostly to domestic clients, large commercial banks concentrate on foreign debtors. Thus, the three banking groups focus on different business areas.

Consequently, performance and risk ratios vary across the three banking groups. On the one hand, savings and mutual cooperative banks are active

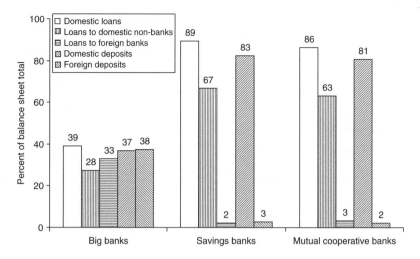

Figure 4.1   Balance-sheet structure of German banking groups

in regionally limited markets, whose performance can easily be evaluated. Consequently, credit risks can easily be monitored and estimated. On the other hand, rural areas are greatly affected by economic monoculture. Therefore, there is a risk of dependency and so-called 'bulk risks'. In contrast, commercial banks possess better opportunities to diversify credit risk owing to their international business relations. Due to their global presence, commercial banks are also able to exploit international return differences.

In net terms, savings and mutual cooperative banks performed better than the commercial banks during the past two decades. Not only did they achieve a higher average return on equity, but also the volatility of equity returns was much lower than that of commercial banks (see Figure 4.2). At least from an empirical perspective, the business model of regionally oriented banks has proved its worth.

We summarize our first findings with regard to German banking groups as follows:

1. single banking groups are very differently positioned.
2. the risk of big banks is on average not compensated by appropriate returns; and
3. small entities can successfully sustain their position in the banking market.

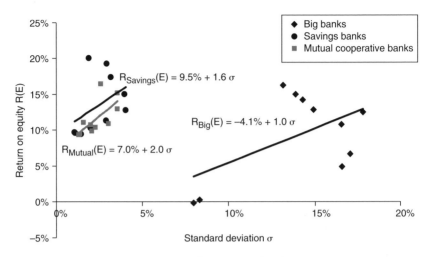

*Figure 4.2   Capital market lines for German banking groups, 1994–2007
(five-year moving averages)*

3   TRACES OF THE FINANCIAL CRISIS

The international financial crisis has put German banks under extreme pressure. As shown in Table 4.2, banking profits declined sharply in 2008, with a loss of about €25 billion. The financial crises had a different effect on the three banking groups. Commercial banks, in particular big banks, suffered most from the crisis. Savings and mutual cooperative banks, although they also reported a decline in earnings, were still profitable.[4]

Writedowns on credits, securities, and outstanding accounts were a decisive factor in explaining the different performances of the banking groups (so-called 'valuation yield'). Compared to 2007, the valuation expenses of all banking groups increased by more than 50 percent and amounted to €37 billion in 2008. Commercial banks had to increase their provision for risks by about €5 billion (more than 100 percent). The big banks accounted for half of this amount.

In contrast, savings and mutual cooperative banks got off lightly. Valuation expenses of the savings banks increased by €0.4 billion, and those for mutual cooperative banks increased by €0.9 billion. The direct consequences of the financial crisis were considerably more transparent for these two groups of institutions. This asymmetry will be of vital importance for the following argumentation.

Table 4.2   Performance of German banking groups in 2007/2008 (€m)

	Operating result before valuation		Operating result		Profit for the financial year before tax	
	2007	2008	2007	2008	2007	2008
All banking groups	44.060	28.419	20.457	−8.148	20.531	−25.011
Commercial banks	19.806	2.356	14.927	−7.768	18.726	−16.443
Big banks	11.887	−4.974	9.081	−12.015	15.290	−17.833
Savings banks	8.499	8.577	4.123	3.685	3.759	2.171
Cooperative mutual banks	5.475	5.996	2.761	2.380	2.880	2.054

4   DECISION FIELDS OF BUSINESS POLICY

Many different factors have to be taken into account in order to determine an appropriate banking business strategy. We focus on some crucial factors that affect banks' profitability.

Prerequisites for Investment Banking

The German banking system is characterized by universal banking. Nevertheless, some banks have a narrower focus of operation, which is the main difference between the different banking groups.

In a narrow sense, investment banking requires efficient structures within a bank, which possess the following characteristics:

- pronounced market knowledge;
- well-developed international experiences;
- highly qualified staff; and
- above-average refinancing volumes.

The importance of these requirements becomes clear if a capital increase of a listed company or an initial public offering of a medium-sized enterprise is taken as an example. In the case of an equity issue, thorough planning is required. In this context, the bank provides an expert report regarding the stock market development. The more often the bank has conducted operations of this kind, the better it gets at making such valuation estimates. It is apparent that a specialized and experienced staff is required for this purpose. Such employees are more likely to be found in big banks, where they are well paid and, therefore, show higher employee retention.

Especially in narrow markets, an accompanying underwriting by the bank is necessary, that is, there is a possibility of a sequential sale of the newly issued shares to the public by the underwriter. This is only assured in cases where the investment bank possesses appropriate access to capital markets in order to refinance the required volumes. In the light of these requirements, investment banking is not lucrative enough for small banks.

Options in Commercial Banking

In contrast to investment banking, the transaction volumes in the field of commercial banking are more straightforward. Nevertheless, in this business segment a bank must have appropriate structures and proficiencies in order to stay competitive. For example, if a bank wants to focus on retail banking customers, it must take into account higher sales and marketing expenditures.

Small lot sizes and highly intensive consulting services depress the spreads, which can only be improved through a standardized volume business. The variety of products and customer expectations can be conciliated through cooperation with insurance companies and building societies. Benefits of the orientation on private customers include the opportunity to attract private investments at a relatively low cost. In cases of a dynamic lending business, an attractive interest rate spread can be generated.

Another target group of commercial banking is craftsmen and freelancers. Even smaller banks can support business start-ups in this segment, providing appropriate financial service packages. Their role facilitates access to clients and the opportunity to cross-sell products and services. One disadvantage of such an orientation towards private customers is in the difficulty of estimating risks. Moreover, in regions with limited economic diversification, bulk risks may occur.

Traditional corporate banking represents one of the cornerstones of commercial banking. Thorough and up-to-date industry knowledge is considerably helpful to regionally oriented credit institutions. Among the drawbacks are the strong need for consultation and very intensive market monitoring. In addition, room for maneuver is possibly limited by long periods of commitments.

Regional Orientation

Strategic decisions concerning the regional orientation of a bank is of vital importance. In principle, the following options exist. The bank can be:

(i) centralized; (ii) regionally oriented; or (iii) virtual.

The centralization strategy requires a compromise between potential advantages from being close to the clients and high costs of a comprehensive office network. In practice, the greater the distance to the central institution, the lower is the branch office density. As a result, decision-making processes become longer and customer relations suffer from the lack of competence of local branch managers.

Banks with a regional focus underline their customer proximity through a high density of branch offices. Although flat hierarchies with sufficient on-site decision authorities strengthen customer retention, they also entail remarkably high personnel costs. In addition, the quasi-fixed costs of opening a branch office in a sparsely populated area reduce returns.

Internet banking helps to decrease personnel expenses significantly. A so-called 'direct bank' anonymously takes standardized orders without any direct customer contact. The crucial benefit of internet banking for clients is the almost unlimited availability of access to banking products and services. Furthermore, there are no consultancy fees. However, clients are solely responsible for their individual transactions.

Especially in the electronic banking segment, almost all financial service providers are represented, with more or less extensive offers. In this respect, there are many possibilities for combining several basic alternatives. Nevertheless, the regional priorities of the particular banking groups differ significantly.

Corporate Philosophy

The three dominant banking groups in Germany are primarily different with respect to their corporate philosophy. Commercial banks follow the distinctive strategy of profit maximization. They are primarily oriented on their shareholder value. Return on equity also represents a prominent target parameter that is often associated with consistent cost orientation.

In contrast, savings banks act on behalf of a statutory public contract. They are committed to public welfare. Thus, they have a special position within the banking system. Although profit maximization is not a primary business objective of savings banks, cost-covering revenues are intended and presumed. However, the absolute level of periodical net income is not their main objective. Nevertheless, profits should be high enough to ensure an appropriate growth to meet capital requirements.

A basic characteristic of mutual cooperative banks is the membership of single investors in a syndicate (terminable on demand). In Germany, the rights and duties of registered cooperatives' members are regulated by law. Their goal is to make a profit, and to share it with their members.

Commercial Profile

The past six decades have demonstrated that the completely different corporate philosophies of the three banking groups successfully coexisted in a competitive environment. Commercial banks, savings banks, and mutual cooperative banks offer special business models, which differ from one another in some properties that are briefly outlined here. The results of the analysis can be represented in a radar diagram of the various business profiles (see Figure 4.3).

As previously mentioned, the choice of our comparison criteria may not be complete. Furthermore, our more or less subjective assessment of the realizations within the banking groups is of course open to debate. Nevertheless, the presented business profiles allow a first impression about the main focuses of the strategic business operations of German banks.

Each category is normalized from 1 to 5, so that the highest impact in a single category is assigned a value of 5. Figure 4.3 presents the differences and similarities between the particular banking groups concerning their business model. A 'typical' credit bank is characterized by the goal of making profits, the relative strength of investment banking, and the access to refinancing potential. Comparative advantages of savings banks and mutual cooperative banks are strong customer orientation and they serve as banks for (average) private clients. The closest proximity of all the banking groups can be found in the area of (medium-sized) corporate customer services.

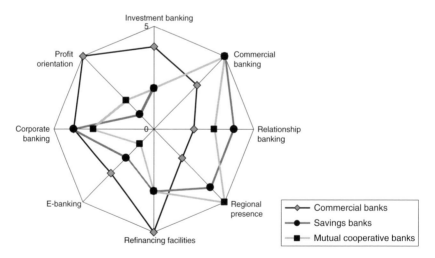

Figure 4.3   Business profiles of German banking groups

5 CONCLUSION

Compared to other international banking systems, the German banking system is at a disadvantage by being extremely difficult for foreigners to comprehend. The legal specifics of public savings banks and mutual cooperative banks are not immediately evident to outsiders. Frequently, a thorough study of the respective regulations is necessary. Poor knowledge of the real competitive relationships of the banking system constitutes a common reason for a misconceived evaluation of the German financial markets.

Monopoly- and oligopoly-like market structures in economically less prosperous regions are not the consequence of government subsidies to savings banks, but, as Figure 4.3 showed, a consequence of the conscious and strategically targeted retreat of the big banks from rural areas.[5] Different business profiles and strategies of single bank groups are the actual causes of the observed market structures, not the legal framework. This coexistence of banks with different business focuses proved to be an invaluable stabilization factor during the financial crisis. The feared knock-on effects could not be observed in Germany. The great number of small- and medium-sized banks significantly reduced the danger of systematic risks. The German Council of Economic Experts (GCEE) has emphasized in a special report (2008) that the current faults at the international financial markets were much better absorbed by the German banking system than in the USA or other industrialized countries.

This, however, does not imply that the current German financial market structure is established on a continuing basis. Access to the German banking market is open for national as well as for international providers. A prerequisite for a permanently successful competitive position is a business model which is attractive and innovative enough to close existing gaps in customer supply.

NOTES

1. See, for example, Brunner et al. (2004), as well as GCEE (2004 und 2008).
2. See Gischer et al. (2007).
3. See GCEE (2008).
4. See Bundesbank (2009). The German banking groups included in Table 4.2 are only those that are relevant for our chapter. Therefore, the list of banking institutions is not complete.
5. For a more extensive discussion see Gischer and Stiele (2009).

REFERENCES

Brunner, A., J. Decressin, D.C.L. Hardy and B. Kudela (2004), 'Germany's three-pillar banking system – cross country perspectives in Europe', International Monetary Fund Occasional Paper 233, Washington, DC.

Bundesbank (2009), 'The performance of German credit institutions in 2008', *Monthly Report*, **61**, September, 33–62.

German Council of Economic Experts (GCEE) (2004), 'External successes – internal challenges', Annual Report 2004/05.

German Council of Economic Experts (GCEE) (2008), 'The German financial system: improving efficiency – enhancing stability', Special Report, June.

Gischer, H. and M. Stiele (2009), 'Competition tests with a non-structural mode: the Panzar–Rosse method applied to Germany's savings banks, *German Economic Review*, **10**, 50–70.

Gischer, H., P. Reichling and M. Stiele (2007), 'Germany's three-pillar banking system from a corporate governance perspective', in B.E. Gup (ed.), *Corporate Governance in Banking: A Global Perspective*, Cheltenham, UK and Northampton, MA, USA: Edward Elgar, pp. 234–51.

5. No free lunch – no decoupling, the crisis and Hungary: a case study

Júlia Király and Katalin Mérő

1 INTRODUCTION

The financial crisis hit the developed countries first. In the summer of 2008, one of the main topics in blogs and journals was whether there would be a decoupling effect, and whether the emerging markets would be affected by the crisis. Then came the Lehman shock and the decoupling story was soon replaced by the recoupling story. Hungary was one country that was severely hit by the Lehman shock after more than a year of relative calm.

In traditional contagion theories, contagion is basically geographical in nature, and non-epicentre countries can primarily be affected by a crisis through foreign trade relations. In the recent approaches, money and capital markets are the determining channels of contagion. The literature investigates several possible channels of contagion, and highlights the spillover effects, the importance of portfolio decisions and the close 'inter-linking' of markets (Kaminsky et al., 2003; Schinasi and Smith, 2000). However, there is still no consensus regarding the underlying reasons for, and the strength and exact effect of the contagion spreading through global financial markets. Some suggest that the crises were triggered and their fast spread was fostered by the rapid capital market liberalisation forced onto the developing countries, while others think that the crises were less devastating in the liberalised markets, and recovery there was also quicker.[1]

The analysis of contagion that is not built directly on economic relations has strengthened, particularly since the Russian crisis, as the starting event in that crisis – the Russian state suspending the payments on its bonds – resulted in much more severe consequences in (seemingly) very remote markets than the Mexican and Asian crises in 1994–95 and 1997, respectively. On the one hand, the crisis had a strong impact on the economies of remote countries (such as Hong Kong, Brazil and Mexico), which did not have a close relationship with the Russian economy, and on the other, it strongly affected the markets of risky products of developed countries as well. Following the outbreak of the Russian crisis, risks were revalued on a global scale, all risky investments depreciated, risk premia soared, and investors turned to lower-risk products (flight to quality). This was the crisis that – mainly through the Long Term Capital Management (LTCM) episode – drew attention to the danger that high-leverage financing may result in contagion, as the shortage of market liquidity caused financing problems then as well, and high-leverage funds were simultaneously pulled out of geographical regions which seemingly did not have any relationship with one another.

In this sense, the crisis in 2007 is most similar to the Russian one, with one significant difference: the crisis spread from the financial markets of the developed countries to the financial markets and economies of the emerging countries. As Stanley Fisher suggested: 'In contrast to most of the financial crises of the previous decade, which started in emerging market countries, this crisis got underway in the centre of the global system – in the United States – and spread outwards. In the words of Guillermo Ortiz, Governor of the Banco de Mexico, in August 2007: This time it wasn't us' (Fischer, 2009).

The chapter analyses the effects of this special crisis on a vulnerable economy, namely on Hungary in the pre- and post-Lehman period and then summarises the actions of the authorities, specifically those of the Magyar Nemzeti Bank (MNB, the Hungarian central bank) and the Hungarian Financial Supervisory Authority (HFSA).

2   THE CRISIS AND HUNGARY

The Pre-Lehman Period: Side-effects of the Tornado

Typical emerging economies were not directly exposed to the subprime mortgage market. Neither US mortgage bonds nor other toxic assets had spread in the emerging markets. That is why the 'decoupling theory' evolved: if toxic assets and the subsequent losses could be avoided, then neither the financial markets nor the real economy should suffer from the consequences of the financial turmoil.

Nevertheless, due to the strong integration of financial markets, these countries were affected by the side-effects of the crisis, basically through two channels. On the one hand, funding costs increased, due to the liquidity squeeze and the increased liquidity premium (Király et al. 2008). On the other, market turbulence affected almost all countries, as the financial turmoil that emerged in the structured product markets slowly spread to other market segments.

In the case of countries integrated into the international financial system, exposure to external financial contagions depends greatly on the given country's fundamentals or, more exactly, on the assessment of such by investors. Of course, this assessment is subjective and changing, and is able to drift away from reality, especially in the event of market panics. This can explain the paradoxical phenomenon that although the subprime mortgage loan market afflicted the US economy the most, investors still considered US government securities to be the safest option, withdrawing their investments from regions and countries deemed volatile, where this resulted in a sharp increase in the risk premium.

In mid-2007, opinion regarding Hungary was quite unfavourable, due to the fiscal deficit, which was very high by European standards, the low growth rate, the high current account deficit and mounting external debt. In this market atmosphere, it did not even matter that most of the important indicators were already showing improvement in terms of their dynamics, and that – in contrast to many other countries – the increase in household mortgage loans which suddenly received special attention had not entailed a rapid increase in real estate prices, that is, no real estate price bubble had evolved. Markets ignored positive news in the same way that they had not 'punished' the deterioration in Hungary's macroeconomic indicators amidst the conditions of improving international risk appetite in previous years.

The increase in risk premium can appear in individual assets to various degrees, and the distribution of an external shock partly depends on the monetary policy regime of the given country as well. In the case of a currency board system, the exchange rate and the domestic interest rate level are given, and thus an increase in the premium cannot appear in these items. In countries that apply a free floating system, it is usually depreciation of the exchange rate which absorbs the greater part of the increase in the premium. This explains the fact that while the forint temporarily depreciated and domestic yields increased, the depreciation seen in 2007–08 proved to be a minor episode. In the summer of 2008 the Hungarian forint was stronger than ever before. The risk premium provided through the increased yield curve covered the risk appetite of investors. The credit default swap (CDS) spread of the country increased – but did not jump, as it deteriorated rather slowly (see Figure 5.1).

In March of 2008 there was a sudden jump, due to the frictions in the government bond market. It was that period of the crisis when contagion reached the T-bond markets, resulting in renewed turbulence all over the world. In Hungary, extreme price fluctuations and widening interest rate swap spreads were accompanying features (see the MNB's 'Report on Financial Stability', April 2008). During the summer of 2008

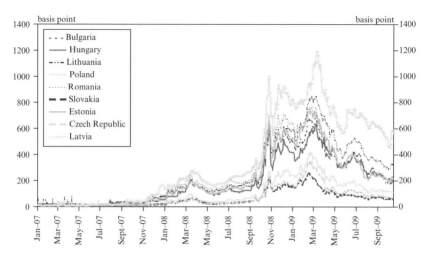

Source: Thomson Financial Datastream.

*Figure 5.1   Developments in selected countries' five-year CDS spreads
(January 2007–November 2009)*

the market turbulence seemed to be over, and foreign investors bought more Hungarian government paper than they sold during the spring turbulence.

Parent banks, as significant players on the European market, experienced the liquidity freeze and the increasing funding cost, although the majority of them did not have significant toxic asset exposure. Only KBC has had to write off substantial losses in the past two years, due to toxic assets, amounting to €4 billion. The exposure of the other bank groups amounted to only a few hundred million euros, and no related large losses have been revealed as of yet. Most parent banks, therefore, were not affected directly by the crisis via toxic assets, but the risk premia moving higher due to the increasingly widespread lack of confidence on financial markets, and drying up liquidity have made funding more difficult for all banks. The share prices of parent banks have fallen, albeit only slightly, while bank CDS premia have increased compared to the period of prosperity preceding the summer of 2007. Contracting money and capital market opportunities affected ties with subsidiaries as well: the direct financing of subsidiaries decreased overall – and funding through swaps gained a more prominent role.

This also meant that in the banking system, which is highly dependent on external funding, the loan/deposit (L/D) ratio by far exceeded 100 per cent; the duration of funding shortened, the maturity mismatch increased and the forex (FX) mismatch on the balance sheet also increased because of swap financing. By contrast, the risk of liquidity withdrawal increased due to intra-group fund reallocations in the banking systems ensuring intra-group funding (for example, in the Czech Republic and Slovakia). Parent banks did not constrain the activity of their subsidiaries, but did increase the cost of funding and replaced direct lending with swap lines, while at the same time shortening the duration of funding. This made the Hungarian banking sector more vulnerable. Nevertheless, in the year following the crisis until October 2008, the liquidity of the forint and FX swap markets had not deteriorated in comparison with the pre-crisis period. The daily functioning of Hungarian money markets seemed to be frictionless. The only signal of the crisis was a slight increase in the cost of funding in all markets. There was no material reaction in the overnight forint yield to news from abroad, nor was any extraordinary collateralised central bank credit extended. Domestic banks were affected by the increase in liquidity risks through the pricing and shortening of foreign interbank and capital market sources. The main effect was the shortening of maturities across all types of funding, since the drying-up effect on the capital markets made longer-term funds unavailable or very expensive for local banks. CDS spreads, which are used for the approximation of the prices of long-term liabilities, showed a very significant increase. The 150–200 basis point rise in CDS spreads observable since July 2007 is attributable to the increase in credit risks on the one hand and to the weakening of confidence in ratings on the other (see Figure 5.2).

All in all, during the pre-Lehman period the Hungarian financial sector did not undergo a serious shock. Banks' profits were increasing rapidly, and the average return on equity (ROE) was above 20 per cent. The growth rate of credit did not decrease, and indeed new extremely risky products appeared in the market: Japanese-yen (JYP)-based mortgage loans and unit-linked insurance-related mortgages. At the same time, broker-based selling increased to more than 50 per cent of total mortgage turnover. More than 90 per cent of new mortgage loans were denominated in Swiss Franc (CHF), and the average loan to value (LTV) ratio slowly climbed (at mid-2008 more than 50 per cent of total loans had an LTV of more than 70 per cent). Moreover, following initial tightening, commercial banks relaxed their lending criteria. Imbalances were slowly accumulating.

The Post-Lehman Period: The Avalanche Begins

On 15 September 2008, the failure of Lehman Brothers meant that 'anything can happen from now on' to investors, who had already been

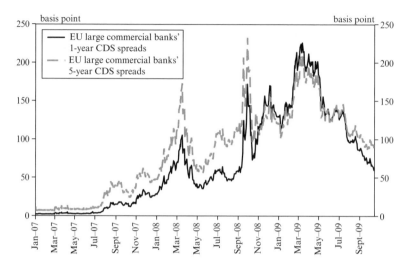

Source: Thomson Financial Datastream.

*Figure 5.2   Developments in short- and long-term risk premia, January
2007–November 2009*

gradually unwinding their positions. Price movements became chaotic
and non-linear with jumps. In each segment of the financial market, only
tail events could have been detected, as low-probability, high-loss events
became the order of the day.

Investors distinguished only two types of investment – 'risky' and
'safe' – with the earlier continuous spectrum between the two disappearing. The liquidity of markets deemed risky dried up, as bid–ask
spreads widened, prices moved chaotically, and quotations ground to
a halt on several markets. Risk premia in markets deemed safe (the US
and German government bond markets) fell to irrational lows, and on
markets deemed risky almost all other stock or bond markets soared to
irrational heights. The liquidity of markets most closely related to the
financial intermediary system collapsed, along with the share prices of
financial mediators. The prices of markets deemed to be even slightly
risky plunged. The volatility of all markets increased, and market liquidity dried up.

Not only did market liquidity disappear, but also funding liquidity.
Deleveraging exploded with an avalanche-like unwinding of positions,
with the ensuing panic and irrational investor behaviour becoming widespread. A desperate fight for evaporating financing liquidity was to ensue.
But nobody was providing funding liquidity any more:

> By September 2008 it seemed that the crisis was ongoing but not worsening. However, following the bankruptcy of Lehman Brothers (unsupported by the authorities) in mid-September, there was a sharp worsening of market conditions and the process of deleveraging became disorderly as counterparty risk perceptions ballooned. This began what can now be seen as the systemic period of the crisis. (Davis, 2009)

For a moment, the financial intermediary system was literally paralysed; interbank interest rates surged to unrealistic levels. Interbank interest rates followed a completely separate path, detaching themselves from central bank base rates and yields of safe government securities. More precisely, this meant that price signals no longer had a role to play. Liquidity for terms of over one day was no longer available at any price. The interbank market dried up, and financial intermediation collapsed. Central bank interventions could only keep some liquidity in the system by injecting it in larger and larger doses, while the US and European banking markets were increasingly being replaced by bilateral relationships between individual banks and the central bank. The once liquid and efficient banking system switched over to an expensive and ineffective mode of operation.

Shattered confidence in the banks was best reflected by the fact that the information content of the generally used capital adequacy ratio became devalued, as investors switched their attention to the strength of 'real' and 'immovable' capital: core tier 1 capital adequacy replaced capital adequacy as the focal point, and apparently investors would have liked every unit of bank investment or loan to be backed by one unit of capital. The world was gripped by panic about leverage still persisting and, as a consequence, funds disappearing with a sudden stop threatening to follow.

The severe declines in prices on the stock exchanges affected the banking sector most acutely. Market uncertainty left no actor unscathed. Global presence and an extensive network of subsidiaries (advantages in times of great moderation and ample liquidity) suddenly became a drawback, with large complex banking groups becoming synonymous with lack of transparency, and consequently gigantic losses were successively revealed at all such banks. The share prices of European bank groups with substantial international exposure plunged by 15–30 per cent in the two weeks following the failure of Lehman. They tried to regain lost depositor confidence by raising the ceiling on deposit guarantees and with unlimited payment guarantees ensured by the state.[2]

Emerging countries were even more deeply affected by the Lehman shock than the developed countries (Dooley and Hutchison, 2009), as share prices plunged more steeply, government security risk premia skyrocketed, CDS spreads became volatile and floating currencies lost much of their value (see Figure 5.3).

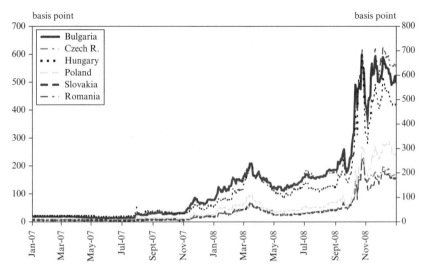

Source: Thomson Datastream.

Figure 5.3   Sovereign CDS spreads in some CEE countries (January 2005–January 2008)

The crisis was to affect each country but to varying degrees, with turbulence stronger in countries which were deemed more vulnerable, for example, the Baltic countries, Bulgaria, Romania and Hungary. When assessing vulnerability, investors primarily took into account a country's dependence on foreign financing (see Figure 5.4).

Investor analyses sharpening the market's focus on the vulnerabilities of the region appeared as early as the beginning of October. Fitch downgraded the three Baltic states on 3 October, drawing attention to the vulnerability of emerging Europe.

The indebtedness of the private sector was growing at a much faster pace than internal savings, a process further exacerbated in Hungary by the government's debt. This went hand in hand with a sharp spike in the banking sector's L/D ratio and a rise in the banking sector's foreign funds. In the eyes of foreign investors, an unquestionable sign of this vulnerability was the high ratio of FX-denominated loans.

The threat of a sudden stop, that is, the possibility of external financing no longer being available and the start of capital outflows, was considered by investors as a reality. Lack of market confidence in Hungary reached such a level that on 9 October 2008 the country's money markets – the FX swap market, the government bond market and the FX spot market

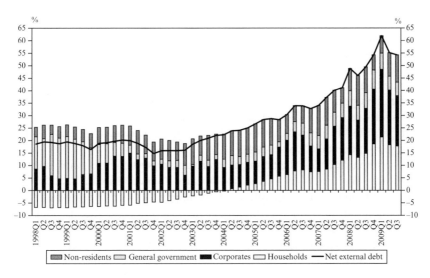

Source: MNB.

Figure 5.4 Net external debt/GDP in Hungary (1998Q1–2009Q2)

– were practically paralysed, the stock exchange index and prices started plummeting and the country found itself faced with the worst nightmare of a financial crisis. Vigorous government and central bank measures and the large IMF–EU package (€20 billion), however, helped stabilise the country and improve its external assessment.

One fundamental factor in the 'Hungarian crisis' was the freezing of the swap market. Among the countries in the region examined, the Hungarian market was the most heavily dependent on short-term swap market financing, and, as described above, longer, on-balance sheet financing progressively substituted dependence on the swap market from the middle of 2007. In October 2008, the faltering operation of European interbank markets in the post-Lehman period did not leave this segment (which is insignificant in a European dimension, but pivotal in Hungary) unaffected. The sudden drop in limits on the swap market (a clear sign of lacking interbank confidence) endangered the day-to-day operation of the banking system.

Regarding the region's vulnerabilities, the reliance on external funding and the high ratio of FX-denominated loans were crucial, but the threat of a possible withdrawal of funds by parent banks had already emerged. Stabilising the situation was impossible without the intervention of parent banks: in the period following October, parent banks' financing increased in both relative and absolute terms. The rollover of maturing foreign funds was ensured mainly by parent banks, and an increasing contribution was observable in both direct financing and FX swap financing-based liquidity generation. However, the conditions of available liquidity (that is, maturity and cost) deteriorated. Higher funding costs were the result of two main opposing factors: while short-term euro-denominated interbank rates fell due to the monetary easing in the euro area, this was largely over-compensated by rising Central and Eastern European (CEE) countries' and parent banks' CDS spreads.

The impairment of the financial intermediary system also paralysed the economy. Warning signs started to appear with increasing intensity in the post-Lehman period from autumn 2008, in parallel with the radical fall in funding liquidity. Global economic growth slowed dramatically, and US and European growth prospects gradually deteriorated. Official forecasts had to be adjusted practically every month, and the deep recession on the two continents became apparent by early 2009. The two most important problems were liquidity and economic stimulus measures. As a result of the European Central Bank's (ECB's) policy focusing strictly on the euro area, banks operating in the non-euro area (although based in the EU) could not access euro liquidity, or if they could, it was at best through their parent banks. For the holders of bonds denominated in local currency, these securities did not mean extra liquidity, so demand for these instruments fell dramatically. The other problem lay in the clearly protectionist nature of the economic stimulus packages, which focused on stimulating their own economies.

Stabilisation of their own banking systems was the top priority of every government, and hence they did not necessarily promote the strengthening of cross-border financing. Home-country policy clearly restrained Central European subsidiary banks' propensity to take risks and the objectives formulated by parent banks increasingly included pushing down the L/D ratio (and simultaneously reducing dependence on foreign parent banks' funds) and limiting risk-weighted assets, that is, shifting lending towards the least risky segments. This meant restraining corporate lending and FX-denominated lending by subsidiaries. All this clearly led to a deterioration in the assessment of the region.[3]

The 2009 recession gravely affected the CEE region and Hungary in particular. Demand in key export markets fell, so traditional commercial openness resulted in not only a slowdown in growth but also a serious decline in GDP. Recession, coupled with currency depreciation, resulted in a strong deterioration in the portfolio quality of local banks. Although no significant portfolio quality deterioration was observed until the beginning of 2009, there were signs that the share of non-performing loans

(NPLs) was increasing. The unexpectedly deep recession and the threat of portfolio deterioration reminded analysts of the banking crisis caused by the transition crisis in the 1990s, when NPLs approached 25–30 per cent. Despite accurate central bank analyses forecasting a maximum NPL rate of 10–12 per cent for 2010, analyst rumours spread rapidly, significantly undermining the assessment of the region and bank groups with substantial exposure in the region.

Investor analyses drawing attention to the region's 'especially risky position' and to the extremely large Eastern European exposures of certain Western European bank groups – namely Austrian, Italian and Belgian bank groups – and the resulting 'terribly high' losses were to appear as early as the beginning of February. These reports referred to Eastern Europe as the riskiest region – which was further reinforced by the headlines of respected economic newspapers: 'Eastern Europe: Argentina on the Danube?' (*The Economist*, 2009a); 'Eastern European crisis may put us all in the goulash' (King, 2009); 'Eastern Europe's woes: the bill that could break up Europe' (*The Economist*, 2009b); 'Subprime Europe' (Ahamed, 2009); 'Failure to save East Europe will lead to worldwide meltdown' (Evans-Pritchard, 2009).

The impact now hit the entire region. Irrespective of the degree of vulnerability, the CDS spreads of every country jumped above October levels, yields rose in government security markets and currencies weakened (except for Slovakia, a euro area member, and Bulgaria, which operated a currency board system) (see Figure 5.5).

The joint assessment prompted the region's countries to take concerted action. The region's central banks and supervisory authorities[4] made their voices heard one after the other. The countries in the region and the countries of the parent banks started the so-called Vienna Initiative – a dialogue between international financial institutions (the IMF, the World Bank, the European Bank for Reconstruction and Development, the European Investment Bank and the International Finance Corporation) and commercial banks active in the region so as to ensure coordination on cross-border issues and continued lending to the region. The commitment of parent banks and international institutions contributed to the improving global climate and helped to rekindle investors' interest in local government paper. By the end of summer 2008, CEE financial markets had calmed down, and CDS spreads fell significantly, dropping below the pre-Lehman level in the case of Hungary, for example. During autumn 2009 these countries were still facing a severe recession, but were enjoying the final or temporary boom on the global financial markets.

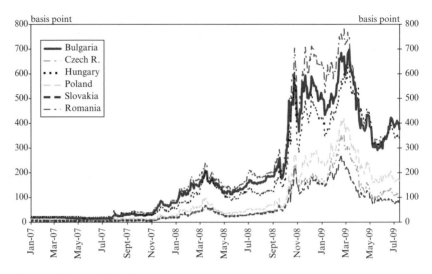

Source: Thomson Datastream.

*Figure 5.5   Sovereign CDS spreads in some CEE countries (January
             2005–October 2009)*

3   CRISIS RESPONSE OF THE AUTHORITIES

The MNB Responds to the Crisis

During the first phase of the crisis, as the macro imbalances did not stop
accumulating, the MNB called the attention of the major players to the
emerging systemic risk and warned about the risk of FX-denominated
loans. In its financial stability reports since 2003, the MNB had published
in-depth analyses on the causes and possible consequences of FX lending
and the rapid rise in household indebtedness, but these concerns did not
trigger regulatory action. Even during the first part of the crisis, the regulatory authorities – along with the major political forces – were convinced
that a growth path with increasing FX-denominated liabilities could be an
equilibrium path for a country in accession. That is why the post-Lehman
shock hit the country with brutal impact in October 2008.

The immediate liquidity crisis following the seizing up of the short-term
FX markets required the central bank to intervene as a system-wide lender
of last resort. The MNB assumed a central role in resolving the problems
of the swap market, recognising that in the current crisis situation it must

also play the role of 'FX lender of last resort', in addition to ensuring the usual local currency funding. The MNB established swap lines and repo lines with foreign central banks (ECB, Swiss National Bank (SNB)) and introduced swap tenders for the domestic banks, while the IMF–EU loan package played an important role in increasing international reserves, thus reducing external vulnerability and providing more room for the provision of FX liquidity. Soon not only the FX liquidity, but the forint liquidity of the banks also disappeared, due to the accumulated huge swap positions and the increasing margin requirements. The MNB then lowered reserve requirements to the ECB level, broadened the scope of eligible collateral (for example, municipal bonds were accepted) and enhanced its basic lending facilities with new instruments, providing 2- and 6-month forint funding to the banks via tenders (beside the 'normal' overnight funding) and overnight, 3- and 6-month FX swaps. These new measures, which were introduced step by step between October and December, significantly eased the liquidity tensions. Meanwhile, based on the daily data the MNB was closely monitoring the forint and FX liquidity needs of the commercial banks, and contributed to the safe liquidity risk management of the sector. The 6-month FX swap aimed to mitigate the possible financial accelerator effect and required the participating banks to keep their corporate exposure at the pre-crisis level.

The other major issue the central bank faced during the turbulent October days of 2008 and then during the 2009 March crisis in the CEE countries was the rapid depreciation of the forint. In October, during the liquidity turbulence the widening swap spreads were threatening, since huge speculative positions had been accumulated at almost zero price, that is, market players could short sell the Hungarian currency almost for free. The pressure on the exchange rate was enormous, and the forint lost almost 10 per cent of its value in 4 days. When it seemed clear that market forces were unanimously pushing the forint down, the central bank moved to increase the base rate by 300 basis points. The Monetary Council had to take this step despite the approaching recession, because further forint depreciation could have caused a sudden stop, due to the existing liquidity crisis. The abrupt shift immediately had a positive effect on the market, as the exchange rate then stabilised close to the pre-Lehman level.

The second shock was bigger: in the first quarter of 2009 the currencies of most of the CEE countries were falling in unison, losing more than 15 per cent of their value. This time, the situation was aggravated by the actions of the euro area member states. European governments and central banks created large packages aimed at stabilising the banking system and stimulating the economy. Their effects, however, were strongly tinged with protectionism and, in more than one case, it was an explicit condition that the additional funding could only be used to finance the domestic players of the economy. Introversion was also strengthened by the ECB's liquidity expansion programmes – the gradual extension of collateral was particularly detrimental to the non-euro area member states – as the programme did not extend to securities denominated in the currency of these member states. Therefore, in the post-Lehman period, the umbrella made available for euro area countries was deliberately not extended to EU countries not yet members of the European Monetary Union (EMU), which raised the spectre of disruption in the EU: 'Crisis management in the euro area also had the unintended consequence of putting non-euro area new member states at a disadvantage. These are unhealthy developments and, without decisive action, a new political and economic divide within Europe may emerge' (Darvas and Pisani-Ferry, 2008). Under these circumstances in the spring of 2009 the main threat was not the liquidity crisis, since by that time the measures taken by the central banks had significantly improved the liquidity shock-absorbing capacity of the commercial banks. Rather, the real danger was a solvency shock: a significant portion of unhedged customers, especially retail customers, could not pay the sharply increasing instalment on their loans and a severe deterioration in banks' portfolios could have occurred. Since the depreciation was not due to specific country reasons, and trade volumes were almost negligible, that is, small trades could move exchange rates, the MNB ruled out a repeated increase in the base rate. Instead, the communication of the MNB determined:

> The Monetary Council will make efforts to bring financial market developments back into line with the outlook for the real economy. To this end, the Bank intends to encourage banks to increase their recourse to its forint and foreign currency liquidity-providing instruments introduced recently, will soon be converting EU funds in the market and stands ready to use the full range of monetary policy instruments at its disposal. (MNB Press Release, 8 March 2009)

The message hit the target: in line with the easing in the international arena the Hungarian FX crisis was successfully averted. To make the picture transparent, the MNB published the results of the top-down stress test exercise, according to which under the baseline macroeconomic scenario, the capital buffer of the banking system as a whole would remain adequate, and modest capitalisation needs would emerge at individual banks in 2010. The shock-absorbing capacity of the banking system was strong, and the accumulated profit and the commitment of the parent banks would cover the potential losses.

The focus of monetary policy changed during this turbulent period. The 'business as usual' inflation targeting framework was supplemented by financial stability issues, that is, a new macroeconomic approach evolved. Traditional information technology (IT) models, mainly based on classical dynamic stochastic general equilibrium (DSGE) models assume frictionless financial intermediation, and do not take into consideration financial stability issues, while all central banks learned a lesson during the crisis: financial instability may cause an endogenous shock to the system, and the financial accelerator mechanism may even deepen the recession. The MNB in its approach attempts to combine 'classical' IT principles with the lessons of the crisis: financial stability should be built in a macro framework.

The HFSA Responds to the Crisis

Initially, the Supervisory Authority's greatest difficulty in managing the crisis arose from the fact that the outbreak and evolution of the crisis coincided with the implementation stage of the Capital Requirement Directive (CRD).[5] Introducing the new capital regulations and monitoring banks' preparations almost entirely engaged the attention of the HFSA's supervisory staff. The implementation of the CRD required close cooperation between the HFSA and the banks. Banks had to come up with new risk measurement and management methods and integrate them into their daily operations, and the Supervisory Authority was to establish a new set of related requirements and its control methodology, while simultaneously monitoring banks' preparation. On the other hand, for banks opting for more advanced methods of capital regulation a validation procedure had to be conducted, which was a criterion for introducing such advanced methods. In this respect, the crises erupted in the midst of the HFSA's peak performance focusing on CRD. This chronological coincidence made it even more difficult for the Supervisory Authority to take notice of the early warning signs of the crisis and to manage the crisis itself, not only in Hungary, but also throughout the EU.

The first supervisory reactions to the US crisis phenomena of 2007 addressed four key aspects:

The first and foremost task was to measure the direct impacts on bank portfolios, that is, to assess the quantity of structured securities affected by the US subprime crisis held by Hungarian banks directly or indirectly, through subsidiaries or investment funds belonging to the banking group, in their portfolios. The survey carried out by the HFSA showed a reassuring picture: the toxic securities affected by the crisis accounted for a negligible share of the Hungarian banking sector's portfolio.

The second aspect was to strengthen supervision of banks' liquidity management. Rethinking banks' liquidity regulation had already led to serious arguments in the EU just before the crisis erupted. At that time, the bone of contention was that banks and their advocacy organisations found the Basel II directive too strict, as it referred the proper management of liquidity risks and the assessment of capital adequacy to the scope of the second pillar (supervisory authority review). This kind of coupling has been questioned repeatedly by many, because the requirement of excess capital provides a solution for only part of the liquidity risks. This saves banks from the insolvency risk generated by the income-reducing effect of liquidity risks. At the same time, interlinking liquidity and capital regulations does not provide any protection against liquidity shocks at all, and is not suitable as a means of preventing liquidity shocks caused by risk management deficiencies or improper business models either. Initially, the main reason behind contesting such interlinking was to criticise the excessive severity, since for banks the capital requirement is the most expensive instrument of banking regulation. As the liquidity impacts of the subprime crisis became more and more serious, the criticism took a 180-degree turn, laying increasing emphasis on the fact that by referring liquidity risks to the second pillar supervisory authorities felt at ease, and paid little attention to whether the banks' liquidity management practices were actually appropriate and if they were capable of handling the liquidity requirements that had been substantially different as a result of the change in the business model.

Note that rethinking the liquidity regulation of banks became a priority issue immediately before the outbreak of the subprime crisis, at the initiative of the industry itself, and with a sign that was opposite to what was first conceived as a consequence of the emerging subprime crisis. The years of ample liquidity led the European Banking Federation (EBF), the European advocacy organisation of banks, to draw the conclusion that in several countries the liquidity regulation of banks is too rigorous, as companies with global liquidity management are also expected to properly manage the liquidity of individual banks at a national level. Moreover, the EBF also disapproved of the phenomenon that the legal obstacles to the cross-border movement of collateral assets presented a barrier to cross-border liquidity management. Therefore, at the time of the outbreak of the subprime crisis, various levels of working groups had already been set up and given the mandate to rethink the issue of liquidity risk management, liquidity regulation and liquidity supervision comprehensively. However, the content of that mandate underwent a material change as it became increasingly evident that the subprime crisis starting from the United States spilled over to become a global liquidity crisis, thus ending the era of ample, practically unlimited liquidity. It was no longer the goal to adopt a much more permissive regulatory and supervisory practice than the existing one, which would also be acceptable for the international banking community, but to assure that banks' liquidity risk management and supervision were prudent enough, even in the case of eventual market turbulence and in times of scarce liquidity. In this regard, the issue of the mobility of collateral became less important, while that of the methodology of the banks' liquidity continuity planning grew more important.

In Hungary, the liquidity regulation of banks does not contain any specific quantitative requirements, there is no compulsory level of liquid assets, and there are no maturity mismatch limits. The only obligation prescribed in the regulation is that the credit institution is required to continuously guarantee its immediate liquidity and must have relevant internal regulations and a plan. In addition, it is obvious that in Hungary the supervisory authority's capital adequacy supervision process also includes the assessment of the sound management of liquidity risks and their capital coverage. A common feature of risks referring to the scope of the second pillar is that due to their nature they are not normally associated with a specific universally applicable quantitative requirement, only the principles of capital determination are laid down at the regulatory level. In the pre-Lehman period this method of liquidity supervision was a generally accepted practice, which is reflected in the publication of the Basel Committee on Banking Supervision issued under the title 'Principles for Sound Liquidity Risk Management and Supervision' issued in September 2008 (BCBS, 2008), as well as in the HFSA's Pillar II Guidelines (HFSA 2008a).

The third aspect focuses on the identification of risks arising at the level of the banking system and specification of the related supervisory requirements. For this, the CRD Pillar II Supervisory Review and Evaluation Process (SREP) provided a new opportunity and instrument. In the framework of Pillar II, banks and the Supervisory Authority are required to engage in a dialogue in order to agree what capital level the Authority requires banks to maintain in excess of the amount of capital formally calculated in the first pillar. Under the SREP, the HFSA reviews the bank's risk profile, as well as its internal capital calculation and capital allocation mechanism, and determines the level of the regulatory capital accordingly.

The SREP does not have a single methodology: it is up to the supervisory authorities of the individual countries. This is also true within the member states of the EU, in spite of the fact that the Committee of European Banking Supervisors (CEBS, 2006) published its 'Guidelines on the Application of the Supervisory Review Process under Pillar II'. This, however, is rather general, as it allows quite a high degree of freedom as to how the individual member states apply these guidelines. When

Table 5.1   HFSA classification of portfolio segment

Portfolio segments of banks	Required excess capital
JPY-denominated lending	50–100% of the capital requirement under Pillar I
Retail loans provided on loose conditions (e.g. lending without certification of income or own contribution, retail lending with LTV ratio above 80%, etc.)	50–100% of the capital requirement under Pillar I
Lending to debtors resident in a country with a lower sovereign credit rating than Hungary	Capital calculated on the basis of the specific method determined by the Supervisory Authority

the HFSA was considering elaboration of its own SREP methodology, it made a decision that the HFSA guidelines would always contain an appendix, which would not only provide a general description of what types of risks should be potentially covered by excess capital on the basis of what considerations, but it would specify the portfolio segments that the Supervisory Authority regarded as being highly risky in the given year, and it would also set a quantitative requirement with respect to the excess capital needed to cover such risks. This approach made it possible to identify the portfolio segments affected by the crises equally in the case of each institution, in a way that both the Authority and the institutions were to pay special attention to them, and to ensure that the required capital buffer cover the higher risks and/or the higher capital costs keep banks away from the given high-risk activity.

In the appendix to Pillar II Guidelines published for the first time in May 2008 the HFSA classified the several portfolio segments into the high-risk category, and prescribed the obligation to maintain excess capital to cover them (HFSA, 2008b) (see Table 5.1).

Identification of the first two portfolio segments are closely related to the loosened standards of retail lending. As presented in Section 2, in the pre-Lehman period only a few signs of the financial depression were perceivable in Hungary, so retail lending, which resulted in an irresponsible and excessive credit expansion, continued, predominantly in the Swiss franc, and to a lesser extent in the euro and the Japanese yen. At this point, the Supervisory Authority considered only JPY-denominated loans to be highly risky, as the exchange rate of the Swiss franc had been in close correlation with that of the euro for a longer period, and in Hungary, especially in the case of long-term loans, the risk of euro loans was deemed to be assumable in the light of Hungary's accession to the euro area as a medium-term target. On the other hand, the reason behind the requirement of excess capital prescribed for debtors resident in countries with a lower credit rating than Hungary was that the largest domestic bank had a number of subsidiaries based outside the EU (in Russia, Ukraine, Serbia and Montenegro), where it was almost impossible to assess the potential impact of the crisis. Within the preset limits the amount of the required excess capital had to be determined depending on the bank's risk awareness and the level of development of its risk measurement and management system.

The fourth aspect was a continuous emphasis on responsible lending and proper information of consumers. In parallel with the relaxation of lending standards, even before the crisis started, the HFSA had called banks' attention to the fact that they were required to provide their clients with detailed information on the risks they were to assume by taking out a loan. To this end, it issued a Recommendation (HFSA, 2006), which did not have a binding force, but was the strongest regulatory document issued by the Supervisory Authority upon the authorisation of the law. In addition, in 2007 the HFSA introduced a new instrument, the so-called 'Dear CEO' letter, which drew the attention of the leaders of the supervised institutions to issues that it thought carried unusually high risks. This is how the Dear CEO letters on JPY-denominated loans and FX loans with currency option were issued (HFSA, 2007).

In the pre-Lehman period, when there was still strong trust in decoupling, these supervisory measures seemed sufficient to manage the crisis, and apparently there was no need for more-powerful, specific actions.

The risk level skyrocketed after the Lehman shock, generating new requirements for the Supervisory Authority as well. The task to be performed immediately was to settle the position of property investment funds and provide for increased supervision of the liquidity of banks on a daily basis.

As one of the first spillover effects of the financial crisis, also in reaction to the paralysis of the interbank money market, banks tried to improve their liquidity by attracting deposits with preferential interest rates, which were much higher than the earlier rates. This resulted in a rearrangement of savings, as investors started to withdraw their capital from investment funds and transfer them to bank deposits. This process affected property investment funds to a particularly high degree, as their portfolio has lower liquidity than that of other investment funds, and if they were to undergo a massive asset fire sale, this would give impetus to the rapid collapse of real estate markets. The liquidity of several large funds was affected, which eventually led to the intervention of the supervisory authority. On 10 November 2008, the HFSA suspended the trading of property investment funds and funds of property investment funds for 10 days (HFSA, 2008c). During this period, the funds had to modify their fund management rules in a way that they were required to change the T+3 days delivery generally applied in the course of repurchases to T+90 days, as permitted by the law. Also, a quick amendment to the laws made it possible to convert open-end property investment funds into closed-end property investment funds. In order to make sure that during the process of such conversion investors' interests suffer the least possible injury, the HFSA issued a Dear CEO letter (HFSA, 2008d) on the principles applicable during the conversion of open-end property investment funds to closed-end property investment funds. This focused on the information and transparency rules required for supporting investors' decisions. In the case of conversion, the fund had to offer the investors the opportunity to repurchase their investments at the value revalued with respect to the date of the conversion, unless they wanted to participate in the conversion.

The rearrangement of savings improved the banks' liquidity to some extent, but was far from sufficient to make up for the domestic and foreign interbank market. To monitor the tight liquidity situation continuously, on a daily basis, and in order to enable the Supervisory Authority to react to ad hoc issues arising in connection with the crisis quickly and in a targeted way, the HFSA set up an operational and a professional working group in October 2008. The operational working group was responsible for exchanging information both with the supervised institutions and with those partner supervisory authorities that controlled the owners or subsidiaries of the Hungarian financial institutions, with the aim of preventing the crisis situation. The operational working group's task was to evaluate the daily liquidity and cash-flow data, the disclosure of which was introduced by the Authority after the Lehman shock. The professional working group was responsible for supporting the operational working group in terms of methodology, analysis and monitoring. This working group specified the structure of the data to be disclosed, and determined what indicators had to be continuously created and monitored on the basis of the data available for the supervisory authority, and carried out an analysis of such up-to-date information. A daily analysis of systemic risk was performed with respect to the largest banks, which the working group evaluated. Initially, the two working groups met on a daily basis, but later on, after the most turbulent stage of the crisis was over, their meetings were held less frequently. After nearly 6 months of operation the working groups were dissolved.

Furthermore, due to the predominance of foreign banks in the

Hungarian banking market, it was of key significance to assure markets that the parent banks have an unbroken commitment towards their Hungarian subsidiaries. To ensure the stability of the market, in October 2008 the HFSA sent a letter to the parent banks of the eight largest foreign-owned Hungarian banks, in which it asked them to make a declaration regarding their long-term commitment towards their Hungarian subsidiaries. Seven of the eight banks issued a Letter of Support, in which they undertook to provide for the conditions required for the operation of their subsidiaries.

Already in the post-Lehman period, the first annual review of the specific excess capital requirements associated with the SREP risky portfolios was undertaken (HFSA, 2009). In the course of this review the Supervisory Authority confirmed that it would maintain the excess capital requirements it had specified in the 2008 Guideline. Moreover, it also prescribed that the capital requirement of FX risks had to be calculated using the Value at Risk model, the application of which would be compulsory for the Supervisory Authority. This was essential because as a result of skyrocketing exchange rate volatility the standard method used by the regulation significantly underrated foreign exchange risk, and a majority of banks applied the standard method to determine the regulatory capital. Parallel with this, the Authority carried out a comprehensive portfolio analysis in the eight largest banks representing a systemic risk. As a result, it prescribed the obligation to maintain excess provisions in several cases. The screening highlighted the weaknesses of bank portfolios, particularly in the case of real property development project loans, and pointed out several regulatory arbitrages. All in all, however, the views on the large banks were in line with our conceptions.

As the financial crisis was slowly coming to a standstill, in Hungary as well as in other parts of the world, the first lessons were learned in the area of supervision, and a package of laws aimed at increasing the efficiency of the HFSA's future operations was adopted. In this package, taking into acount the pre-declared aspects, including independence, transparency and accountability, effectiveness and efficiency, integration of micro- and macroprudential considerations, and crisis resilience, proposals were made for establishing the decree-making authority of the HFSA, for setting up a Stability Council consisting of the top officers of the Ministry of Finance, the Supervisory Authority and the MNB with substantial intervention rights, and for extending the regulatory authority of the MNB, in order to enable it to mitigate macroprudential risks. In the near future, the directions and steps of regulation will be determined on the basis of a continuous processing and joint consideration of the lessons learned from the crisis.

4 CONCLUSION

During the pre-Lehman period the financial turbulence had a mild effect on the Hungarian economy: the cost of funds increased slightly, credit expansion continued, maturities of foreign funds significantly shortened, liquidity risk increased and macro imbalances slowly accumulated. The MNB and the Supervisory Authority were aware of the accumulating risks, but it was not possible to take strong action, because the Ministry of Finance, which was responsible for regulation, opposed direct intervention in the market forces.

The post-Lehman shock hit the vulnerable Hungarian economy with brutal force. Financial markets froze, financial intermediation slowed down, the country faced a long, U-shaped recession, and external funding was at risk. The joint actions of the MNB, the HFSA and the government first eased the financial tensions, then in different ways, due to the differences among the institutions, they tried to manage the crisis jointly.

The liquidity crisis could have been eased partly, with the contribution of the two authorities. The looming solvency problems were detected by the authorities, but the shock-absorbing capacity of the local banks was still strong, and thus no extra intervention was required.

However, the final lessons of the crisis are still to be drawn and the consequences are to be transformed into reshaping the prudential framework. The first step has been taken – the microprudential competence of the supervisors and the macroprudential competence of the MNB has been increased.

NOTES

1. The two best-known partners in the debate are: Joseph E. Stiglitz, Nobel Prize winner and former Vice President of the World Bank, today one of the best-known critics of the absurdities of globalisation, on the one side, and Stanley Fisher (not yet, but potential Nobel Prize winner) former First Deputy Managing Director of the IMF, who has faith in the stabilising power of global financial markets and their effect facilitating catch-up, on the other.
2. The Irish government was the forerunner on 30 September. At first, it sparked intense protestations on an international scale, but was followed by a raising of deposit protection ceilings in almost all of Europe, with governments undertaking political guarantees too.
3. Bloomberg (2009): 'Regional markets weakened after EU leaders rejected both a proposed support package totalling €180 billion and an accelerated euro adoption process at an EU summit yesterday'.
4. 24 February Coordinated statement on currency weakness. 'The central banks of the Czech Republic, Hungary, Poland, and Romania released coordinated statements calling recent currency weakness unjustified and raising the possibility of intervention in FX markets if their currencies continued to weaken. CE-3 currencies appreciated

slightly, following the statements' (Joint statement of the Supervisory authorities of Bulgaria, Czech Republic, Hungary, Poland, Romania and Slovakia).

5. The CRD is a set of directives that integrate the Basel II capital regulations into the European legislative system. The new capital regulations had to be implemented by the EU member states in the course of 2007, and they were introduced in Hungary as from 1 January 2008.

REFERENCES

Ahamed, L. (2009): 'Subprime Europe', *The New York Times*, 7 March, available at: http://www.nytimes.com/2009/03/08/opinion/08Ahamed.html?_r=2 (accessed 22 March 2010).

Basel Committee on Banking Supervision (BCBS) (2008): 'Principles for Sound Liquidity Risk Management and Supervision', September, available at: http://www.bis.org/publ/bcbs144.htm (accessed 22 March 2010).

Bloomberg (2009), 'EU spurns calls for Eastern aid', 2 March, available at: http://www.bloomberg.com/apps/news?pid=20601095&sid=a3Pdn_WBTDwe&refer=east_europe (accessed 8 June 2010).

Committee of European Banking Supervisors (CEBS) (2006): 'Guidelines on the Application of the Supervisory Review Process under Pillar II', January, available at: http://www.c-ebs.org/getdoc/00ec6db3-bb41-467c-acb9-8e271f617675/GL03.aspx (accessed 22 March 2010).

Darvas, Z. and Pisani-Ferry, J. (2008): 'Avoiding a new European divide', Bruegel Policy Brief, Issue 2008/10.

Davis, E.P. (2009): 'The lender of last resort and liquidity provision – how much of a departure is the subprime crisis?', Brunel University and NIESR, London, paper presented at the Conference 'Regulatory Response to the Financial Crisis', London School of Economics, 19 January.

Dooley, M.P. and Hutchison, M.M. (2009): 'Transmission of the US subprime crisis to emerging markets: evidence on the decoupling–recoupling hypothesis', NBER Working Paper 15120, National Bureau of Economic Research, Cambridge, MA, June.

Economist, The (2009a), 'Eastern Europe: Argentina on the Danube?', 19 February, available at: http://www.economist.com/opinion/displayStory.cfm?story_id=13144925 (accessed 22 March 2010).

Economist, The (2009b), 'Eastern Europe's woes: the bill that could break up Europe', 26 February, available at: http://www.economist.com/displaystory.cfm?story_id=13184655 (accessed 22 March 2010).

Evans-Pritchard, A. (2009): 'Failure to save East Europe will lead to worldwide meltdown', *Daily Telegraph*, 14 February, available at: http://www.telegraph.co.uk/finance/comment/ambroseevans_pritchard/4623525/Failure-to-save-East-Europe-will-lead-to-worldwide-meltdown.html (accessed 22 March 2010).

Fischer, S. (2009): 'Preparing for future crises', presented as the lunchtime speech at the 33rd Annual Symposium of the Federal Reserve Bank of Kansas City, on 'Financial Stability and Macroeconomic Stability', at Jackson Hole, WY, 21 August.

HFSA (Hungarian Financial Supervisory Authority) (2006): Recommendation No. 9 of 2006 (XI. 7) of the Board of the Hungarian Financial Supervisory

Authority on the principles of retail crediting provision of preliminary advice to clients and consumer protection, available at: http://www.pszaf.hu/en/left_menu/regulation/pszafen_recommendations/pszafen_recommendations_20061204_1.html (accessed 25 March 2010).

HFSA (2007): Dear CEO Letter No. 8/2007 for the Chief Executive Officers of credit institutions and financial enterprises providing Japanese yen-based loans, as well as forex loans with currency options, available at: http://www.pszaf.hu/data/cms1290653/pszafen_dearceo8_2007.pdf (accessed 25 March 2010).

HFSA (2008a): The Supervisory Review Process, Guidelines, February, available at: http://www.pszaf.hu/data/cms1288349/The_Supervisory_Review_Process_(SRP)___Guidelines.pdf (accessed 25 March 2010).

HFSA (2008b): Information on the high-risk portfolios and the related capital surplus requirements treated with high priority in the framework of the Supervisory Review Process (SREP), May, available at: http://www.pszaf.hu/data/cms1288348/Kock__zatos_portfoli__k_2008_eng.pdf (accessed 20 June 2008).

HFSA (2008c): Resolution No. J-III-200/2008, November.

HFSA (2008d): Dear CEO letter No. 7/2008, available at: http://www.pszaf.hu/data/cms1588076/PSZ__F124_vezkorlev_7_2008_Eng.pdf (accessed 25 March 2008).

HFSA (2009): Information on the high-risk portfolios and the related capital surplus requirements treated with high priority in the framework of the Supervisory Review Process (SREP), May, available at: http://www.pszaf.hu/data/cms1288348/Kock__zatos_portfoli__k_2009_eng.pdf (accessed 20 June 2009).

Kaminsky, Graciela L., Reinhart, Carmen M. and Végh, Carlos A. (2003), 'The unholy trinity of Financial Contagion', NBER Working Paper 10061, available at: http://www.nber.org/papers/w10061 (accessed 8 June 2010).

King, I. (2009): 'Eastern European crisis may put us all in the goulash', *The Times*, 19 February, available at: http://business.timesonline.co.uk/tol/business/columnists/article5762544.ece (accessed 8 June 2010).

Király, J., Nagy, M. and Szabó, V.E. (2008): 'Analysis of a special sequence of events – the beginning', MNB Occasional Paper, Magyar Nemzeti Bank, 76, September.

Schinasi, Garry J.S. and Smith, R. Todd (2000), 'Portfolio Diversification, leverage and financial contagion', IMF Staff Papers, **47**(2).

PART III

Asia and Australia

6.   An analysis of the ripple effects of the global financial crisis on the South Korean economy and the recovery*

Jungeun Kim, Kyeong Pyo Ryu and Doowoo Nam

1   IMPACTS OF THE GLOBAL FINANCIAL CRISIS

After the US subprime crisis started about the end of 2006, the South Korean economy continued to be in a sound basic economic condition for some time. The bankruptcy of Lehman Brothers on September 15, 2008 triggered the serious financial crisis throughout the world, and the uncertainty surrounding the Korean economy also increased significantly. The instability in the global financial system began to seriously affect the Korean financial markets, incurring the unfavorable movements in its interest rates, exchange rates, and stock prices. This adversely affected the real sector, lowering employment, consumption and investment in the Korean economy. To make matters worse, the world economic downturn caused by the turmoil in the global financial markets slowed down its exports. But the turmoil of the Korean economy was not as serious as that of the United States due to the low delinquency rate in consumer loans, the low degree of securitizing the loans for project financing related to large-scale real estate development, and various regulations on the soundness of financial institutions. Thanks to the efforts of the Korean government to stabilize the foreign exchange market and to prevent the economic depression through decisive fiscal policy measures including tax cuts, in just one year after the Lehman Brothers débâcle, the Korean financial markets and the economic indicators for its real sector started to return to the pre-débâcle levels.

As shown in Figure 6.1, the collapse of Lehman Brothers in 2008 had a large negative effect on the Korean economy. While the business recession, due to the subprime mortgage crisis at the end of 2006, in the developed countries surfaced in 2007, the Korean economy, along with other newly

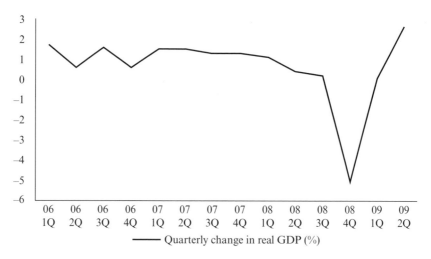

Source: Korean Statistical Information Service.

Figure 6.1   Quarterly changes in real GDP (Q1.2006–Q2.2009)

emerging countries, maintained a relatively high growth during the period. The annual real GDP growth rate was 5.2 percent in 2006 and 5.1 percent in 2007, but it fell to 2.2 percent in 2008. In particular, the growth rate in the fourth quarter of 2008 right after the bankruptcy of Lehman Brothers well demonstrates its impact on the Korean economy.

This sudden change in the Korean economy, like that in other newly emerging countries, was mainly the result of 'deleveraging'. The bankruptcy of Lehman Brothers spread a sense of urgency in the credit markets around the world, causing international investors to quickly liquidate their risky assets mainly at the newly emerging financial markets. The US financial institutions, facing financial difficulty amid the subprime crisis, exacerbated the situation by also acting promptly to liquidate their foreign investments. The withdrawal of capital invested in the foreign financial markets by the US financial institutions reached to a total of $92 billion for the three months from June 2008 (Jeong, 2009). This amount far exceeds the total of $64 billion during the financial crisis in East Asian countries, Brazil and Russia in the late 1990s. The record counterflow of foreign investment dragged the financial markets of most newly emerging countries into turmoil, and many of those countries in Asia, Eastern Europe and Central and South America experienced the rapid outflow of capital from their securities markets, leading to the fall in their currency value and stock prices.

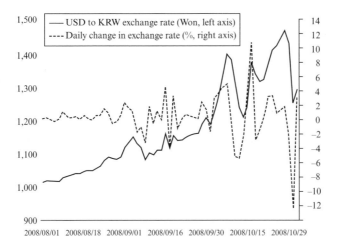

Source: ECOS Database, Bank of Korea.

Figure 6.2   KRW/US$ exchange rate: level and daily changes (August–
October 2008)

The Korean financial markets also became more volatile. The range of fluctuations in the various financial indexes, including the exchange rates and stock prices, recorded the highest level. As seen in Figure 6.2, the exchange rate of the Korean won against the US dollar skyrocketed to 1,373 won by 133.5 won (or 10.8 percent), the largest ever one-day drop in the value of the Korean won, on October 16, 2008. In addition, on the same day, as shown in Figure 6.3, the Korea Composite Stock Price Index (KOSPI) recorded 1,213.78, a decrease by 126.5 points (or −9.4 percent), which is also one of the largest one-day drops in KOSPI history.

Since the bankruptcy of Lehman Brothers, the downtrend in various indexes for domestic demand, including employment, consumption and investment, of the Korean economy was obvious. A favorable tone in its exports could not be maintained, either, as seen in Figure 6.4. A red light was turned on after all for the Korean economy, with the downturn in both the coincident composite index (CCI), an indicator of current business conditions, and the leading composite index (LCI), which forecasts economic conditions for the following six to nine months, for several months in a row.

Also, perception of the Korean economy from overseas turned negative. International credit rating agencies such as Moody's and Standard and Puor's (S&P) continued to downgrade the ratings of Korean commercial banks in October 2008. Specifically, Moody's announced the downgrading

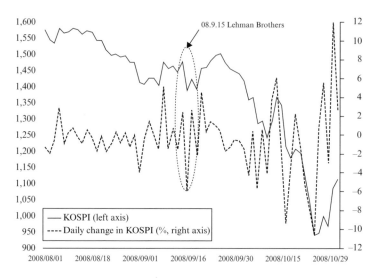

Source: ECOS Database, Bank of Korea.

Figure 6.3   KOSPI: level and daily changes (August–October 2008)

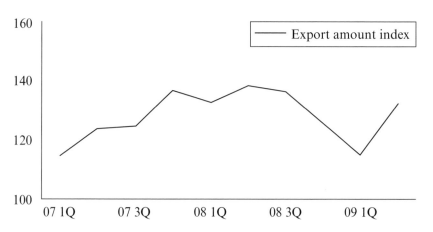

Note: The base year of the index is 2005 where its level is set as 100.

Source: ECOS Database, Bank of Korea.

Figure 6.4   Quarterly changes in export volume index (Q1.2007– Q2. 2009)

of all Big Four commercial banks in Korea (Kookmin Bank, Woori Bank, Shinhan Bank and Hana Bank) from 'stable' to 'negative' on October 1, and S&P announced the inclusion of seven Korean financial firms (Korea Exchange Bank, Shinhan Card and Woori Financial Group, the first financial holding company in Korea, in addition to the Big Four) in the 'credit watch' list on October 15 (Chang et al., 2008). Consequently, the Korean banking industry's ability to raise foreign capital deteriorated.

The purpose of this study is twofold. One is to analyze the impacts of the global financial crisis on the Korean economy by investigating the changes in indexes for its financial and real sectors before and after the collapse of Lehman Brothers on September 15, 2008. The other is to examine how the Korean economy coped with all the difficulties during the global financial crisis. The chapter is organized as follows. Sections 2 and 3 examine the changes in the financial and real sectors of the Korean economy amid the global financial crisis. Section 4 summarizes the policy responses of the government to overcome the difficulties and Section 5 concludes.

2   IMPACTS ON THE FINANCIAL SECTORS

The Banking Industry

The credit crunch resulting from the instability of the global financial markets spread into the Korean financial markets. As a consequence, the funding capacity of the Korean financial institutions was seriously reduced in both domestic and overseas capital markets; and the management of liquidity in both the Korean won and the foreign currencies became their utmost concern. When the influx of deposits stagnated, the Korean banks attempted to expand the issuance of certificate of deposits (CDs) and bonds. However, the demand for the bonds, which were deemed to be getting riskier, decreased at the height of the global financial turmoil. This means that the cost of raising funds from both domestic and overseas sources rose significantly for the Korean banking industry. As the cost of funds was hiked up, the interest rates on consumer and commercial loans also increased, which put a heavy financial burden on households and businesses, especially the small- and medium-sized enterprises. The real estate market was held in check for lack of sufficient funds, and concerns escalated over a shaky situation in the project financing related to large-scale real estate developments. The average interest rates on business loans rose by 0.7 of a percentage point to 7.3 percent in August 2008, up from 6.6 percent in the previous month.

The single most important source of these problems in the banking industry was the aggravation of its capacity of funding from overseas sources. Since 2006, Korean commercial banks had increased the short-term foreign-currency borrowing by $93 billion in order to cope with the demand for hedging against foreign exchange losses by Korean shipbuilders and exporters. The efforts of those banks to secure US dollars, in order to prepare for rollover not being rendered, led to rumors of a foreign currency liquidity crisis and a foreign debt crisis, and played a major role in exacerbating the difficulties of the Korean economy. In October 2008, Korea's credit default swap (CDS) premium more than quadrupled, jumping to almost 7 percent,[1] which, in turn, aggravated the foreign currency liquidity problem in the banking industry and Korea's economy. At the height of the rumors, the government issued a press release stating that the portion of the borrowing for the shipbuilders and exporters could not be viewed as debt since it would be automatically erased when they received payment.

Considering the properties of short-term foreign debts and the structure of foreign borrowing by Korean banks, it was recognized that the liquidity crunch could be successfully resolved. As of September 2008, Korea's foreign exchange reserve was $240 billion, which is far greater than the short-term foreign debts of $146 billion owed by the Korean banking industry. The size of the reserve could also cover the extreme case that foreign investors would pull out their money from the Korean stock market all at once, an amount that was then estimated at $180 billion. Furthermore, the three-month foreign currency liquidity ratio of Korean banks was 100.5 percent, far exceeding the guidelines of 85 percent set by the banking regulatory authority, in September 2008.[2]

The Foreign Exchange Market

The value of the Korean won against the US dollar depreciated considerably compared with other major currencies, and its volatility also increased greatly. The won–dollar exchange rate skyrocketed from 936.1 won per dollar at the end of 2007, to 1,239.5 won on October 15, 2008, to 1,570 won in early March 2009. This means that the value of the Korean won depreciated by 24.5 percent against the US dollar between the end of 2007 and October 15, 2008. This rate of depreciation far exceeded the depreciation of the Korean won against the euro (2.7 percent) and the pound (13.7 percent) during the same period, currencies that were also seriously affected by the global financial crisis. In addition, the volatility, which is measured by the standard deviation of daily changes in exchange rates, of the exchange rate between the Korean won and the US dollar increased significantly by 2.8 times from 0.65 percent in the first half of 2008 to 1.83

percent in the period of July 1 – October 15, 2008. This increased level of volatility was almost twice that of other major currencies such as the euro and the pound.

The causes of this instability of the Korean won value against the US dollar can be analyzed mainly in the following three aspects. First, there was a massive selloff by foreign investors in the Korean stock market in an attempt to secure liquidity amid the global financial turmoil. During the 10-month period from January to mid-October 2008, foreign investors net-sold a total of $34.8 billion, which far exceeded the size of net selling, $29.2 billion, for the entire year of 2007 (Financial Supervisory Service, 2008).[3] The size of investment withdrawn by foreign investors on such a stock sellout accounted for 46.6 percent of the total withdrawal of foreign investment ($74.7 billion dollars) from seven Asian countries.[4] Second, the spot foreign exchange market seriously contracted following the dollar liquidity crunch, and Korea's foreign exchange market had been heavily US dollar oriented. For instance, in the second quarter of 2008 the daily trading volume was, on average, $39.9 billion for the Korean won *vis-à-vis* the US dollar, which accounted for 96.8 percent of the total trading volume, $41.2 billion, for the Korean won *vis-à-vis* foreign currencies (Chang et al., 2008). In a situation where the foreign exchange market itself shrank, a rapid rise in the exchange rate of the Korean won against the US dollar was inevitable due to the expectation of the stronger dollar and the massive buying of foreign exchange futures by Korean investment and trust companies following bearish global stock markets. Third, with the continuous current account deficit, the Korean economy suffered the deepening shortage of the dollar as overseas borrowing became more difficult since the credit crunch was spreading over the global financial markets. Between January and August 2008, the current account deficit increased to $12.6 billion due to the soaring prices of raw materials, but the amount of overseas borrowing fell to $24.2 billion, a decrease by $13.5 billion as compared with the same period of the previous year.

The Stock Market

Compared with the beginning of the year, the KOSPI, an index of the Korea Stock Exchange, dropped sharply by 37.7 percent as of October 16, 2008 and the total market value of listed stocks also plunged to $656.1 billion, a decrease of 31.4 percent as of the end of September 2008. In the same period, the stock price indexes and the total market value fell by 33–34 percent and 10–26 percent, respectively, in major developed countries like the United States and Japan (Chang et al., 2008). As shown in Figure 6.5, the volatility of the Korean stock market increased whenever

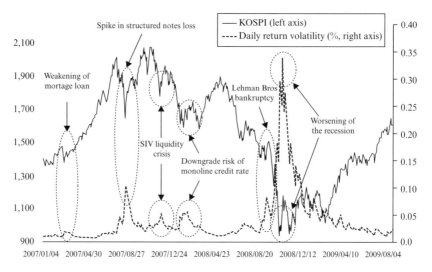

Note: The daily volatility of the KOSPI is derived from GARCH (1,1) model.

Source: Korea Information Service (KIS) Value Database.

Figure 6.5   *Changes in daily volatility of the KOSPI (January*
2007–August 2009)

there was bad news came from the United States about the recession.
The average daily volatility increased from 0.014 percent in 2007 to 0.017
percent as of October 17, 2008.

The downturn of the Korean stock market coupled with its increased
volatility was largely due to a massive net selling by foreign investors to
enhance their liquidity position following the large charge-offs by US and
European financial institutions. Concerns over a global recession further
exacerbated the situation. In addition, a rapid increase in the short selling
by foreign investors, including hedge funds, played a significant role in
the increased volatility of the Korean stock market. The portion of equity
held by foreign investors fell to 27.4 percent as of October 14, 2008 from
32.3 percent at the end of 2007, and the proportion of foreigners' trading
in total stock trading rose to 28.1 percent for January–August 2008,
from 24.7 percent for 2007. One of the implications is that the trading by
foreign investors, mainly in blue-chip stocks, controlled the direction of
the Korean stock market.

3   IMPACTS ON THE REAL SECTORS

In early 2007, the global financial crisis triggered by the US subprime mortgage débâcle, put the global economy into a slump and increased the uncertainty in the global financial markets. The Lehman Brothers' collapse in September 2008 deepened the financial turmoil and directly affected the Korean financial market where the foreign currency liquidity decreased and the financial market volatility increased. The contraction of the world economy, coupled with the turbulent domestic financial markets, eventually affected the real sectors of the Korean economy, reducing imports and exports, production, and consumption and investment. Overall, the impact on the real sectors of the Korean economy led to a recession.

Business Indexes and Foreign Trade

In September 2008, the CCI, an indicator of current business conditions, fell to 99.8 below the level of 100 for the base year, 2005. It continued falling until March 2009. On the other hand, the LCI, which is used to forecast economic conditions for the following 6–9 months,[5] also exhibited a continuous downtrend from March 2008 and started to rise in February 2009. Overall, the Korean economy has rallied since early 2009.

Korea's exports also declined from the fourth quarter of 2008, and then recovered in the second quarter of 2009. Compared with the situation during the economic crisis of 1997, it is interesting to note that the amount of exports to all of Korea's major trading partners fell during this period of the global financial crisis, for example, China (–23.9 percent), the EU (–16.7 percent), Japan (–11.8 percent), the United States (–6.0 percent), while exports to regions other than East Asian countries like Japan and China showed no sign of letdown during the 1997 economic crisis (National Assembly Budget Office, 2009). This was due to the deteriorating terms of trade. Korea's main export products were low- and mid-priced ones with high price elasticity. However, the rigid price elasticity of imported raw materials resulted in lower profits for exporters. The Korean economy, which is heavily dependent on foreign trade, suffered from the problems of high unemployment and lower investments.

Industry Production, Investment and Consumption

As shown in Figure 6.6, the global financial crisis deepened in 2008, the fourth-quarter industrial production index of the Korean economy declined 11.3 percent from the same period a year earlier. The domestic real sectors suffered a full-scale slump. The figure also shows that the

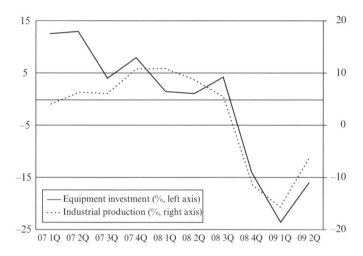

Note: The base year of the index is 2005 where its level is set as 100.

Source: ECOS Database, Bank of Korea.

Figure 6.6   *Quarterly changes in industrial production and equipment*
investment Indexes (Q1.2007–Q2.2009)

equipment investment index fell from the first quarter of 2008, and it continued a downtrend reaching a 16.8 percent decrease in the fourth quarter
from a year earlier. However, the rate was lower than during the 1997
economic crisis (37.7 percent decrease), and the index started to rebound
from the second quarter of 2009.

Figure 6.7 provides quarterly changes in the private consumption index.
The index also entered a downward trend in the first quarter of 2008 and
started to pick up in the second quarter of 2009.

In the aftermath of the global financial crisis, all economic indicators
on domestic demand, including industrial production, investment, consumption, employment and so on, dropped. However, since the second
quarter of 2009, the real sectors of the Korean economy have shown signs
of recovery.

4   POLICY RESPONSE TO THE GLOBAL FINANCIAL
CRISIS

In this section, we examine the measures that the government has taken
to minimize and overcome the repercussions of the global financial crisis

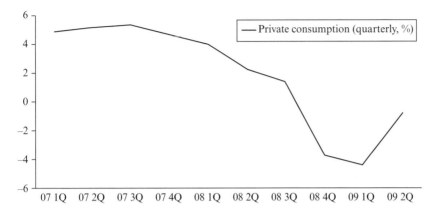

Source: ECOS Database, Bank of Korea.

Figure 6.7 *Quarterly changes in private consumption index*
(Q1.2007–Q2.2009)

triggered by the subprime mortgage débâcle. The measures are categorized as the financial stabilization policy, the restructuring policy and the economic stimulus plan.

The Financial Stabilization Policy

The Bank of Korea (BOK) executed a series of bold cuts in its benchmark interest rates,[6] in order to stabilize the market psychology, which had become unstable amid the global financial turmoil, and to induce the downward stabilization of market interest rates.[7] The rates were reduced from 5.25 percent in September 2008 to 2 percent in February 2009. Furthermore, to cope with the credit crunch in the banking industry, the government provided liquidity for the financial markets by expanding the purchases of repurchase agreements from financial institutions, the early retirement of Monetary Stabilization Bonds issued by the BOK ($0.6 billion on October 23, 2008), and the direct purchases of government securities in the secondary market ($0.9 billion on November 19, 2008). Also, a bond market stabilization fund, totaling $9 billion, was established to revitalize the bond market. The government also provided the capital for several banks to stabilize the banking system: the Korea Development Bank ($1.2 billion), the Industrial Bank of Korea ($0.9 billion) and the Export–Import Bank of Korea ($0.56 billion).

The result of the actions by government and the BOK was greater financial stability in the domestic financial markets. As can be seen in Figure

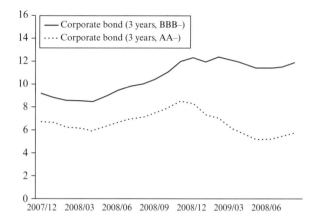

Source: ECOS Database, Bank of Korea.

Figure 6.8   *Monthly changes in the corporate bond yields by credit rating*
              (December 2007–June 2009)

6.8, the upward trend in the yields on corporate bonds starting from early
2008 due to the credit crunch in the domestic financial market was reversed
in late 2008. In particular, the yields on corporate bonds with a high credit
rating (AA–) clearly showed a downward trend from December 2008 and
dropped to a level even lower than before the global financial crisis.

In order to stabilize the foreign exchange market, the government and
the BOK attempted to secure foreign currency liquidity by entering into
foreign currency swap agreements with the central banks of its major
trading partners. These include the Federal Reserve Bank, the Bank of
Japan, and the People's Bank of China. Table 6.1 shows the amount of
foreign currency secured through these agreements in addition to the
source of short-term foreign currency liquidity from the IMF.

The government's measures to stabilize the foreign exchange market,
coupled with the global financial markets settling down somewhat, had a
slow but steady effect. Having soared from August 2008, the exchange rate
of the Korean won against the US dollar showed a downward trend and
was stabilized in mid-2009. The exchange rate peaked at 1,570 won per
dollar early in March and dropped to 1,195 won in September 2009.

The Restructuring Policy

The government implemented a strong structural reform policy on the
financial and industrial sectors. It evaluated the credit risk of companies

Table 6.1   Foreign currency liquidity secured from other countries and IMF

	Federal Reserve Bank	Bank of Japan	People's Bank of China	IMF
Pledged resources	$30 billion	$5 billion → increased to $30 billion	$33 billion (180 billion yuan)	$22 billion of short-tem liquidity
Date agreed	October 30, 2008	December 12, 2008	December 12, 2008	–
Maturity	April 30, 2009 → extended to October 2009	April 30, 2009	3 years	–

Source: National Assembly Budget Office (2009).

in the construction and shipbuilding industries, which were more seriously hit by the global financial crisis than any other industries, twice in 2009 and tried to normalize the management of those companies and improve their financial structure. In order to enhance financial resources needed for such restructuring, the government established a bank capital replenishment fund, a restructuring fund, and a financial stabilization fund. These funds would enable relatively healthy financial institutions to replenish their capital proactively, and play a role in strengthening the financial system together with the deposit insurance fund, established to deal with weak financial institutions, of the Korea Deposit Insurance Corporation (KDIC).

The Economic Stimulus Plan

In order to cope with the global financial crisis and international gas price hikes, the government has tried to maximize the effect of its economic stimulus packages by drawing up and executing the expansionary national budget simultaneously with tax cuts since the second half of 2008. It has also attempted to pump up local economies through the revitalization of the real estate market, the expansion of social overhead capital (SOC) investments, a project called 'Green New Deal' and a job creation project. In this context, the residential real estate sector was also substantially deregulated.

5   CONCLUSION

The government and the Bank of Korea aggressively coped with the insta-bility of its domestic capital and foreign exchange markets and the rapid contraction of its real sectors in the aftermath of the turmoil in the global financial markets and the recession of the world economy. In particular, since the collapse of Lehman Brothers in September 2008, the government has taken various policy measures to minimize the repercussions of the global financial crisis. As the crisis deepened and the real sectors of the world economy also seriously contracted after the Lehman Brothers' débâcle, many countries around the world implemented a lenient monetary policy including a series of interest rate cuts and an expansionary fiscal policy to stabilize their financial markets and to stimulate their economy. The Korean government took the same policy measures. Thanks to these efforts, since the first half of 2009, Korea's financial markets have been stabilized to some extent and the real sectors of the economy have improved slowly but steadily.

An average leading business index of 30 member countries of the Organisation for Economic Co-operation and Development (OECD) rose to 95.7 in June 2009 from 94.5 a month earlier, an increase for four consecu-tive months. The index of every member country has improved, which is a sign of recovery in the world economy. Also, in the second quarter of 2009 the GDP growth rate of the EU was only –0.1 percent better than an estimate (–0.5 percent growth). In this external environment, the Korean economy has been doing better and recovering faster than have its major trading partners like the United States, China and the EU. A US investment bank, Goldman Sachs, raised a forecast growth rate of the Korean economy (–1.7 percent → –0.6 percent for 2009 and –0.6 percent → 3.7 percent for 2010).

Note that the Korean government has progressively implemented its expansionary fiscal policy since the onset of the global financial crisis in 2008; however, there is some concern about its fiscal soundness, which might contribute to higher market rates of interest. Considering the current state of the Korean economy, interest rate hikes can be a stum-bling block which hinders its full-scale recovery. Therefore, the govern-ment needs to balance the original objectives of its expansionary fiscal policy and, at the same time, minimize the side-effects from the expanded fiscal deficit. In addition, the sustained efforts of the Korean economy would be needed to minimize the ripple effects of financial shocks from overseas by reinforcing the monitoring of domestic and foreign financial markets and improving its financial system. Finally, in a situation where major global financial institutions have made every effort to survive by selling some of their assets, reducing the scale and scope of their opera-tions, and so on, the Korean banking industry needs to carefully consider an aggressive growth strategy through the development of its investment banking sector and the enhancement of its global competitiveness, and the Korean economy to prepare for another sudden liquidity crisis and address a potential inflation issue.

NOTES

* This work was supported by an INHA Research Grant.
1. A CDS premium indicates a country's credit risk, and CDS indexes are benchmarks for protecting bonds against default; investors use them to speculate on credit quality. An increase suggests that the perceptions of credit quality are worsening.
2. The three-month foreign currency liquidity ratio is computed by dividing foreign currency assets maturing in three months by foreign currency liabilities with maturity of less than three months.
3. The volume of net selling is the sum of the KOSPI and the Korea Securities Dealers Automated Quotations (KOSDAQ) markets.
4. For the 10 months in 2008, foreign investors withdrew $74.7 billion of their money from seven Asian stock markets: $34.8 billion from Korea, $12.2 billion from Taiwan, $11.2 billion from India, $11 billion from Japan, $4 billion from Thailand, $0.8 billion from the Philippines, and $0.7 billion from Indonesia (Financial Supervisory Service, 2008).
5. The forecasting of an expansion or slowdown in the economy is based on 10 economic indicators related to employment, production, consumer spending, investments, financial markets and trade.
6. The benchmark interest rate, called the BOK base rate, is a rate applied to transactions, such as repurchase agreements, between the BOK and its counterparts, the financial institutions.
7. Changes in the benchmark interest rate are shown below (National Assembly Budget Office, 2009):

Control date	Aug. 7 2008	Oct. 9 2008	Oct. 27 2008	Nov. 7 2008	Dec. 11 2008	Jan. 9 2009	Feb. 12 2009
Control range (%)	0.25	−0.25	−0.75	−0.25	−1.00	−0.50	−0.50
Target rate (%)	5.25	5.00	4.25	4.00	3.00	2.50	2.00

REFERENCES

Chang, J.C., Y.J. Chun, H.Y. Chun, C.M. Shin, H.Y. Chung, J.S. Yoo, M.J. Sohn and M.W. Kang (2008), 'The global financial crisis and the Korean economy' (in Korean), *CEO Information*, Vol. 677, Samsung Economic Research Institute, October 22.
Financial Supervisory Service (2008), *FSS Weekly Newsletter*, October 20.
Jeong, H.S. (2009), 'Recent evaluation of and prospects for the financial crisis in newly-developing countries' (in Korean), *SERI Economic Focus*, Vol. 226, Samsung Economic Research Institute, January 13.
National Assembly Budget Office (2009), *Impacts of the Global Financial Crisis and Policy Response* (in Korean), April.

7. Promulgation of the US housing market crisis into Asia: impacts and depths

Masanori Amano and Hikari Ishido

1 INTRODUCTION

The US housing market crisis (subprime loan crisis) has left the Asian countries with lingering effects in production and other real as well as financial activities. Only recently have the news articles reported the upward trend in production and real GDP of those countries around the first quarter of 2009. In this chapter, we report and analyze the timing relations and depths of the US-started stagnation, with a focus on selected Asian countries.

The next section gives an overview of the impacts of the US housing market crisis on Asia. Section 3 describes the falls in production growth, between January 2008 and the middle of 2009, to see how the US housing crisis has hit the Asian countries in question, although these falls are not solely due to the US crisis. Section 4 estimates some determinants of production growth of selected Asian countries, where the determinants are US variables as well as some of their own. The countries considered are Japan, Singapore, Thailand, South Korea, Malaysia, China, Indonesia, and India (throughout this chapter 'Korea' indicates 'South Korea').[1] This ordering reflects the size of falls in the growth of industrial production, which were partly due to the US crisis, with Japan posting the largest drop. In the same section, we then present pairwise correlations between stock prices of the US and Asian countries. The last part of this section suggests, using regression analyses and stock price correlations, the transmission mechanism of the US-started crisis to various regions of Asian countries. Section 5 concludes with a summary of the discussion.

2   THE IMPACTS OF THE US HOUSING MARKET CRISIS ON ASIA: AN OVERVIEW

This section gives an overview of the impacts of the US housing market crisis on Asia.[2] The global economic downturn of 2008 originated in the US subprime housing mortgage crisis. By mid-2009, the financial crisis had spread across the Atlantic to many European countries. Both the US and the European Union (EU) are suffering a severe credit crunch. An issue of utmost importance for Asia, therefore, is the extent to which the global financial crisis has affected its financial stability.

On the whole, Asian financial institutions and financial systems do not yet seem to have been shaken by the financial crisis (now on a global scale); nor have Asian housing market price indexes experienced the sharp declines seen in the US or the EU. Despite the sporadic and intermittent episodes of extreme market pressures in Asian money markets, interbank rates have generally remained at or below pre-crisis levels after a spike which followed the collapse of Lehman Brothers in September 2008. This could be due partly to liquidity injections made by Asian central banks, but more fundamentally, it reflects the fact that in Asia, the global credit crisis has not disrupted the flow of short-term loans. The region has thus far been able to cope with the financial turbulence faced by the US and EU financial sectors. A major reason for Asia's relative stability lies in the fact that Asia's financial institutions, unlike their counterparts in the US and Europe, have only limited exposure to subprime and related products. Despite the rapid development of capital markets in recent years, Asian financial systems are still dominated by commercial rather than investment banks, with lower leverages and hence more financial stability.

Worsening global prospects had, however, soured the medium-term outlook for the real sectors of most Asian countries after the US housing market crisis. Overall, economic growth in Asia started to cool in 2008 from the record levels of 2007. This economic downturn had made a negative impact on the pace of poverty reduction in this region. Governments in the Asian region have been fighting against the downturn through fiscal stimulus packages, yet their future impact remains uncertain.

The Asian region's sharp slowdown underlines the risks of excessive dependence on external demand. The current global economic slowdown is having an adverse impact on Asia's real sector. GDP growth is set to decelerate throughout the region as a result of weakening demand for the region's exports (to be discussed in Section 4). In view of this, the policy makers as well as the public of the region are mostly preoccupied with the real sector rather than with the financial sector. Despite some tightening, the credit markets continue to function fairly normally and, unlike the

US and the EU, only a small-scale 'credit crunch' has so far hit the Asian economy.

Nevertheless, some anecdotal evidence from the region suggests that banks have pulled back from lending to riskier borrowers. For example in Japan, loan proposals from domestic small and medium-sized enterprises (SMEs) have been declined with a larger probability, a manifestation of the significant drop in the country's industrial production (discussed later in Section 4). The new Japanese administration (under the Democratic Party of Japan) took a policy initiative in the latter part of 2009 to enable the moratorium of loan repayments within a few years (the impact of such a policy option remains uncertain as of when this chapter was written: October 2009).

In Korea also, there is a large gap between the ability of large-scale firms, on the one hand, and SMEs, on the other, to secure bank loans, even though overall credit conditions have eased. In Singapore, the government, recognizing the tightening of credit lines for smaller firms, has committed itself to facilitating loans to them and to bearing a high share of the risk associated with those loans.

As of late 2009, protectionism also presented an especially significant risk to a global recovery, with serious implications for highly trade-dependent Asian countries. In spite of the World Trade Organization's (WTO's) effort against such protectionism, slowing growth and rising unemployment could give rise to social instability in Asia, potentially leading to a further decline in investment and growth.

All in all, the real-sector impact, albeit displaying some time lag, seems to be much larger than the financial impact. The next section focuses on the real sector, that is, industrial production of Asian economies in preparation for the regression analyses that follow.

3   PRODUCTION FALLS AND THE LINKAGE BETWEEN THE US AND ASIAN ECONOMIES

Figure 7.1 exhibits time shapes of production growth of the USA, Japan, and China, and Figure 7.2 those of India, Korea, and Thailand. Focusing on these economies is expected to highlight the difference in the performance of Asian countries' industrial production.

Figure 7.1 shows that until the start of the housing crisis, US and Japanese growth evolved on a similar level, but the fall of growth in the latter half of 2008 was much larger in Japan than in the US. As the financial crisis deepened, Japan appeared to be able to withstand the financial turbulence. In September 2008, the country's financial sector was in a

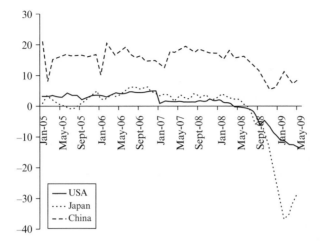

Source: Authors' calculation based on IMF (2009), *International Financial Statistics*,
August 2009 (reproduced in Appendix Table 7A.1).

*Figure 7.1   Growth rates of industrial production (year on year) of the
USA, Japan and China*

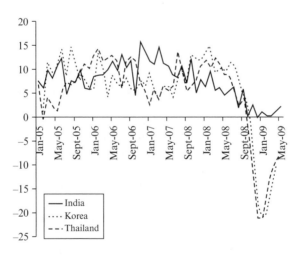

Source: Authors' calculation based on IMF (2009), *International Financial Statistics*,
August 2009, reproduced in Appendix Table 7A.1.

*Figure 7.2   Growth rates of industrial production (year on year) of India,
Korea and Thailand*

sound condition with limited exposure to the risky financial assets. Yet the economy had been weakening even before the collapse of global financial markets. The current account surplus began to narrow in tandem with the appreciation of the yen. Although Japan maintains a trade surplus with the US especially in the field of machinery exports, the yen has appreciated by about 40 percent in real trade-weighted terms since mid-2007, adding strains to the export sector.

In 2008, Japan's exports declined by more than imports, widening the trade gap and leading to a current account deficit of $1.93 billion, the first current account deficit in the past 13 years. Reacting to the slowing economy, Japanese firms reduced their workforces, particularly non-regular workers, in 2008. Consumption plummeted, and the gradual economic recovery (albeit largely unnoticed by domestic consumers) after the 'lost decade' of 1990–2000 as an aftermath of the 'bubble economy' of the latter part of 1980s, has stopped somewhat abruptly.

China's growth, on the other hand, stays at much higher levels and the drop after the crisis is small. Expansionary fiscal and monetary policies, coupled with the obvious fact that it is among the world's fastest growing countries, have been able to mitigate the negative impact arising from the global recession. Industrial production regained momentum early in 2009 as firms resumed making capital investments and accumulating inventories.

Turning to Figure 7.2, we observe that until the crisis, the growth of Korea and Thailand is rather similar (but the latter is slightly higher), and their changing patterns after the crisis also resemble each other. A steep fall in exports caused by the global trade slump drove down industrial production and investment in early 2009, in both Korea and Thailand.

India's growth exhibits a similar level to the other two, but the drop is quite minor. As with most other developing countries, the financial crisis certainly slowed India's economic growth significantly, as reflected in a clear weakening of industrial production. However, the country's robust real sector is shown in its relatively stable industrial performance.

To supplement our discussion so far, Table 7.1 shows how much industrial production fell between January 2008 and the month in which each country recorded the lowest growth in industrial production.

Industrial production is measured monthly, and its growth rate is calculated on a year-on-year basis. It is now commonly thought that the housing crisis started in August 2007, but in the table, the initial starting year of the production fall is set to be in January 2008. For instance, Japan posted a fall of growth in industrial production of 40.9 percentage points; that is, it was –36.9 percent in February 2009 and 4.0 percent in January

Table 7.1   *The size of falls in industrial production growth*

Country	Period	Size of fall
Japan	Jan. 08–Feb. 09	40.9 percentage points (1)
US	Jan. 08–Jul. 09	15.8 percentage points (6)
China	Jan. 08–Apr. 09	9.9 percentage points (7)
Indonesia	Jan. 08–Jan. 09	7.5 percentage points (8)
India	Jan. 08–Dec. 08	6.4 percentage points (9)
Korea	Jan.08–Dec. 08	33.1 percentage points (4)
Malaysia	Jan.08–Jan. 09	27.5 percentage points (5)
Singapore	Jan.08–Mar. 09	40.4 percentage points (2)
Thailand	Jan.08–Jan. 09	34.9 percentage points (3)

Notes
1. (Industrial) production is measured monthly. Growth rates are annual (over the past 12 months).
2. The ending month is that which posted the lowest growth, where the monthly data extend around the middle of 2009.
3. The numbers in parentheses are orders of the size of growth falls.

Sources: Economist Intelligence Unit (online database) and IMF (various years).

2008. As shown in the table, the month with the lowest production growth differs from country to country.

Although the falls in production growth are partly due to domestic business-cycle reasons, the table suggests that the following factors affected the size of the production falls: geographical proximity, trade and financial linkages, and degree of trade dependence of the sampled countries on the US economy and among their own.

Table 7.2 shows the correlation coefficients of stock prices among selected Asian countries as well as the US. While the financial linkage with the US is strong especially in the cases of Japan, Singapore and Thailand, there are some 'intra-Asian' financial linkages among China, India and some neighboring countries. One can also expect an ever-increasing level of autonomous, or intra-regional, industrial linkage in Asia. The US housing market crisis might have triggered a similar anxiety in Asia, but it is the real-sector interdependence, most significantly channeled by trade and investment linkages, that seems to determine its impact in Asian countries.

4   SOME REGRESSION ANALYSES

To see the points raised in the previous section more clearly, we have run single-equation ordinary least squares (OLS) regressions using the

Table 7.2   The correlation coefficient matrix of stock prices

	USA	China	India	Indonesia	Japan	Korea	Malaysia	Singapore	Thailand
USA	–	0.53	0.59	0.53	0.90	0.68	0.70	0.81	0.88
China	–	–	0.89	0.91	0.35	0.89	0.93	0.22	0.50
India	–	–	–	0.96	0.46	0.92	0.91	0.26	0.56
Indonesia	–	–	–	0.33	0.88	0.93	0.32	0.54	
Japan	–	–	–	–	–	0.59	0.51	0.06	0.73
Korea	–	–	–	–	–	–	0.89	0.28	0.68
Malaysia	–	–	–	–	–	–	0.27	0.65	
Singapore	–	–	–	–	–	–	–	–	0.26
Thailand	–	–	–	–	–	–	–	–	–

Source: Economist Intelligence Unit (online database), reproduced in Appendix Table 7A.2.

maximum-likelihood method, with growth rates of industrial production of various countries as dependent variables. The first such specification we have adopted and the regression result are as follows:

$$ipj = -42.000 + 0.011spa + 1.112 ipa - 0.383tba + 0.133tbj + 0.321\text{AR}(1).$$
$$[51] \qquad\qquad (4.675) \quad (5.851) \quad (1.912) \quad (1.912);$$
$$R^2 = 0.97, DW = 2.10. \quad (7.1)$$

In equation (7.1) *ipj* stands for the growth of Japanese industrial production over the previous 12 months, *spa* is the US stock market index (S&P 500), *ipa* is annual growth (%) of US industrial production, *tba* is trade balance (fob export value minus cif import value basis, $US billion), *tbj* is Japan's trade balance (the basis and unit are the same as for the US), and AR(1) implies that the errors follow a first-order autoregressive process.[3] Since the *t*-ratio (in absolute value) for the constant is also not relevant (see note 3), it is not shown in the text. R^2 is the adjusted coefficient of determination. In equation (7.1), the figure in square brackets is the number of observations actually used. The last letters imply country attributions; that is, *a*: the USA, *j*: Japan, *c*: (Mainland) China, *k*: South Korea, *t*: Thailand, *m*: Malaysia, *s*: Singapore, *i*: Indonesia, and *in*: India.

Equation (7.1) is a little surprising because most of the fluctuation in Japanese industrial production is explained by US stock prices, industrial production and trade balance, as well as the Japanese trade balance.

Although the adjusted R^2 is lower, what can be said with regard to Japan also applies to China, except that *tba* does not significantly explain *ipc* (China's growth of industrial production):

Equation (7.2) is the estimation for China, after *tba* (the US trade balance) is dropped:

$$Ipc = 4.25 + 0.01spa + 0.18ipa - 0.15tbc + 0.21AR(1) + 0.05AR(2).$$
[51] $\quad$ (5.37) $\quad$ (0.03) $\quad$ (4.17); $\quad R^2 = 0.77, DW = 1.97.$

$$(7.2)$$

A remarkable point here is that China's trade balance has a negative coefficient with a highly significant *t*-ratio. This might imply that there is a reverse causality running from bigger industrial production–(domestic) consumption to smaller excess trade balance; or that China's domestic consumption is a substitute for foreign countries' consumption.

In a similar estimation for Korea, we obtain a quite different picture from the previous cases. Our Korean specification is as follows:

$$ipk = -13.26 + 0.01spa + 0.98ipa - 0.11tba + 0.0002tbk +$$
$$0.70AR(1) - 0.14AR(2)$$
[50] $\quad$ (0.01) $\quad$ (2.79) $\quad$ (0.43) $\quad$ (0.59);
$$R^2 = 0.86, DW = 1.88. \quad (7.3)$$

Korea's industrial production growth cannot be explained by US stock prices, its trade balance, or even Korea's trade balance. The only variable that matters is the growth of US industrial production. The correlation coefficient between stock prices of the US and Korea is not so high (see Table 7.2 for more details). Hence one is tempted to infer that Korea's exports to the US are quite high as a percentage of its total exports, but this is not consistent with the Korean figure in Table 7.3 where Korea's (US exports)/(its total exports) ratio ranks only sixth out of seven countries. Various reports written on the country, however, suggest that Korea's industrial production was affected by the credit crunch in 2008 which was triggered by the global financial turmoil and domestically magnified by investors' capital outflow and fear of another Asian financial crisis.[4]

Turning to Thailand, we can see below that all the listed coefficients are significant at the 5 percent level, although the US trade balance is dropped because the coefficient is not significant:

$$ipt = 5.58 + 0.02spa + 0.81ipa - 0.001tbt + 0.62AR(1) \quad (7.4)$$
[52] $\quad$ (2.51) $\quad$ (2.64) $\quad$ (2.64); $\quad R^2 = 0.84, DW = 1.87.$

The high correlation coefficient between stock prices of the US and Thailand (0.88), and the high significance in the coefficients of *spa* and *ipa*, imply that both countries maintain a strong linkage financially as well as through the commodities trade. As in China's case, Thailand's trade

Table 7.3   Share of exports to the US in total exports

Rank	Country	Share of exports to the US in total exports (average of 2005–08, %)
1	Japan	21.0
2	China	19.8
3	Malaysia	16.6
4	India	14.4
5	Thailand	13.6
6	Korea*	13.4
7	Indonesia	10.6
8	Singapore	9.2

Note: *Korea's figure is the average of 2006, 2007 and 2008.

Source: Economist Intelligence Unit (online database).

surplus reduces its production growth, small in degree but significantly. It may be conjectured here as well that the causality ran from production (consumption) to trade balance or that domestic and foreign consumptions competed with each other.

The following is the specification for Malaysia:

$$Ipm = -16.15 + 0.002spa + 0.715ipa - 0.231tba + 0.28\text{AR}(1). \quad (7.5)$$
$$[51] \qquad\qquad (0.54) \qquad (4.01) \qquad (2.89);$$
$$R^2 = 0.780,\ DW = 1.85.$$

In the case of Malaysia, although US stock prices have no significant effect, US industrial production and trade balance have significant impacts, which implies that Malaysia serves as a supplier of refined and crude oil as well as materials derived from other underground resources.

Singapore's specification is:

$$ips = 2.02 - 0.003spa + 1.34ipa + 1.55tbs + 0.02\text{AR}(1). \quad (7.6)$$
$$[53] \qquad (0.26) \qquad (2.55) \qquad (1.15);\ R^2 = 0.31,\ DW = 1.90.$$

Singapore's growth of production exhibits somewhat distinct features because trade balances of the US and of its own, as well as US stock prices, have no significant effects on it. Table 7.2, however, records high correlations between the two countries' stock prices, suggesting the strong financial linkage between them. Note also that the size of the fall in Singapore's growth of industrial production is the second largest next to Japan.

Indonesia's specification is:

$$ipi = -11.79 + 0.15spa - 0.19ipa - 0.001tbi + 0.52AR(1). \quad (7.7)$$
$$[51] \qquad\qquad (1.46) \quad (0.70) \quad (1.71);$$
$$R^2 = 0.32, DW = 2.00.$$

The time shape of Indonesia's industrial production is autonomous and similar to Singapore's, because stock prices, production, and the US trade balance are independent of its industrial activity. The only factor affecting its production is the trade balance of its own country, in a weak way ($p = 0.09$).

We now turn to India, where US stock prices correlate strongly with India's production, suggesting a financial linkage between the two:

$$ipin = -2.21 + 0.01spa + 0.18ipa + 0.0004tbin - 0.05AR(1). \quad (7.8)$$
$$[53] \qquad\qquad (3.22) \quad (1.32) \quad (3.06);$$
$$R^2 = 0.54, DW = 1.86.$$

Furthermore, India's trade balance strongly affects its industrial activity, but the overall US trade balance cannot explain India's production significantly.

To examine whether (and how much) Japanese or Chinese domestic variables have affected the growth of US industrial production, we ran the following two regressions, first using Japanese (7.9), and then Chinese (7.10) variables (listed on the right-hand side):

$$ipa = -1724.08 + 1.60E - 5spj + 0.14ip - 0.004tbj + 0.70AR(1) +$$
$$0.30AR(2). \quad (7.9)$$
$$[51] \qquad\qquad\qquad (0.95) \qquad\qquad (2.12) \quad (0.18);$$
$$R^2 = 0.96, DW = 1.96.$$

In (7.9), US production growth is explained only by Japanese production growth, confirming the close linkage of real activity of the two. It is somewhat surprising to see that US production has not been explained by its own trade balance (which is not listed on the right-hand side).

The final question is whether China's domestic activity influenced US domestic production:

$$ipa = 6.25 - 0.0003spc + 0.01ipc + 0.002tbc + 1.06AR(1). \quad (7.10)$$
$$[52] \qquad\quad (0.0002) \quad (0.01) \quad (0.01);$$
$$R^2 = 0.96, DW = 2.27.$$

Equation (7.10) provides clues to this question; surprisingly, none of China's variables explains US production. The above two estimations were conducted to see whether reverse causality from either the Japanese or the Chinese economy existed. But what was found was bilateral causality between real economic (as well as financial, see Table 7.2) activity of the US and Japan. In other words, the US economy was quite independent or autonomous in nature.

Table 7.2 exhibits pairwise correlation coefficients between two countries' stock prices. An interesting observation that emerges from the table is that one can group three pairwise countries that have high correlations, as follows:

1. High correlation countries centering on the US: US–Japan (0.90), and US–Thailand (0.88).
2. High correlation countries centering on China: China–India (0.89), China–Indonesia (0.91), and China–Malaysia (0.93).
3. High correlation countries centering on India: India–Indonesia (0.96), India–Korea (0.92), and India–Malaysia (0.91).

These groupings, together with regression analyses (7.1)–(7.10), may be interpreted as follows: the housing crisis that started in the US spread into Japan, China, and Thailand through real as well as financial avenues. Financial crises thus created in Asia were spread from China and India (and also Japan) into the rest of the Asian countries with which this chapter is concerned. However, real and financial woes thus created in Asia did not affect the US, probably because the size of the US economy is far larger than that of the other countries, whose export ratios (exports/ GDP) are some of the smallest.[5]

Finally, Table 7.3 shows the average number of (exports to the US)/ (total exports), from 2005–08 for each Asian country. The five highest averages are for Japan (21.0 percent), China (19.8 percent), Malaysia (16.6 percent), India (14.4 percent), and Thailand (13.6 percent). Although we need to take into account the size of each country, these figures seem to support (at least partly) the observations mentioned in the previous paragraph.

5   CONCLUSIONS

This chapter has examined the impacts and depths on some Asian countries of financial-housing crises which originated in the US economy. As is well recognized, there are two avenues through which US crises have been transmitted into Asia: real activity through trade relations and financial activity through financial transactions.

The countries that experienced big drops in production growth are, in descending order, Japan, Singapore, Thailand, Korea, Malaysia, and China; the least affected countries are Indonesia and India.

Further, we can classify countries pairwise using stock price correlations; thus, the countries maintaining the highest correlations with the US are Japan and Thailand. Next, the countries having the highest correlations with China are Malaysia, Indonesia, and India. Finally, the countries showing the highest correlations with India are Indonesia, Korea, and Malaysia.

In view of the above groupings and characterizations, the following promulgation mechanisms of the crises can be proposed. Both the financial and real impacts of the crises were transmitted from the US to Japan. What was conveyed from the US to China and Malaysia was largely real influence, which was transmitted via trading activity. Other Asian countries (except for Japan) were affected financially in the form of declining stock prices, which were mediated through China and India. India has not been affected as much, which is probably due to its small export dependency rate (0.13, see note 4), in spite of its fairly large ratio of (exports to the US)/(total exports).

Overall, a policy recommendation on the basis of the above findings would be that Asia's regional policy makers have to make serious medium- and long-term commitments to try to boost the region's real sector, while they might have to struggle for their short-term objectives of checking a future occurrence of another Asian financial crisis.

NOTES

1. We planned to include the Philippines and Taiwan in the sample, but could not do so because of limited data availability.
2. The description in this section largely draws on ADB (2009a, 2009b) and Png (2008).
3. To avoid serially correlated errors we assume that errors follow either AR(1) or AR(2) processes; also, to get away from heteroskedasticity, we use White-heteroskedasticity-consistent standard errors. As the DW ratio (as well as Breusch–Godfrey's LM (Lagrange Multiplier) test, which is not shown here) imply, low t-values (high p-values) of AR(1) and AR(2) terms do not necessarily imply that the error term entails serial correlation. Hence t-values for AR(1) and AR(2) are not shown. See, for example, Johnston and DiNardo (1997, Chs 6 and 7) for AR(i) processes and Breusch–Godfrey serial correlation tests.
4. Takayasu (2009), for instance, describes the behavior of foreign as well as domestic investors' capital outflow in the latter half of 2008.
5. Our estimates of these figures are as follows: USA: 0.09, Japan: 0.13, China: 0.03, Indonesia: 0.31, India: 0.13, Korea: 0.53, Malaysia: 0.76, Singapore: 0.19, and Thailand: 0.63. (The figures are on an annual basis of 2007 or 2008, except for India which is for 2006, computed from the IMF.) The average of the above nine countries is 0.31.

REFERENCES

Asian Development Bank (ADB) (2009a), *Asian Development Outlook 2009: Rebalancing Asia's Growth*, Manila: ADB.

Asian Development Bank (ADB) (2009b), *Asian Development Outlook 2009 Update: Broadening Openness for a Resilient Asia*, Manila: ADB.

International Monetary Fund (IMF) (various years), *International Financial Statistics*, Washington, DC: IMF.

Johnston, J. and J. DiNardo (1997), *Econometric Methods*, 4th edn, New York: McGraw Hill.

Png, Ivan (ed.) (2008), *Financial Crisis 2008*, Singapore: Saw Centre Financial Studies.

Takayasu, Yuichi (2009), 'Kankoku ni okeru Keizai Kouzou no Henka to Sekai Kin-yu fuan niyoru Eikyo' (Change in Korea's economic structure and the impacts of global financial fear), *Waarudo Torendo* (World Trend), vol. 166, pp. 6–9.

Appendix Table 7A.1   Growth rate of industrial production of the USA and selected Asian countries (Jan. 2005 = 100)

	USA	China	India	Indonesia	Japan	Korea	Malaysia	Singapore	Thailand
Jan-05	3.2	20.9	7.5	2.0	0.9	6.7	5.7	10.7	5.9
Feb-05	3.1	7.6	5.9	10.6	3.9	-0.9	-0.2	-10.7	1.3
Mar-05	3.6	15.1	9.8	7.2	2.2	4.4	5.9	8.9	11.7
Apr-05	3.0	16.0	8.1	3.5	0.7	2.1	2.2	4.1	9.1
May-05	2.8	16.6	10.8	4.7	0.4	1.2	1.5	1.9	10.8
Jun-05	4.3	16.8	12.2	3.2	-0.2	5.2	3.8	11.2	14.1
Jul-05	3.6	16.1	4.7	-0.8	-1.2	7.4	1.7	6.1	8.7
Aug-05	3.7	16.0	7.6	1.7	0.1	6.6	4.8	11.8	14.9
Sept-05	2.1	16.5	7.2	-1.1	0.9	7.2	7.2	22.3	11.1
Oct-05	2.6	16.1	9.8	-5.4	2.5	8.1	6.1	18.9	7.7
Nov-05	3.3	16.6	6.0	0.2	3.4	11.4	8.5	21.1	7.8
Dec-05	3.6	16.5	5.7	-7.6	4.9	10.2	2.2	5.4	6.1
Jan-06	3.3	9.8	8.5	-6.5	1.9	13.0	4.1	0.0	5.8
Feb-06	3.0	20.1	8.8	-6.9	2.3	14.5	7.4	35.7	13.3
Mar-06	3.7	17.8	8.9	-9.6	3.7	11.6	4.9	24.0	10.1
Apr-06	4.4	16.6	9.9	-3.8	3.1	12.3	4.4	1.9	4.0
May-06	4.0	17.9	11.7	-4.0	3.7	12.9	5.9	10.1	8.8
Jun-06	4.3	19.5	9.7	-0.7	5.3	12.0	6.4	22.4	6.8
Jul-06	4.7	16.7	13.2	0.4	6.1	6.4	6.2	19.9	6.2
Aug-06	4.6	15.7	10.3	-2.9	6.2	11.6	4.3	5.4	8.0
Sept-06	4.4	16.1	12.0	1.4	5.5	12.6	3.0	6.4	5.5

Appendix Table 7A.1 (continued)

	USA	China	India	Indonesia	Japan	Korea	Malaysia	Singapore	Thailand
Oct-06	4.7	14.7	4.5	-9.1	6.6	11.7	-1.6	3.6	5.7
Nov-06	4.9	14.9	15.8	14.2	4.9	7.0	7.8	16.4	8.0
Dec-06	5.1	14.7	13.4	16.0	4.5	5.3	6.4	5.8	6.5
Jan-07	0.9	13.6	11.6	8.6	3.3	2.6	3.9	15.5	9.3
Feb-07	1.7	12.6	11.0	3.6	4.0	6.0	-1.4	5.3	5.2
Mar-07	1.4	17.6	14.8	9.3	3.4	3.5	-1.0	0.0	3.8
Apr-07	1.5	17.4	11.3	9.2	1.1	6.4	1.9	22.0	6.3
May-07	1.6	18.1	10.6	6.6	3.7	5.5	3.2	16.6	6.2
Jun-07	1.2	19.4	8.9	5.1	2.5	6.5	-0.2	-10.6	4.0
Jul-07	1.3	18.0	8.3	4.7	2.2	13.7	1.7	24.9	7.6
Aug-07	1.2	17.5	10.9	5.0	4.4	8.9	0.6	14.7	10.2
Sept-07	1.8	18.9	7.0	2.4	2.7	5.4	1.5	-3.0	8.9
Oct-07	1.5	17.9	12.2	5.6	3.9	6.9	5.2	3.4	13.0
Nov-07	2.3	17.3	4.9	4.6	2.0	7.7	2.8	-2.9	12.1
Dec-07	1.7	17.4	8.0	3.3	2.3	10.9	7.2	-4.0	11.8
Jan-08	2.2	16.4	6.2	5.8	4.0	11.9	9.6	8.3	13.9
Feb-08	1.1	15.4	9.5	9.5	3.9	10.2	9.7	10.2	14.9
Mar-08	0.9	17.8	5.5	2.5	2.5	12.3	2.7	17.8	9.2
Apr-08	-0.1	15.7	6.2	3.5	2.3	11.1	4.5	-5.3	10.0
May-08	-0.4	16.0	4.4	4.0	2.3	8.9	2.6	-13.5	9.1
Jun-08	-0.7	16.0	5.4	2.4	0.2	8.6	2.3	2.3	11.3

Jul-08	−1.0	14.7	6.4	2.8	−0.2	5.9	5.0	−21.9	11.0
Aug-08	−2.2	12.8	1.7	2.9	−5.7	3.1	1.2	−12.0	7.7
Sept-08	−6.4	11.4	6.0	−0.8	−4.0	3.9	−2.0	3.3	4.3
Oct-08	−4.7	8.2	0.1	6.1	−9.0	−2.1	−3.1	−12.2	2.4
Nov-08	−6.5	5.4	2.5	0.6	−14.1	−12.5	−7.9	−6.7	−7.7
Dec-08	−8.9	5.7	−0.2	−1.9	−21.8	−21.2	−15.9	−13.4	−18.6
Jan-09	−10.9	7.9	1.0	−1.7	−30.0	−21.1	−17.9	−26.3	−21.2
Feb-09	−11.3	11.0	0.2	0.9	−36.9	−15.2	−12.5	−11.8	−19.9
Mar-09	−12.5	8.3	0.3	1.3	−35.1	−11.4	−12.6	−32.6	−14.6
Apr-09	−12.7	7.3	1.2	1.5	−30.7	−9.1	−11.5	0.8	−9.7
May-09	−13.5	8.9	2.2	n.a.	−27.6	−7.7	n.a.	2.1	−10

Source: Economist Intelligence Unit (online database).

Appendix Table 7A.2   Stock market price indices of the USA and selected Asian countries (Jan 2005 = 100)

	USA	China	India	Indonesia	Japan	Korea	Malaysia	Singapore	Thailand
Jan-05	100.0	100.0	100.0	100.0	100.0	100.0	100.0	100.0	100.0
Feb-05	101.9	109.6	102.4	102.8	103.1	108.4	99.0	101.1	105.7
Mar-05	100.0	99.0	99.0	103.3	102.5	103.5	95.1	102.2	97.0
Apr-05	98.0	97.2	93.9	98.6	96.7	97.6	96.0	100.9	93.9
May-05	100.9	89.0	102.4	104.1	99.0	104.0	94.0	103.1	95.2
Jun-05	100.8	90.7	109.7	107.4	101.7	108.0	96.9	105.6	96.3
Jul-05	104.5	91.0	116.5	113.1	104.5	119.1	102.3	112.3	96.3
Aug-05	103.3	97.7	119.1	100.5	109.0	116.1	99.8	108.5	99.4
Sept-05	104.1	97.0	131.7	103.3	119.2	130.9	101.3	110.0	103.0
Oct-05	102.2	91.8	120.4	102.0	119.5	124.1	99.5	105.8	97.3
Nov-05	105.8	92.3	134.1	105.0	130.6	139.0	97.8	109.7	95.2
Dec-05	105.7	98.3	143.3	111.3	141.5	147.8	98.3	112.0	101.7
Jan-06	108.4	105.4	151.3	117.9	146.2	150.1	99.8	115.1	108.7
Feb-06	108.5	109.0	158.2	117.8	142.3	147.1	101.4	118.4	106.0
Mar-06	109.7	108.8	172.1	126.6	149.8	145.8	101.2	120.8	104.4
Apr-06	111.0	120.9	183.7	140.1	148.5	152.2	103.6	124.6	109.4
May-06	107.5	137.8	158.6	127.3	135.8	141.3	101.3	113.7	101.0
Jun-06	107.5	140.5	161.8	125.4	136.2	138.8	99.9	116.2	96.6
Jul-06	108.1	135.5	163.9	129.4	135.7	139.1	102.2	116.7	98.4
Aug-06	110.4	139.4	178.4	136.9	141.7	145.0	104.6	118.4	98.4
Sept-06	113.1	147.1	190.0	146.9	141.6	146.9	105.7	122.6	97.7

Oct-06	116.7	154.4	197.7	151.5	144.0	146.3	107.9	128.9	102.8
Nov-06	118.6	176.3	208.9	164.5	142.9	153.5	118.0	135.4	105.3
Dec-06	120.1	215.9	210.3	172.7	151.3	153.7	119.7	142.5	96.9
Jan-07	121.8	234.1	214.9	168.1	152.6	145.8	129.8	149.1	93.2
Feb-07	119.1	241.9	197.3	166.6	154.6	151.9	130.6	148.1	96.4
Mar-07	120.3	267.5	199.4	175.2	151.8	155.7	136.1	154.2	96.0
Apr-07	125.5	322.5	211.6	191.3	152.8	165.3	144.3	160.4	99.6
May-07	129.6	344.5	221.8	199.4	157.0	182.3	147.1	167.5	105.0
Jun-07	127.3	320.5	223.5	204.7	159.3	186.9	147.8	169.3	110.7
Jul-07	123.2	374.8	237.2	224.8	151.5	207.2	150.0	169.3	122.5
Aug-07	124.8	438.0	233.7	210.0	145.5	200.8	139.1	161.9	115.8
Sept-07	129.3	465.9	263.7	225.7	147.4	208.6	145.9	176.8	120.5
Oct-07	131.2	499.8	302.6	252.9	147.0	221.3	154.4	181.6	129.2
Nov-07	125.4	408.6	295.3	257.2	137.7	204.3	152.5	168.0	120.5
Dec-07	124.3	441.3	309.4	262.8	134.4	203.3	157.8	166.1	122.2
Jan-08	116.8	367.7	269.2	251.4	119.4	174.2	152.1	142.3	111.7
Feb-08	112.7	364.7	268.1	260.5	119.5	183.5	148.1	144.4	120.5
Mar-08	112.0	291.2	238.6	234.2	110.0	182.6	136.2	143.5	116.4
Apr-08	117.4	309.8	263.7	220.6	121.6	195.6	139.7	150.2	118.5
May-08	118.5	288.0	250.4	233.9	125.9	179.5	139.3	152.3	118.8
Jun-08	108.4	229.4	205.3	224.8	118.4	171.0	129.6	140.6	109.5
Jul-08	107.3	232.8	219.0	220.6	117.5	158.0	127.0	139.8	96.3

Appendix Table 7A.2 (continued)

	USA	China	India	Indonesia	Japan	Korea	Malaysia	Singapore	Thailand
Jul-08	107.3	232.8	219.0	220.6	117.5	158.0	127.0	139.8	96.3
Aug-08	108.6	201.2	222.2	207.3	114.8	155.2	120.2	130.7	97.4
Sept-08	98.7	192.6	196.2	175.4	98.9	119.3	111.2	112.5	85.0
Oct-08	82.0	145.2	149.3	120.3	75.3	115.3	94.3	85.6	59.4
Nov-08	75.9	157.1	138.7	118.9	74.7	120.5	94.5	82.7	57.3
Dec-08	76.5	153.9	147.1	129.7	77.8	120.5	95.7	84.1	64.1
Jan-09	69.9	167.1	143.7	127.6	70.2	124.5	96.5	83.3	62.4
Feb-09	62.2	174.8	135.6	123.0	66.5	113.9	97.3	76.1	61.5
Mar-09	67.6	199.1	148.1	137.2	71.2	129.3	95.3	81.1	61.5
Apr-09	73.9	207.1	173.9	164.9	77.5	146.7	108.2	91.6	70.1
May-09	77.8	220.9	223.1	183.4	83.6	149.0	114.0	111.1	79.8

Source: Economist Intelligence Unit (online database).

138

8. How Australia survived the global financial crises

Chris Bajada and Rowan Trayler

1 INTRODUCTION

The first major effect of the US subprime mortgage market was felt in Australia around August 2007 when the Australian mortgage lender RAMS announced that it was unable to sell $6 billion[1] of its securitized debt in the global financial market. The RAMS financing model depended on selling home loans in Australia, securitizing these and then selling the securitized debt in international financial markets. Following this announcement, the RAMS share price fell $0.82c to $0.57c. The announcement had an immediate detrimental flow-on effect on the share prices of other financial institutions including the Macquarie, Adelaide and St George banks, as well as several other highly geared non-bank companies such as Centro Properties.

One year later, in August 2008, the shares of Australia's largest child-care provider ABC Learning Centres were put into a trading halt as it had failed to provide its annual results to the share market. There was speculation at the time that the company would be placed into liquidation as it was rumored that its auditor Ernst & Young wanted to review several of the previous year's accounts. The market speculated that this would result in problems that would contravene ABC Learning's bank loan covenants. ABC Learning had expanded rapidly in the previous years, borrowing almost $3.5 billion, of which $1.5 billon was due for repayment in two years. The state of the global debt markets was considered by the market to be a major obstacle for ABC Learning's capacity to refinance its debt. With the collapse of international debt markets and the imminent collapse of ABC Learning, the Australian government announced that it was working through contingencies to keep the 100,000 Australian children within their day-care programs. This is one of a number of examples that highlight the government's timely response to events resulting from the global financial crisis (GFC).

In the lead up to the GFC, the Australian economy was well placed to weather out the ensuing storm. Australia was in its sixteenth consecutive year of strong growth, supported primarily in more recent years by the boom in the mining sector. The terms of trade, partly in response to higher export prices, had improved substantially over the few years leading up to the GFC. This occurred alongside increasing incomes and historically low levels of unemployment. The strong economic performance translated into a rising share market, an appreciation of the Australian dollar against most major trading currencies, including the US dollar, and significant increases in wealth and consumer confidence.

The federal budget (Australian Treasury, 2007) projected a positive outlook for the Australian economy, driven primarily by a strong labor market, low levels of unemployment, a sustained period of economic growth, moderate levels of inflation, and strong business investment, following an average 8.4 percent growth in the preceding 10 years. The budget forecast outlined continuing economic growth, increases in export volume, productivity increases and a rising level of workforce participation. The government also forecast a budget surplus over the next three years, following on from 10 successive years of budget surpluses.

In 2009, one year after the start of the GFC, the Treasurer, in his speech to the Australian Business Economists, reported that the Australian economy was the only one of 33 advanced economies around the world that had not gone into recession as a result of the GFC (Swan, 2009). Compared with other OECD countries, the size of Australia's stimulus package as a percentage of GDP was by far the largest. A measure of how successful the stimulus package has been in mitigating the effects of the GFC and steering the economy towards its pre-GFC growth path is the focus of this chapter. The rest of this chapter is structured as follows. Section 2 provides a chronology of the government's response to the GFC while Section 3 provides an assessment on the success of the stimulus package. Section 4 examines the effects of the bank guarantee on the financial system and Section 5 concludes.

2   AUSTRALIAN GOVERNMENT RESPONSES TO THE GLOBAL FINANCIAL CRISIS

Most OECD countries initiated significant fiscal stimulus packages to mitigate as far as possible the effects of the GFC on their economies. However, the amount spent varies widely across each of these countries. The amount forecast to be spent for the 2008–10 period in Australia is 2.6 percent of GDP, which far exceeds the OECD average, and ranks Australia's stimulus package at the top of the OECD list of countries (OECD, 2009b).

Although there were signs of financial turmoil from mid-2007, it was not until the rapid deterioration of the global financial markets in September 2008, precipitated by the nationalization of Fannie Mae and Freddie Mac and the bailout of Lehman Brothers and others, that governments around the world initiated significant action to alleviate the tightening of credit markets and to stimulate their economies. On 19 September 2008, the Australian government enacted a ban on short selling of shares following similar moves in other countries. The Reserve Bank of Australia dropped the benchmark interest rate by 1 percentage point, the largest in 17 years. Then on 12 October 2008, with a worsening of availability of credit in the global financial markets, the government announced a number of measures to support the Australian financial system and the economy. The first major measure was in response to governments abroad raising the level of guarantees for bank deposits as well as fears of a run on a regional Australian Bank similar to that experienced in the United Kingdom with Northern Rock. The Australian government announced that it would guarantee all deposits and offshore borrowings of Australian banks (later extended to include overseas banks operating in Australia). On 14 October 2008, the prime minister announced a '$10.4 billion AUD economic security strategy to support continued positive growth in the national economy, and to provide practical help to households' (Rudd, 2008). The government stimulus plan had five main features:

- $4.8 billion on long-term pension reform involving an immediate payment of $1,000 to each pensioner in December 2008;
- $3.9 billion in support payments for low-and middle-income families involving a one-off payment of $1,000 for each eligible child in their care;
- $1.5 billion investment to help homebuyers purchase their first home. Under this stimulus payment, first-home buyers who buy existing homes would have their current first-home buyers' grant doubled from $7,000 to $14,000 and if it was a newly constructed home the grant would be $21,000. The government estimated that 150,000 first-home buyers would take advantage of this scheme;
- $187 million to create 56,000 new training places in 2008/09; and
- bringing forward the implementation of three nation building funds, set up in previous budgets, and the commencement of an investment in nation building projects during 2009.

The GFC impacted significantly on a number of international non-bank financial organizations operating in Australia. This was especially the case in the Australian automobile industry. GE Finance and General Motors

Acceptance Corporation (GMAC) had advised their Australian clients that they were terminating their funding arrangements requiring all loans to be repaid within six months and leaving over 40 percent of Australian car dealerships without funding for their dealer floor-plan arrangements. On 5 December 2008, the government announced the establishment of a Special Purpose Vehicle to provide liquidity to car dealers experiencing problems in funding due to the withdrawal by GE Finance and GMAC.

In February 2009 the government announced a second stimulus package following forecasts by the International Monetary Fund (IMF) of a further contraction in economic growth by 2 percent in 2009 and the concerns over the slowdown in the Australian mining sector and the Chinese economy. The combination of these factors posed a severe risk for the Australian economy and jobs. The prime minister labeled the announcement as a '$42 billion nation building and jobs plan to support jobs and invest in future long term economic growth' (Rudd, 2009). In the announcement the prime minister indicated that the effects of the stimulus package would add a half a percent to GDP in 2008/09 and 1 percent in 2009/10. The main elements of the stimulus package were:

- Free ceiling insulation for homes with the objective of reducing greenhouse gas emissions in 2020 by approximately 49.4 million tonnes. The government estimated that around 2.7 million homes would use the scheme and save $200 a year in energy costs.
- Build or upgrade a building in every one of Australia's 9,540 schools. The budget for each school would be $200,000 and included a variety of approved works including libraries, halls, science laboratories and language learning centers.
- Build more than 20,000 new social and defense homes.
- A $950 one-off cash payment to eligible families, single workers, students, drought-affected farmers and others most affected by the flow-on effects of the world financial crisis.
- A temporary business investment tax break of 30 cents in every dollar for small and general businesses buying eligible assets before December 2009.
- Significant increases in funding for local community infrastructure and local road projects including the installation of boom gates at railway level crossings and other road improvement projects in accident black spots.

The reductions in interest rates by the Reserve Bank of Australia (RBA) complemented the government's stimulus package. The RBA, like many other central banks around the world, cut interest rates over this period. In

November 2008 the RBA reduced the cash rate by a further 0.75 percent (following a 1 percent drop the month earlier) during which time many of the world's developed economies were in recession. Then again in December 2008 and February 2009, the RBA cut interest rates by 1 percentage point followed by another 0.75 percentage cut on April 2, 2009, reducing interest rates to a historic low of 3 percent.

3   TAKING STOCK: ASSESSING THE SUCCESS OF THE AUSTRALIAN STIMULUS PACKAGE

A stimulus package needs to satisfy a number of criteria if it is to be considered a success. The features of a successful stimulus package ensure that it:

1. effectively mitigates any (severe) downturn expected in economic activity;
2. impacts on economic activity within a relatively short period of time and can be (gradually) withdrawn as the economy begins to recover;
3. comprises various initiatives, which are appropriately timed and have targeted multiplied effects on the real economy; and
4. contributes towards restoring economic activity to pre-downturn conditions.

The remainder of this section will address each of these four issues in turn and in doing so provides an assessment on how successful the stimulus package has been in mitigating the effects of the GFC on the Australian economy.

Scorecard 1 Effectively mitigates the downturn in economic activity
Section 2 outlined the various spending initiatives by the government in response to the global financial crisis. The size of the stimulus package, measuring in excess of 2 percent of GDP, is by far the largest discretionary expenditure as a percentage of GDP of any of the OECD countries. The federal government's commitment to a stimulus package equivalent to 2.6 percent of GDP over the 2008–10 period (OECD, 2009b) is double that of Canada's package, which over the same period is projected to be 1.3 percent of GDP. Both Canada and Poland have committed the second largest stimulus package as a percentage of GDP of all the OECD countries. To put these figures into perspective, the projected size of the packages for Germany, the United States, France and the United Kingdom are 0.8, 0.3, 0.2 and 0.1 percent of GDP, respectively (ibid.).

How has such a significant stimulus package mitigated the severe

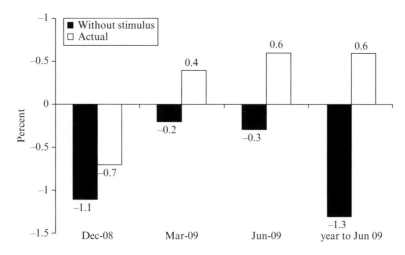

Source: Swan (2009).

Figure 8.1 The impact of the fiscal stimulus of GDP growth

downturn expected in economic activity in Australia and how has this contributed to restoring Australia's economic activity to the pre-GFC conditions? According to Treasury estimates, the timing and size of the fiscal stimulus has meant that Australia avoided a recession in early 2009. Figure 8.1 compares the growth rate of GDP with and without the stimulus package.

As the figure suggests, the growth rate in the December quarter was –0.7 percent, that is, 0.4 percent above that which it would otherwise have been had the government not responded with its stimulus package. In the absence of any fiscal stimulus, GDP growth the following quarter was projected to have been –0.2 percent in March 2009 followed by another negative quarter of economic growth (–0.3 percent) in June 2009. According to Treasury estimates, the fiscal stimulus helped avert a recession, increasing GDP growth from an estimated –0.2 percent (without the stimulus package) to +0.4 percent in March 2009 and from –0.3 percent to +0.6 percent in June 2009. On an annual basis for the year-to-June 2009, the estimated GDP growth, in the absence of any fiscal stimulus, was projected to be –1.3 percent of GDP compared with the actual growth in GDP of +0.6 percent.

Scorecard 2 Short-term impact and capacity for gradual withdrawal
In Table 8.1, each of the various stimulus initiatives are categorized for their short-run impact or speed (column 2) and long-run economic

Table 8.1   The short- and long-run effects of the Australian fiscal stimulus initiatives

Australian fiscal stimulus initiatives	Short-run (impact)	Long-run (impact)
Payments to pensioners	Fast	Low
Payments to low- and middle-income families	Fast	Low
First-home buyer scheme	Medium	Medium–high
Funding for new training places	Medium	Medium
Ceiling insulation and solar hot water rebates	Fast	Low
Social and defense housing improvements and construction	Slow–medium	Medium
Tax, single-income family and back-to-school bonus payments	Fast	Low
Tax breaks for small business	Fast	Medium
School building construction initiatives	Slow–medium	Medium
Science and language center initiatives	Fast	Low
Local community infrastructure projects	Slow	Medium–high
Local road and railway projects	Slow	Medium

impact on economic activity (column 3). The classifications in column 2 are based on a judgment on how quickly each of the stimulus initiatives injected cash into the economy and contributed to employment growth. This is measured on the scale of 'slow', 'medium' and 'fast'. The classification in column 3 is based on the OECD estimates of fiscal multipliers for Australia grouped according to the classifications of infrastructure, government consumption and transfers to household (OECD, 2009a). Each of the fiscal stimulus initiatives are classified as 'low', 'medium' and 'high' according to their likely impact on long-run economic growth. The discussion on the classifications given in column 3 is postponed to the following section.

From Table 8.1 (column 2), most of the fiscal initiatives in the stimulus package were designed to produce significant short-run impacts on economic activity – exactly what is needed during short sharp declines in economic activity and consumer and business confidence. With the exception of some of the more significant infrastructure projects, most of the stimulus initiatives have either occurred as a one-off cash injection in the economy or comprise initiatives that can easily be wound back as the economy recovers from the global economic slowdown. Overall, the nature of the fiscal stimulus appears to satisfy the scorecard criteria that it should 'impact on economic activity within a relatively short period of time and can (gradually) be wound back as the economy begins to recover.

Scorecard 3 Comprises various initiatives, appropriately timed and with a balance of short- and long-term impacts

The effectiveness of any fiscal stimulus initiative during an economic downturn is conditional on the speed and magnitude at which such initiatives impact on the real economy, and much of this has to do with the timing and the types of fiscal initiatives. The stimulus packages outlined in Section 2 and listed in Table 8.1 can be grouped into three broad types of initiatives: (i) cash transfers to low- and middle-income earners; (ii) infrastructure spending on 'shovel-ready' projects; and (iii) spending on more significant longer-term infrastructure endeavors. The sequence of these initiatives occurred in essentially the same order in which they are presented, meaning that the injection of funds to mitigate the initial decline in economic activity occurred rapidly and with some potency. The cash transfers were followed by more significant commitments in construction on projects which the government required to be 'shovel ready' so that their impact is felt relatively quickly but with a longer duration period which the cash transfers would not provide. From Table 8.1 (column 3), most of the fiscal initiatives in the stimulus package provided a suitable mix of strategies for cushioning and steering the economy on a projected growth path towards pre-GFC conditions.

Each of these initiatives and their timing proved to be a potent formula in significantly reducing the likelihood of a recession in Australia – providing the short-term stimulus measures through a process of cash transfers that had an immediate impact on income and consumption, followed by stimulus initiatives that provided for a greater productive capacity over the medium to longer term.

Scorecard 4 Helping to restore economic activity to pre-downturn conditions

As we have already discussed, one of the scorecard items for a successful stimulus package is the extent by which the size of the economic downturn is mitigated over time by a combination of various discretionary fiscal policy initiatives. Our attempt to estimate the impact of the stimulus package, particularly its success in smoothing the economic cycle, is based on comparing projections of economic activity prior to the GFC with the actual economic situation that occurred post-GFC. This approach is different from the previous scorecard measure as it instead tries to gauge the success of the stimulus package by looking at how successful governments

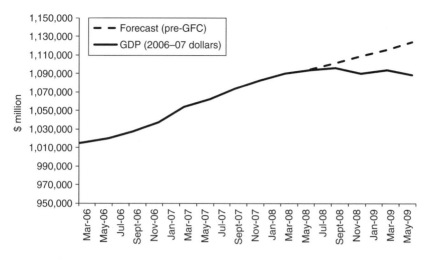

Source: OECD (2009a).

Figure 8.2   GDP: actual and forecast

have been in steering economic activity towards the forecast economic targets estimated prior to the GFC. In essence, this scorecard measure of the success of the stimulus package is not how it has alleviated a recessionary episode, but rather how successful has it been in steering the economy towards the forecast pre-GFC economic growth path.

In Figures 8.2–4 we compare the forecast measures of real GDP, the unemployment rate and real household disposable income against the actual levels of these variables which includes the impact from the government's stimulus package. The dotted line in Figure 8.2 is the forecast value for real GDP estimated by the OECD in early 2008. It is notable in the figure that the decline in real GDP from the impact of the GFC has been quite significant but when compared to other OECD countries (results not presented here) the extent of this downturn is rather insignificant by comparison.

When we compare the forecast and the actual levels of unemployment (see Figure 8.3), the observed unemployment rate has risen moderately above the forecast value. This is significantly different from what economic commentators were predicting at the time. Their predictions were for the unemployment rate to reach 8 percent, admittedly before there was full recognition of the impact of the stimulus package.

Figure 8.4 presents an interesting finding on the impact of the fiscal stimulus package on real household disposable income.

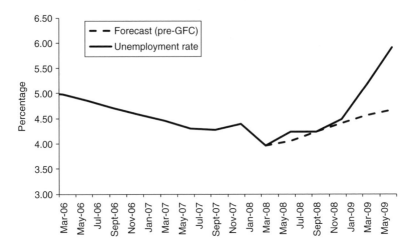

Source: OECD (2009a).

Figure 8.3   Unemployment rate: actual and forecast

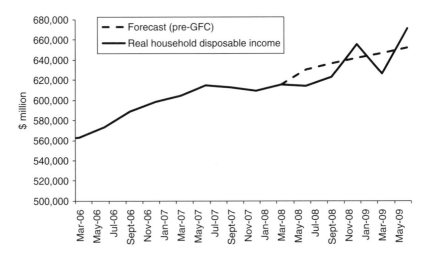

Source: OECD (2009a).

Figure 8.4   Real household disposable income: actual and forecast

In Figure 8.4, the actual level of real household disposable income over the period of the GFC remains within the forecast range. In fact it is notable in this figure that the spikes that occur at the end of 2008 and mid-2009 coincide with the cash transfers paid by the government which

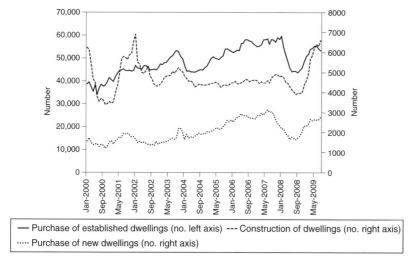

Source: ABS (2009).

Figure 8.5 Construction and purchase of new and existing dwellings

occurred during December 2008 and April 2009. From the figure it appears that the cash transfer payments made by the government were at a level appropriate to reverse the adverse impacts on the level of household disposable income mainly driven by increases in the level of unemployment. The effects on this stimulus package on real household disposable income were of a magnitude that maintained real household disposable income on the forecast growth path.

Figure 8.5 plots the number of new housing construction and purchase of new and existing dwellings from 2000. On 1 July 2000, the federal government introduced the first-home owner grant scheme, which is administered by the various state and territories, to compensate those first-home buyers from the effects of the goods and services tax (GST) introduced at that same time. This commenced as a payment of $7,000 which was considerably increased in October 2008 in response to the GFC. The initiatives under the stimulus package increased this $7,000 subsidy to $14,000 for those who wish to buy an established house and $21,000 for those who purchase a newly constructed home. On the back of the initial subsidy, the number of new dwelling constructions since 2002 has trended upwards, but only moderately. Over the same period, the purchase of new and existing dwellings has also risen. However from mid-to-late 2007, the number of new constructions and the number of purchases of new and existing dwellings fell considerably (–18.9, –24.9 and –19.7 percent, respectively).

From Figure 8.5, the increase in the first-home owner grant in October 2008 had a considerable effect on reducing the downturn in construction and purchases of new and existing dwellings. In fact by June 2009, the falls in the purchase of new and existing dwellings were nearly reversed and the number of new constructions increased substantially above the 2008 level, representing a growth of 69 percent.

Although it is too early to tell how well the stimulus package has rated on the overall performance scorecard, it would appear based on the preliminary evidence presented in this section that the stimulus package has been relatively successful on all four counts. The October 2009 increase in the cash rate by the RBA has been in part driven by significant improvements in domestic economic conditions, including labor market, job vacancies and hiring intentions. These improvements without doubt have been driven, as the evidence suggests, by the stimulus package in conjunction with the corresponding reductions in interest rates during the early phases of the economic downturn in Australia.

4   EFFECTS OF THE BANK GUARANTEE AND THE IMPACT ON BANKING

In response to the lack of confidence in money markets, many countries extended or introduced some form of government guarantee for bank deposit funds. In Australia the government introduced a guarantee of funds lodged with Australian banks as well as for wholesale borrowing arrangements that ultimately would have a major impact on the Australian financial system. Australia was one of the few developed countries that did not have to inject government funds directly into the banking system, unlike the bank bailouts in the United States, the United Kingdom, Germany and France (see Table 8.2). Evaluating the success of the government guarantee, the assistant governor of the Reserve Bank of Australia stated, 'We think that the guarantee has worked well in achieving its purpose which was to unblock key parts of the financial system that were seizing up and to restore confidence' (Lannin, 2009).

But what was the impact of this guarantee on the structure of the financial system? The original intent of the guarantee was to support the smaller and less well-placed financial entities, but what eventuated appears to have been erosion of the beneficial gains from competition and reform achieved over the last 10 years. The effect of the guarantee has resulted in the four major banks in Australia significantly increasing their market share. In July 2009 the four major banks wrote almost all of the $7 billion of new home mortgages that month. Prior to the financial crisis in 2007, the big

Table 8.2   Government support measures for banks, 2008 (selected countries)

Country	Capital injection	Purchase of assets	Total	Total in USD	Total as % of GDP
Australia	nil	A$8	A$8	5.5	0.5
USA	US$250	US$450	US$700	700.0	4.9
UK	£50	nil	£50	73.5	2.6
France	€41	nil	€41	57.6	1.9
Germany	€130	nil	€130	182.8	4.8

Source: Bank of England (2008). Figures are in billions of currency shown, except final column.

four banks had a 60 percent market share and small lenders a 12 percent market share. By 2009 small lenders held less than 1 percent of the market while the big four banks commanded over 90 percent. This can be traced to a number of factors which we discuss below.

The government guarantee applied to deposits of up to $1 million, above that debt raising is guaranteed for a fee based on the risk of the bank. For example, an AA rated bank such as one of the big four Australian banks pays a fee of 70 basis points over the cost of funds while a BBB rated bank such as Bendigo Bank pays a fee of 150 basis points. Many argue that the guarantee arrangements are allowing the big four to dominate the market. Australian banks have used the government guarantee to tap into international debt markets, borrowing $100 billion plus over the nine months to July 2009, which accounted for 10 percent of the global issuance of government-guaranteed bank funds (ABC News, 2009). The big four banks have been the main beneficiaries of this fund raising due to their high credit ratings affording them a competitive advantage in obtaining funds compared with other less highly credit-rated banks – the result of which has led to a downward rigidity in the borrowing rates available to the consumer.

The guarantee raises the issue of a moral hazard dilemma in that the banks may take on excessive risk in their portfolios without the additional funding costs that the higher risk lending should incur. With respect to the guarantee, there is an expectation that the prudential authorities will need to take steps to ensure that the big banks are not investing in more risky asset portfolios.

As a result of the GFC, two of the big four banks have taken over smaller banks in the Australian market. Westpac Bank (fourth largest) merged with St George Bank (fifth largest) to form Australia's largest

Table 8.3　Composition of home mortgage market (%)

Lending institution	Market share August 2007	Market share August 2009
Big four banks	59.1	74.3
Second-tier banks	19.7	10.8
Non-bank lenders	13.2	10.1
Foreign banks	8.1	4.8

Source:　Munro (2009).

bank by market capitalization. The Commonwealth Bank of Australia, the largest Australian bank, was able to acquire Bank West – the Australian subsidiary of troubled HBOS. At the time of these takeovers, the head of the Australian Competition and Consumer Commission indicated that under normal circumstances such takeovers would not have been approved. Therefore the impact of these takeovers plus the effects of the government guarantee has meant a lessening of competition in the home mortgage market. The effects of the mergers, the guarantee, and the move to secure lenders is highlighted in Table 8.3, which compares their effects on the composition of the home mortgage market in 2007 (prior to the GFC) with that in 2009.

Both Westpac Bank and the Commonwealth Bank now account for over 48.5 percent of all outstanding mortgages. Given their size and market dominance there is concern that the big four banks have reduced competition in the Australian market and borrowers may be paying a premium for loans. A similar situation has arisen in the deposit market where the big four are again dominating. The fear is that even after the government guarantee is removed, the big four will hold such a dominant market position that non-bank lenders and second-tier banks will not be able to effectively compete, thereby significantly reducing competition in the market.

5　CONCLUSION

The Australian government acted quickly in response to the global financial crisis by stimulating spending and acting to restore confidence in the financial markets. In this chapter we have highlighted how the financial stimulus package prevented Australia sliding into recession. The fact that Australia is the only one of 33 other OECD countries that averted a recession is testimony to the success of the stimulus initiative (and the complementary monetary policy strategy). Although our economic score-card shows that the stimulus package has been a success and that both the economy and the community have greatly benefited, the outcome of the financial guarantee, while initially preventing any banking collapse has, as several commentators have argued, removed the gains of competition and reform that have slowly evolved over the last 10 years. It will be some time yet before we know for certain whether the Australian financial environment will deliver the benefits of the lessons learnt, past and present.

NOTE

1. Australian dollars unless otherwise indicated.

REFERENCES

ABC News (2009), 'Banks should ditch the guarantee', Podcast radio program, ABC News Radio, Sydney, 28 July, available at: http://www.abc.net.au/news/stories/2009/07/28/2638639.htm (accessed 9 October 2009).

Australian Bureau of Statistics (ABS) (2009), 'Housing Finance, Australia, Table 1. Housing Finance Commitments (Owner Occupation), By Purpose: Australia (5609.0)', Statistical Series 2009, Australian Bureau of Statistics, Commonwealth of Australia, ACT, Canberra.

Australian Treasury (2007), 'Budget Overview', Commonwealth of Australia, ACT, Canberra.

Bank of England (2008), 'Financial Stability Report 24', London, available at: http://www.bankofengland.co.uk/publications/fsr/2008/fsrfull0810.pdf (accessed 5 October 2009).

Lannin, Sue (2009), 'Bank guarantee did its job but should be phased out: RBA', PM podcast radio program, ABC News Radio, Sydney, 28 July, available at: http://www.abc.net.au/pm/content/2008/s2639047.htm (accessed 12 October 2009).

Munro, C. (2009), 'Research confirms big banks dominate mortgage market', Money Manager, Sydney, available at: http://www.moneymanagement.com.au/article/Research-confirms-big-banks-dominate-mortgage-market/504534.aspx (accessed 22 October 2009).

Organisation for Economic Co-operation and Development (OECD) (2009a), 'The effectiveness and scope of fiscal stimulus' (Chapter 3) in *OECD Economic Outlook*, Interim Report, Paris: OECD.

Organisation for Economic Co-operation and Development (OECD) (2009b), *Policy Responses to the Economic Crisis: Stimulus Packages, Innovation and Long-Term Growth*, May, Paris: OECD.

Rudd, K. (2008), 'Economic security strategy', Media Release, 14 October, available at: http://www.pm.gov.au/node/5521 (accessed 5 October 2009).

Rudd, K. (2009), '$42 billion nation building and jobs plan', Media Release, 3

February, available at: http://www.pm.gov.au/node/5331 (accessed 5 October 2009).

Swan, W. (2009), 'One year on: fiscal stimulus and the path ahead', Address to the Australian Business Economists, Sydney, available at: http://www.treasurer.gov.au/speeches/2009/ (accessed 9 October 2009).

PART IV

International regulatory issues

9. A single financial market and multiple safety-net regulators: the case of the European Union

María J. Nieto*

1 FINANCIAL INTEGRATION IN THE EUROPEAN UNION: THE 'CUTTING-EDGE' OF FINANCIAL GLOBALIZATION

In the late 1950, the founding fathers of the European Union (EU) put the member countries on a course toward a single financial market. The main purpose of the Treaty of Rome (1957) was to create a common market where goods, services, people and capital could move freely, including the free provision of financial services. In spite of the political momentum, until the end of the 1970s, not only was the financial sector heavily regulated, but the financial markets were also highly fragmented. Ever since, the integration of the financial markets has been an ongoing project with important landmarks (see Box 9.1) but considerable challenges. The opening of the capital accounts in the late 1980 and particularly the launching of the single currency (the euro) gave a significant thrust to financial integration. At present, the financial integration within the EU is relatively advanced and can be regarded as the 'cutting-edge' of financial globalization (Berrigan et al., 2009).

Integrated money and capital markets need to be supported by a well-functioning and integrated market infrastructure. The European Monetary Union (EMU) fostered this integration because the central banks of the countries that belong to the euro and the European Central Bank (ECB), which together constitute the Eurosystem, have developed facilities in the field of payment and settlement systems. The degree of market integration varies considerably across the different market segments, depending partly on the characteristics of the underlying market infrastructures (ECB, 2009). TARGET is the real-time gross settlement system for the large-value payments and time-critical payments in euros.[1] It was launched in 1999 at the time of the inception of the euro and, since

BOX 9.1   FINANCIAL INTEGRATION IN THE EU:
           ACTIONS TAKEN BY POLICY MAKERS

Deregulation of Entry (1957–1973)
- The spirit of the 1957 Treaty of Rome
- Directive 73/183/EEC on the Freedom of Establishment for Credit Institutions
     The Abolition of Restrictions on Freedom of Establishment and Freedom to Provide Services for Self-employed Activities of Banks and Other Financial Institutions
- Directive 73/239/EEC First Coordinating Directive on Direct Non-Life Insurance
- Directive 76/580/EEC on the Freedom of Establishment in Direct Insurance

Harmonization of Banking Regulations (1973–1983)
- First Banking Directive 77/780/ECC The Coordination of Laws, Regulations and Administrative Provisions Relating to the Taking up and Pursuit of Credit Institutions
     Principle of home country control (branches, most common way to operate internationally)
- Directive 79/267/EEC Coordinating Directive on Direct Life Insurance

Completion of the Internal Market (1983–1992)
- Commission White Paper on Financial Integration (1983)
- Directive 88/361/EEC on the Liberalization of Capital Movements
- Second Banking Directive 89/646/EEC
     Credit institutions authorized in an EU country would be able to establish branches or supply cross-border financial services in other countries without further authorization
     Home country control on solvency (branches and subsidiaries)
     Harmonized capital adequacy standards and large credit exposure rules
- Directive 94/19/EC on Deposit Guarantee Schemes
     Provides for mandatory deposit insurance for all EU banks

Monetary Union (1999)

Financial Services Action Plan (1999–2005) Objective was to develop the legislative and non-legislative framework along *four* objectives:

- A single EU wholesale market
- Open and secure retail banking and insurance markets
- State of the art prudential rules and regulation
- Optimal wider conditions (mainly fiscal rules) for an optimal single financial market

White Paper on Financial Services (2005–2010)

- The pursuit of 'better regulation' (transparent consultation procedures and the undertaking of timely *ex ante* impact assessments of new regulatory proposals)
- Consolidation of existing legislation
- Strengthened supervisory cooperation in the offer of retail financial services (retail financial services and investment funds)

then, it has been the market's preferred system for large value payments in euros (approximately 10,400 banks, including branches and subsidiaries, use TARGET in the EU). It is the backbone of the euro money market. In 2007, the cross-border interbank market exposures were slightly above 30 percent and the securities holding (excluding bank shares) was slightly above 50 percent of the total of the respective asset classes (Tieman and Čihák, 2007). In the commercial paper market and certificates of deposit markets, on the contrary, there is a high degree of fragmentation.[2]

Regarding the integration of bond and capital markets, there are a number of policy initiatives such as the European Directive on Markets and Financial Instruments (MiFID) and the Code of Conduct on clearing and settlement work that are expected to support significant progress on integration of both bond and equity markets by fostering a regulatory level playing field and increasing competition among service providers. Nonetheless, spreads in the government bond market remain sizeable even after controlling for country credit risk as shown in a recent ECB Report (ECB, 2009) indicating some integration problems, while the overall level of issuance in the euro area corporate bond market is lower than in most benchmark countries.

The development of TARGET2-Securities will constitute a major step forward in the delivery of a single integrated securities market for financial services. TARGET2-Securities will provide a single, borderless pool of pan-European securities, as well as a core, neutral, state-of-the-art settlement process. Market users will be able to access these assets through central securities depositories in a way which already embodies agreed harmonization measures in a number of key areas.[3]

Bank mergers and acquisitions (M&As) are another important form of integration of the financial markets in the EU. The cross-border bank consolidation that has occurred to date has not yet reached the point where it is likely to lead to real pan-European institutions in the short term. Moreover, it could be claimed that the current financial crisis has caused the renationalization of some large cross-border financial institutions via government bank capital injections. Until the turn of the century, cross-border banking consolidation had mainly taken place within regional areas in the EU. Indeed, two linkages can be clearly distinguished in the Benelux and the Nordic countries. In particular, in the latter case intra-regional deals represent 90 percent of the total value of the deals within EU15 involving at least one Nordic entity. This ratio is around 60 percent for the Benelux region (European Commission, 2005). However, in the last few years, the acquisition patterns have changed somewhat regarding the geographic location of the target banks that were located far from the home market of the acquirer bank. This was the case of the acquisition of Banca Nazionale d'Lavoro by BNP Paribas in 2006 and Antonveneta by ABN Amro in 2005.

Acquisitions in many Central and Eastern European countries occurred after their banking crises in the early 1990s particularly by the banks in the neighboring EU countries. Other special circumstances have fostered those acquisitions, such as the run-up to EU membership and the privatization process. Three new member states joined Luxembourg (traditionally the country with the most cross-border banking activity) in having over 80 percent of their banking assets in banks from other EU countries, while three other new member countries have almost 60 percent. Four of the new members also rank relatively highly with regard to the percentage of assets from third countries.[4] In sum, the accession of the new members has given added impetus to cross-border banking issues in the EU (Garcia, 2009). Figure 9.1 shows the bank M&A activity in the EU27 from 1997 to 2007.

In the EU, there are no banks with European charters, although Nordea expressed its intention to obtain a *Societas Europaea* or European Company Charter – a possibility that arose first in 2004. This explains the decentralized character of the EU safety net. In sharp contrast with the US experience where the recurrent financial crisis led the authorities to centralize the lender-of-last-resort (LOLR) functions (the Federal Reserve Bank System was created in 1913), the deposit insurance guarantee and the bank reorganization and winding-up functions (the Federal Deposit Insurance Corporation was created in 1934) were created before the development of interstate banking (Garcia, 2009).

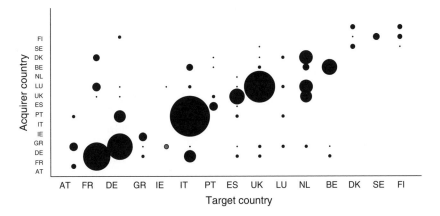

Notes
a.   Size of the bubble is proportional to the size of the deal.
AT Austria; FR France; DE Germany; GR Greece; IE Ireland; IT Italy; PT Portugal;
ES Spain; UK United Kingdom; LU Luxembourg; NL Netherlands; BE Belgium;
DK Denmark; SE Sweden; FI Finland.

Source: Hernando et al. (2009).

Figure 9.1   Bank M&As in the EU (1997–2007)

2   THE INSTITUTIONAL FRAMEWORK TO SAFEGUARD FINANCIAL STABILITY: MULTIPLE REGULATORS AND RESOLUTION AUTHORITIES

The EU's institutional architecture for financial crisis management and resolution reflects two principles: decentralization and cooperation. The performance of financial stability functions[5] relevant for crisis management are based, in large part, on the exercise of national responsibilities by prudential supervisors, central banks, treasuries and deposit insurance schemes. The ECB and the national central banks (NCBs) of the European System of Central Banks (ESCB) have financial-stability-related responsibilities, notably in the field of oversight of payment systems and contribution to national policies on financial stability and prudential supervision. The ESCB comprises the ECB and the NCBs of all EU member states whether they have adopted the euro or not.

The lender-of-last-resort (LOLR) function is a national responsibility.

This is also the case in the euro area, where the provision of emergency liquidity assistance (ELA) is the responsibility and liability of the NCBs. In this regard, the ECB (1999, p. 96) refers to ELA in the following terms:

> Emergency liquidity assistance (ELA) . . . embraces the support given by central banks in exceptional circumstances and on a case-by-case basis to temporarily illiquid institutions and markets . . . The main guiding principle is that the competent NCB takes the decision concerning the provision of ELA to an institution operating in its jurisdiction. This would take place under the responsibility and at a cost of the NCB in question.

This is a unique feature of the Eurosystem in which NCBs have the responsibility of providing ELA without having monetary-policy (as opposed to monetary-operations) responsibilities. However, information flows within the Eurosystem are such that the potential liquidity impact of ELA operations on the monetary aggregates can be managed in the context of the single monetary policy. Regarding the basic functions of the ESCB, the EC Treaty refers to the task of promoting the good functioning of payment systems (article 105(2)), but does not explicitly mention the function of promoting financial stability. However, a broad reference is included in article 105(5) of the EC Treaty: 'the ESCB shall contribute to the smooth conduct of policies pursued by the competent authorities relating to the prudential supervision of credit institutions and the stability of the financial system'. Such broad reference implicitly considers 'financial stability' as a non-basic function of the ESCB. Consistent with article 105(2) of the EC Treaty, the ECB could be expected to act as LOLR via the existing monetary policy operational framework, in the case of a general liquidity freeze as it has done in the context of the present financial crisis. However, it is in the traditional role of LOLR envisaged by Bagehot (1873) that the ECB role of LOLR has been implicitly decentralized to the NCBs (Lastra, 2000). (See Appendix 9A, which summarizes the ECB open market operations in the present financial crisis.)

Consistent with the 'principle of subsidiarity' enshrined in the EC Treaty (article 5), prudential supervision, deposit guarantees and reorganization and resolution procedures are decentralized in the EU.[6] They largely follow the legal structure of financial groups, and in parallel accountability reside primarily at the national level. Table 9.1 shows the responsibilities of home and host countries regarding prudential supervision, deposit guarantees and reorganization and winding-up of banks. Diversity of national laws and regulations on the safety net is constrained by EU directives. The directives set a lower bound on rules affecting safety and soundness and seek to minimally harmonize laws and regulations across member states in order to establish a level playing field, reduce regulatory arbitrage, and limit the possibility of a 'race to the bottom'. Hence, harmonization is an implicit mechanism of cooperation.

A number of cooperation structures are in place for bridging the potential information gaps of coverage between national responsibilities in safeguarding financial stability. These structures range from legal provisions (for example, the Capital Requirement Directive: CRD)[7] to common fora and memoranda of understanding (MoUs). There are three MoUs currently in place on financial crisis management of cross-border banks in the EU, one between central banks and supervisors and two others additionally involving national treasuries.[8] There are also generally bilateral MoUs among prudential supervisors. The MoUs consist of sets of principles and procedures that deal specifically with the identification of the authorities responsible for crisis management (central banks, prudential supervisors and ministries of finance) and the required flows of information between all authorities and the practical conditions for sharing information at the cross-border level. The 2008 MoU also includes supervisors of insurance and securities sectors as well as market infrastructures. In addition to these MoUs, EU banking supervisors and central banks also adopted in 2001 the MoU on cooperation between payment systems overseers and banking supervisors, which sets out arrangements for cooperation and information in relation to large-value payment systems. The provisions of the MoUs are not legally binding; however, the fact that the 2008 MoU on financial crisis management is, for the first time, public makes the explicit pre-commitments more likely. An *ex ante* commitment can affect the outcome by raising the cost of reneging on the commitment. It could be argued that pre-commitment raises this cost by making any decision to renege transparent to all parties involved.

Against this background, achieving a balance between member state sovereignty and financial stability in the EU is becoming increasingly difficult as the European financial system integrates (Garcia and Nieto, 2007). Moreover, the existing cooperation mechanisms fall short of fully internalizing the potential negative externalities that result from the existing national orientations of the financial safety nets and financial-sector policies (Nieto and Schinasi, 2007).

3   THE ACADEMIC *QUA* POLICY LITERATURE ON COOPERATION INCENTIVES IN THE EU

During the first years of EMU, policy makers deemed that the existing coordination arrangements between safety-net regulators were sufficient. However, the introduction of the euro encouraged the development of

Table 9.1 Supervision, deposit insurance and resolution authorities' jurisdiction in the EU

	Prudential supervisor[1]	LOLR (individual banks)	LOLR (market)	Deposit insurance regulators[2]	Reorganization and winding-up authority[3]
Banks locally incorporated Parent banks authorized in home country	Home country authorizing parent bank (consolidated supervision – solvency)	Home country	ECB	Home country	Home country
Subsidiaries of parent banks headquartered and authorized in another EU country	Home country authorizing parent bank (consolidated supervision – solvency) Host country authorizing the subsidiary ('solo' basis)[4]	Host Country	ECB	Host country	Host country
Branches Branches of banks headquartered and authorized in other EU country	Home country of head office (consolidated supervision – solvency) Host country[5] (liquidity)	Host country	ECB	Home country (possibility of supplementing the guarantee by host country)[6]	Home country

Notes

1. Directive 2006/48/EC of the European Parliament and of the Council of 14 June 2006 relating to the taking up and pursuit of the business of credit institutions (recast), *Official Journal of the European Communities*, 30 June 2006, No. L 177.

2. Directive 94/19/EC of the European Parliament and of the Council of 30 May, 1994 on deposit-guarantee schemes, *Official Journal of the European Communities*, 31 May 1994, No. L135/5 and Directive 97/9/EC of the European Parliament and the Council of 3 March 1997 on investor-compensation schemes, *Official Journal of the European Communities*, 3 May 1997, No. L 84/22.

3. Directive 2001/24/EC of the European Parliament and of the Council of 4 April on the reorganisation and winding up of credit institutions, *Official Journal of the European Communities*, 5 May 2001, No. L 125.

4. Directive 2006/48/EC of the European Parliament and of the Council of 14 June 2006 relating to the taking up and pursuit of the business of credit institutions (recast) Art. 44 '[It] shall not prevent the competent authorities of the various Member States from exchanging information in accordance with this Directive and with other Directives applicable to credit institutions. That information shall be subject to the conditions of professional secrecy'.

5. Directive 2006/48/EC of the European Parliament and of the Council of 14 June 2006 relating to the taking up and pursuit of the business of credit institutions (recast) (art. 43.1): '[It] shall not affect the right of the competent authorities of the host Member State to carry out, in the discharge of their responsibilities under this Directive, on-the-spot verifications of branches established within their territory'.

6. Directive 94/19/EC of the European Parliament and of the Council of 30 May, 1994 on deposit-guarantee schemes, *Official Journal of the European Communities*, 31 May 1994, No. L 135. (art. 4): 'Admission shall be conditional on fulfillment of the relevant obligations of membership, including in particular payment of any contributions and other charges'.

Source: Garcia and Nieto (2005, updated).

165

pan-European markets and cross-border financial institutions underlining the limitations of the existing institutional arrangements. Against this background, in 2004 the EU policy makers explicitly recognized, for the first time, the limitations of the existing decentralized institutional framework. The political recognition came long after the academic debate that had been highlighting for many years that the nationally oriented existing institutional setting provided incentives for delayed action and potentially increased losses for the taxpayer (Prati and Schinasi, 1999; Goodhart, 2000). Freixas (2003) described the existing framework as 'improvised cooperation', conveying the view of an efficient although adaptative exchange of information and decision making.

In the particular case of the *prudential supervision* of banks, the incentives are such that the interdependence of supervisors operating across borders creates a principal–agent relationship between the taxpayers of one country as principal and the various supervisors of the rest of the banking group as agents – assuming that supervisors act as perfect agents on behalf of their national taxpayers (Holthausen and Ronde, 2005; Mayes et al., 2008). However, this view is challenged. In a cross-country setting, the principal–agent problems are made substantially worse because some of the principals may not have direct authority over the agent, as when a supervisory authority in one country may expose the taxpayers in another country to losses. When conflicts arise among the principals (governments/taxpayers), the agent (supervisor) is likely to follow the perceived interests of its own country's principals. This is likely to increase the fiscal costs of bank resolution, which, in turn, would further complicate the sharing of resolution costs among countries ('burden sharing') (Eisenbeis and Kaufman, 2006).

Over the past five years, European policy makers have adopted several initiatives aimed at improving the explicit cooperation among safety-net regulators in the EU as presented in the previous section (Schinasi and Teixeira, 2006). But it was the financial crisis that started in August 2007 that gave momentum to more ambitious reforms. In October 2007, the ministers of finance agreed on a comprehensive approach that, for the first time, considered the simultaneous reform of the entire EU safety net.

There is a dearth of literature that provides much analytical guidance on these issues of coordination and, in particular, for assessing the existing architecture's ability to safeguard financial stability in the EU. Freixas (2003) argues that information asymmetries and country differences in prudential supervision capabilities in the EU will most likely lead to suboptimal decision making and outcomes that can be improved upon through cooperative decision making and centralized information. Nieto and Wall (2006) also defend the idea that centralization of private information on the financial condition of cross-border banks is a precondition for effective supervisor prompt corrective action policy.

Nieto and Schinasi (2007) examine model-based benchmarks for assessing the ability of Europe's existing institutional architecture – including its decision-making processes – to efficiently allocate resources to safeguard the EU financial system against systemic threats to stability – such as the insolvency of a pan-European bank. The approach is that of the 'economics of alliances', developed by Olson (1965) to analyze the nature of decision making by a group of countries (NATO: North Atlantic Treaty Organization) desiring to create a common (military) deterrence against an outside (nuclear) threat. This approach is applicable to settings where collective and cooperative decision making in the production of public goods could lead to welfare-improving outcomes relative to decentralized decision making. Both NATO and the EU share two characteristics relevant for the application of 'economics of alliances': a large number of member countries and the need for providing multiple public goods. Nieto and Schinasi apply this approach to the provision of European financial stability as a transnational public good within the EU.

These authors characterize the existing cooperation mechanisms and the ongoing process of cooperative and coordinated decision and policy making as an iterative process in which EU countries gradually and selectively internalize some of the negative externalities associated with cross-border financial problems and instability. This ongoing process can thus be seen as one way of moving towards a more desirable European approach to safeguarding EU financial stability.

As examples of the different degrees of internalization of potential negative externalities, the case of the European payment system is almost complete for the large-value payments (TARGET2). By contrast, the process of internalization is far from complete in the case of safety nets for European cross-border banks and, thus, there remain potentially large negative cross-border externalities that may not be captured by the agglomeration of existing national-oriented safety nets for banks. For example, the enhanced role of the consolidating supervisor will result in a significant 'loss of control' over domestic bank assets by host-country supervisors in a number of the EU countries (Luxembourg, Finland, the Czech Republic, Hungary and Poland) without giving up parallel responsibilities, for example, in deposit insurance guarantees and bank reorganization and winding-up. In turn, the responsibilities of some prudential supervisors for banks' safety and soundness (Belgium and Spain) will increase considerably without a corresponding increase in the responsibilities of other safety-net regulators.

Finally, Nieto and Schinasi highlight the need to tackle previously discussed reforms in various strands of the academic literature such as those referred to in the first paragraph of this section that openly consider the possibility of centralization of the safety-net functions.

Regarding the question of the order of centralization of safety-net regulators, Khan and Santos (2002) analyze the consequences of the allocation of the LOLR and supervisory functions in the euro area for the degree of forbearance in closing problem banks and for the level of diligence in prudential supervision as well as the consequences of the order of centralization of LOLR and prudential supervision. The authors conclude that the lack of centralization of LOLR and supervision in an integrated banking market increases forbearance and reduces the diligence of prudential supervision. At the same time, centralizing these regulatory functions will tend to reverse these effects. Moreover, they show that the centralization of supervision (and not LOLR) presents the advantages of increasing supervisors' incentives to invest in monitoring and reduces the financing cost of the LOLR.

Although there is a growing consensus among academics and policy makers on the non-assumption of responsibilities of micro-prudential supervision by the ECB, the EC Treaty (article 105(6)) and the ESCB Statute (article 25.2) leave open the possibility that the ECB might gain responsibility for the prudential supervision of credit institutions and other financial entities, with the exception of insurance companies. In order to assign these responsibilities, a qualified majority of the EU Council must decide in favour.[9] At the time of writing (2009), the European Commission published its proposal for the structure of European financial supervision based on the de Larosière Group (2009) recommendations created in the context of the present financial crisis to lay out a framework to take the EU forward. The adopted structure consists of a macro-prudential supervisory framework centered around the European Systemic Risk Council (ESRC) chaired by the ECB president and consisting of NCBs of the EU member states as well as a micro-prudential supervisory framework, the European System of Financial Supervisors (ESFS), consisting of a steering committee, three sectoral European supervisory authorities (ESAs) and the network of national supervisors in the fields of banking, insurance and pensions as well as securities.

4   CONCLUSIONS

The process of European financial integration has experienced a significant progress in the past 15 years. In particular, the EMU has been one of the most important benchmarks of this process because the central banks of the member countries and the ECB have developed integrated market infrastructures. While the benefits of European financial integration are numerous and far reaching, integration of financial markets is not without risks. In particular, the risk of contagion and the possibility of development of systemic crisis of regional or pan-European scale.

Policy makers have increasingly been recognizing the 'efficiency' gaps in providing for EU financial stability in the context of a decentralized architecture for regulation, supervision and financial stability. Recognition of this gap has led to some tangible efforts to capture some of the potential efficiency gains through legally binding mechanisms, policy coordination committees and MoUs. As noted in Nieto and Schinasi (2007), this ongoing iterative process of cooperation and coordination can be interpreted as having already internalized some of the EU potential negative externalities.

Nonetheless, the first global financial crisis has highlighted the limitations of the decentralized approach. National governments have scrambled to provide public fund guarantee schemes and precautionary recapitalizations of fundamentally sound financial institutions, putting at risk the very objective of the single financial market. The efficiency gaps of the EU safety net have put at risk the long-term European objective of a single market and highlighted the inconsistency of having national safety nets in an increasingly integrated financial market where the provision of European financial stability is considered as a transnational public good. The bridging of those gaps requires ambitious reforms that would have an impact on national sovereignty and hence they need national government support. The launching of the euro was the first surrender of sovereignty by European countries in times of peace. The political commitment to the launching of EMU gave a credible exit to the fixed exchange rate arrangements that existed in the EU since 1979 (European Monetary System). As was the case with EMU, the reform of the existing institutional setting for safeguarding financial stability requires the surrender of areas of national sovereignty that would make credible the long-term political commitment of having a single financial market.

NOTES

*   The opinions stated herein are those of the author and do not necessarily reflect those of Banco de España.
1.   *T*rans-European *A*utomated *R*eal-time *G*ross settlement *E*xpress *T*ransfer system (TARGET). The second generation launched in November 2007 (TARGET2) was designed to meet new demands from its users, including those from new member states that had joined the EU most recently.

2. The Eurosystem has fostered their integration via the market-led Short Term European Paper (STEP) initiative aimed at developing a pan-European short-term paper market through the voluntary compliance of market participants with a core set of commonly agreed standards. This initiative was launched in June 2006.
3. See http://www.ecb.int/paym/t2s/html/index.en.html.
4. Data are lacking for a number of individual new member states because the ECB does not publish data when the number of subsidiaries or branches is less than three.
5. The ECB has defined financial stability, 'as a condition in which the *financial system* would be able to withstand shocks, without giving way to cumulative processes which impair the allocation of savings to investment opportunities and the processing of payments in the economy' (emphasis added).
6. EC Treaty Establishing the European Community (article 5): 'The Community shall take action . . . only if and in so far as *the objectives of the proposed action cannot be sufficiently achieved by the Member States* and, can therefore, by reason of the scale or effects of the proposed action, be better achieved by the Community' (emphasis added).
7. The CRD comprises Directive (2006/48/EC) of 14 June 2006 relating to the taking up and pursuit of the business of credit institutions, OJ L 177/1, 30 June 2006 and Directive (2006/49/EC) of 14 June 2006 on the capital adequacy of investment firms and credit institutions, OJ L 177/201, 30 June 2006.
8. Press releases available, respectively, at: http://www.ecb.int/press/pr/date/2003/html/pr030310_3.en.html, http://www.eu2005.lu/en/actualites/documents_travail/2005/05/14 ecofin_mou/index.html and http://www.ecb.int/pub/pdf/other/mou-financialstability 2008en.pdf. The 2001 MoU on cooperation between payment systems overseers and banking supervisors, press release available at: http://www.ecb.int/press/pr/date/2001/html/pr010402.en.html.
9. According to the new constitutional treaty (Treaty of Lisbon).

REFERENCES

Bagehot, Walter (1873 [1962]), *Lombard Street: A description of the Money Market*, Homewood, IL: Richard D. Irwin.

Berrigan, John, Vitor Gaspar and Patrick Pearson, (2009), 'Notes on the future of banking regulation in Europe', in D. Mayes, R. Pringle and M. Taylor (eds), *Towards a New Framework for Financial Stability*, London: Central Banking Publications, pp. 499–508.

Eisenbeis, Robert and George Kaufman (2006), 'Cross-border banking: challenges for deposit insurance and financial stability in the EU', Presented at the Third Annual DG ECFIN Research Conference September 7–8, 2006, Brussels, mimeo.

European Central Bank (ECB) (1999), Annual Report, Frankfurt-am-Main, available at: http://www.ecb.int/pub/pdf/annrep/ar1999en.pdf (accessed 30 May 2009).

European Central Bank (ECB) (2009), 'Financial Integration in Europe', April, Frankfurt-am-Main, available at: http://www.ecb.int/pub/pdf/other/financial integrationineurope200904en.pdf (accessed 30 May 2009).

European Commission (2005), 'Cross-border consolidation in the EU financial sector', SEC (2005), 1398.

Freixas, X. (2003), 'Crisis management in Europe', in J.J.M. Kremers, D. Schoenmaker and P.J. Wierts (eds), *Financial Supervision in Europe*, Cheltenham, UK, and Northampton, MA, USA: Edward Elgar, pp. 102–19.

Garcia, Gillian G.H. (2009), 'Sovereignty versus soundness: cross-border/interstate banking in the European Union and the United States: similarities, differences and policy issues', *Contemporary Economic Policy*, **27** (1), January, 109–29.

Garcia, G. and María J. Nieto (2005), 'Banking crisis management in the European Union: multiple regulators and resolution authorities', *Journal of Banking Regulation*, **6** (3), 215–19.

Garcia, Gillian G. and María J. Nieto (2007), 'Preserving financial stability: a dilemma for the European Union', *Contemporary Economic Policy*, **25** (3), 444–58.

Goodhart, C.A.E. (ed.) (2000), *Which Lender of Last Resort for Europe?*, London: Central Banking Publications.

Hernando, Ignacio, María J. Nieto and Larry D. Wall (2009), 'Determinants of domestic and cross border bank acquisitions in the EU', *Journal of Banking and Finance*, **33** (6), June, pp. 1022–32.

Holthausen, Cornelia and Thomas Ronde (2005), 'Cooperation in international banking supervision', Discussion Paper Series 4990, Center for Economic Policy Research, London.

Khan, Ch. M. and J.A.C. Santos (2002), 'Allocating lending of last resort and supervision in the euro area', ch. 19 in V. Alexander, J. Melitz and G.M. von Furstenberg (eds), *Monetary Union: Why, How, and What Follows?*, Oxford: Oxford University Press.

Lastra, R. (2000), 'The role of the European Central Bank with regard to financial stability and lender of last resort operations', in Goodhart (ed.), pp. 197–212.

Mayes, David, María J. Nieto and Larry Wall (2008), 'Multiple safety net regulators and agency problems in the EU: is prompt corrective action partly the solution?', *Journal of Financial Stability*, **4** (3), 223–57.

Nieto, M.J. and Garry Schinasi (2007), 'EU framework for safeguarding financial stability: towards an analytical benchmark for assessing its effectiveness', International Monetary Fund Working Paper Series, WP/07/260, Washington, DC, November.

Nieto, María J. and Larry Wall (2006), 'Preconditions for a successful implementation of supervisors' prompt corrective action: is there a case for a banking standard in the EU?', *Journal of Banking Regulation*, **7** (3–4), 191–220.

Olson, Mancur (1965), *The Logic of Collective Action*, Cambridge, MA: Harvard University Press.

Prati, Alessandro and Garry J. Schinasi (1999), *Financial Stability in European Economic and Monetary Union*, Princeton Studies in International Finance No. 86, Cambridge, MA, August.

Schinasi, Garry J. and Pedro Gustavo Teixeira (2006), 'The lender of last resort in the European single financial market', in Gerard Caprio, Jr., Douglas D. Evanoff and George G. Kaufman (eds), *Cross-Border Banking: Regulatory Challenges*, Hackensack, NJ: World Scientific Studies in International Economics, pp. 349–72.

Tieman, Alexander and Martin Čihák (2007), 'Internationally active large banking groups', in Jörg Decressin, Hamid Faruqee and Wim Fonteyne (eds), *Integrating Europe's Financial Markets*, Washington, DC: International Monetary Fund, pp. 142–55.

APPENDIX 9A   ECB OPEN MARKET OPERATIONS IN THE PRESENT FINANCIAL CRISIS

The Eurosystem operational framework for monetary policy implementation comprises three instruments: open market operations (OMOs), minimum reserve requirements (remunerated) and standing facilities. The Eurosystem has traditionally conducted two types of OMO: liquidity provision against eligible collateral (one-week and longer maturities) and the collection of fixed-term deposits used to temporarily absorb liquidity. There are two types of standing facilities; banks can place liquidity in the deposit facility on an overnight basis at a rate of 1 percentage point below the policy rate, while they can borrow overnight against eligible collateral via the marginal lending facility at a rate which is 1 percentage point above the policy rate.[1] The Eurosystem operates with 1,700 banks, although only between 300 and 500 operate on a regular basis.

In the context of the present financial crisis, the Eurosystem has adjusted its existing framework with the aim of ensuring that the very short-term interbank money market rates are close to the policy rate decided by the Governing Council of the ECB. The measures adopted are as follows: (a) expansion of the list of assets eligible as collateral to include marketable debt instruments denominated in currencies other than the euro; debt instruments issued by credit institutions; subordinated debt instruments when they are protected by an acceptable guarantee; marketable and non-marketable assets rated BBB– (with the exception of asset-backed securities); (b) enhancement of the provision of longer-term refinancing extending the maturity up to one year. These operations are conducted as fixed rate tender procedures with full allotment; (c) provision of liquidity principally but not exclusively in US dollars through foreign exchange swaps; (d) narrowing of the corridor of standing facilities from 2 percentage points to 1 percentage point around the interest rate on the main refinancing operation (this was a temporary measure adopted on October 9, 2008 and reversed to normal on January 21, 2009); and (e) full allotment at the interest rate on the main refinancing operation of the weekly main refinancing operations, which were carried out through a fixed rate tender procedure (this was also a temporary measure). Last but not least, at the time of writing (2009), the ECB is deploying unconventional monetary policy tools such as the acquisition of banks' covered bonds.

The Eurosytem OMOs were broadly successful in maintaining the average level of very short-term interbank money market rates close to the policy rate during this period of high volatility (ECB, 2008). The effectiveness of these measures shows up in the narrowing of money market spreads during the first months of 2009.

Note

1. See ECB (2006) for information on the original list of eligible collateral.

References

European Central Bank (ECB) (2006), 'The implementation of monetary policy in the euro area: general documentation on Eurosystem monetary policy instruments and procedures', Frankfurt-am-Main, available at: http://www.ecb.int/pub/pdf/other/gendoc2006en.pdf (accessed 30 May 2009).
European Central Bank (ECB) (2008), *Monthly Bulletin*, May, available at: http://www.ecb.int/pub/pdf/mobu/mb200805en.pdf (accessed 30 May 2009).

10. The global financial crises: back to basics, bank supervision in developing countries*

Thomas Lutton and Joseph Cauthen

1 INTRODUCTION

The global financial crisis (GFC) established an incontrovertible fact. Regulators in developed countries with access to the latest technology and management information systems were caught by surprise. As a group, regulators failed to anticipate the onset and scope of the GFC of 2008 and 2009. Despite a variety of sophisticated on- and off-site early warning and risk assessment systems, manned by thousands of examiners adhering to a supervision by risk (SBR) examination process, risks went undetected until they ultimately materialized as losses. Many depository and non-depository financial institutions took what turned out to be extremely risky positions. They became dangerously illiquid if not insolvent under the not-so-watchful eye of regulators and rating agencies who were supposed to be monitoring risk. Risk-based pricing, risk-based supervision, risk-based assets, and risk management overall took a convincing hit in the eyes of financial regulators in less-developed economies.

Although the fundamental causes of the GFC will be the focus of research studies for many years, bank supervisors and regulators in developing countries do not have the luxury of time to address what appears to be a fundamental question. If the 'more advanced' safety and soundness monitoring processes proved so deficient in developed economies, what risk assessment and monitoring processes should they pursue?

To place this question in context, many central banks have been struggling to implement Basel II economic capital measures. They have had difficulty in estimating the parameters of unconditional loss distributions for market, credit, and operational risk components of economic capital although the majority of African countries, for example, have embraced an SBR process. Nevertheless they find themselves unable to estimate economic capital.

In the wake of the GFC, bank supervisors in developing countries conclude that the implementation of Basel II in its current forms has failed to provide adequate risk assessments and early warnings. Many countries now faced with both primary and secondary impacts of the GFC that threaten the financial condition of their banks, have begun to consider a more modest and direct approach to risk assessment that blends both on- and off-site supervision. For lack of a better term, this 'back to basics' (BTB) approach emphasizes the use of conventional financial soundness indicators (FSIs) that builds upon the experience of examination staffs.

'FSIs' has come to mean a collection of monthly financial ratios and other indicators that affect the *expected discounted net cash flow* and the *volatility of net cash flow* for each bank. The International Monetary Fund (IMF) uses the term 'financial soundness indicators' to connote both macroeconomic and microeconomic financial condition indicators. In this chapter we confine our use of FSIs to financial soundness indicators for regulated depository financial institutions. The literature on FSIs spans much of the last decade.[1]

FSIs such as non-performing loans to total loans, returns on equity and assets, and capital to asset ratios without risk weights, and other comparatively simple and easily measured financial ratios and indicators have now become available on a monthly basis for off-site analysis. What sets this approach apart from the complexity of the fair valuation procedures, contingent claims analysis, internal risk-based analytics, and loss distribution approaches apparent in many developed countries, is that the BTB approach is simple, flexible, and synthesizes a variety of current data to produce the most basic safety and soundness risk metric – the conditional probability of insolvency.

Unlike economic capital measures that require the estimation of loss distributions and the subtraction of unexpected and expected losses, under BTB, regulators need not estimate market risk, credit risk, and operational risk for each bank, or relegate on-site risk assessments to the qualitative risk assessments in SBR.

With BTB, regulators can obtain and use cardinal risk measures to determine the timing of the next on-site examination and how changes in FSIs and the portfolio of banks can reduce the probability of insolvency. Indeed, regulators in less-developed economies have begun to reacquaint themselves with a risk assessment process that actually has more dimensions and better synthesizes information for risk assessments.

This BTB approach integrates on-site with off-site examination assessments. It relies on an individual bank scoring system. The Uniform Financial Institutions Rating System (UFIRS) was adopted in the US by the Federal Financial Institutions Examination Council (FFIEC) in 1979.

In December 1996, the FFIEC updated the UFIRS.[2] The revised system was effective from January 1, 1997. Today the system is more widely recognized by its acronym, 'CAMELS'.[3]

The term, 'CAMELS', refers to six components of a bank's financial condition: Capital adequacy (C), Asset quality (A), Management (M), Earnings (E), Liquidity (L) and Sensitivity to market risk (S). At first the system was employed only by on-site examiners. Over the years with advances in management information systems, the C, A, E, L components may be scored using off-site techniques with monthly data. This permits a monthly monitoring of each bank. Both the M and S components continue to remain the responsibility of on-site examination and reflect scores given during the most recent exam.

Given the proprietary nature of the data, however, CAMELS scores and scoring procedures have remained unavailable to academic inquiry although research staffs in federal regulatory agencies have published some evaluations of the scoring procedures.[4] Other countries have since developed similar scoring systems. Examples include ORAP (France), PATROL (Italy), RAST (Netherlands), RATE and TRAM (United Kingdom), and so on. All focus on recent FSIs which in large part are derived from quarterly or monthly income and balance-sheet data.[5]

Examiners assign ratings for each component in addition to aggregating the components to produce an overall rating of a bank's financial condition. The ratings are assigned on a scale from 1 to 5. Banks with ratings of 1 or 2 are considered to be less risky, while banks with ratings of 3, 4, or 5 present moderate to extreme risks. Risks here can be viewed as the conditional probability of future losses sufficiently large as to precipitate insolvency.

Although such ratings have been implemented for almost three decades, there is little direction found in IMF or BIS documents, or individual country examiners' handbooks, that dictates precisely how ratings are to be constructed. Each regulator seems to have developed its own method of producing scores, often appealing to a committee or subjective assessment. Note the direction provided to bank examiners by the FDIC:

> The composite rating generally bears a close relationship to the component ratings assigned. However, the composite rating is not derived by computing an arithmetic average of the component ratings. Each component rating is based on a qualitative analysis of the factors comprising that component and its interrelationship with the other components. When assigning a composite rating, some components may be given more weight than others depending on the situation at the institution. In general, assignment of a composite rating may incorporate any factor that bears significantly on the overall condition and soundness of the financial institution.[6]

Clearly the overall condition and soundness of the financial institution appropriately reflect the concerns about solvency, but how precisely is this determination of aggregate score actually made? This lack of direction and overt appeal to subjective assessment does provide flexibility but it raises an important question in the aftermath of the GFC. To what extent did the failure to ascertain risk before the fact result from subjective judgments and lack of analytical rigor in the aggregation of the CAMELS ratings?

Many banks that became insolvent had low CAMELS scores only months prior to insolvency. It certainly becomes difficult to learn from past mistakes in risk assessments if a sliding scale with subjective assessments becomes the standard for each aggregation.

Bank supervision in many countries has begun to seek more consistency and analytical rigor in scoring methods. This can be achieved through systematic application of standards, quantification, and aggregation rules. Such a process creates an ability to document scores, compare on- and off-site assessments, learn from past mistakes, and test the validity of the assessment process. Moreover the process need not be overly complex.

Quantifying the CAMELS scoring requires an explicit application of trigger points, step functions, critical values or some parametric rules of thumb to ensure a systematic and objective assignment of ratings. Although scoring models are not new and date back several decades, the more recent availability of reasonably current and accurate data suggests that off-site examination classification of CAMELS components may provide greater surveillance capabilities than a system that relied solely on less-frequent on-site exams. In some African countries, like Lesotho, the data used to monitor CAMELS are available on a weekly basis. Moreover, in contrast to the FDIC's statement of policy concerning aggregation, BTB approaches see virtue in using simple weighted averages for aggregation, understanding that the weights can certainly change over time. However, if the weights do change, they should change for all banks to ensure equal treatment.

It should be noted, therefore, that the BTB approach is at least complementary to, if not a departure from, the SBR approaches advocated by developed economies over the last decade.[7] SBR typically requires nine different ordinal risk assessments based largely on on-site qualitative assessments and processes.[8] Although consistent with Basel II approaches, the SBR has been found wanting in the aftermath of the GFC and appears to be undergoing a dramatic reappraisal by regulators in many developing economies.[9] In particular, the process does not provide any systematic way to aggregate the different risk assessments into an overall assessment of whole bank risk. Another limitation of the SBR process is that it provides no way to assess systemic risk. Whether BTB is a complement to or a departure from SBR can be debated, but the BTB process clearly attempts to more explicitly quantify risk in terms of the conditional probability of insolvency. Moreover, it does so with comparatively simple risk assessment tools.

2 BTB: FINANCIAL SOUNDNESS INDICATORS

The BTB approach starts with recently validated data obtained from regulated financial institution income and balance sheets consistent with International Accounting Standards Board (IASB) accounting principles. Such data obtained provide the basis for constructing an off-site system that synthesizes information to produce a simple and easily implemented early warning system designed to pick up changes in financial conditions on a monthly basis (Figure 10.1).

The central banks in different countries have begun to hire off-site examination specialists to complement their on-site examination staffs. Such specialists use the off-site FSIs to produce CAEL components: Capital adequacy (C), Asset Quality (A), Earnings (E), and Liquidity (L), and combine them with on-site Management (M) and Sensitivity to market risk (S) measures to construct aggregate CAMELS scores.

Figure 10.1 provides a systematic overview of the financial condition monitoring process that starts with the current FSIs (monthly updates) and on-site FSIs (M & S ratings from the last exam). Together these FSIs are used to construct CAMELS components using comparatively simple weighted averages. The components are then aggregated to construct the aggregate CAMELS. The probability of insolvency becomes a monotonically increasing function of CAMELS scores. In terms of stress tests and monitoring of risks, one can observe changes in FSIs, CAMELS, and probabilities of failure to produce before the fact risk assessment.

FSIs need not be limited to historic ratios or levels. FSIs can be reconstructed as trends and outputs from pro-forma models or projections provided as pre-commitments. Such FSIs permit the CAMELS scoring to be more forward looking. Some countries have even begun to use projected macroeconomic conditions consistent with outputs from the research departments of central banks as inputs to the set of FSIs used in scoring models.

3 THE BTB APPROACH: DEPOSITORY INSTITUTION FSIS

In 2002, the International Monetary Fund (IMF) published the first in a lengthy list of papers on the subject of FSIs. The object of that and

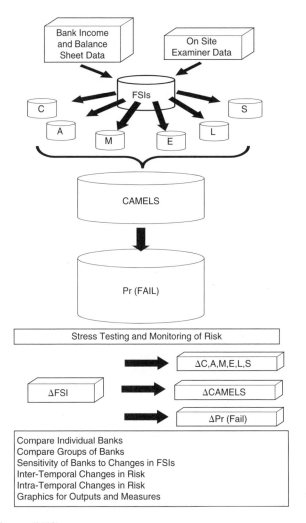

Source: Thomas (2009).

Figure 10.1 Schematic for the BTB approach

subsequent papers was to identify a basic set of FSIs that could provide a consistent basis for financial regulation and monitoring of safety and soundness. After many surveys of member countries, the IMF developed a comparatively simple set of 'core and encouraged' FSIs. Over time this core set of FSIs has grown to include 12 core and 14 encouraged FSIs for depository institutions (see Table 10.1).

Table 10.1   Financial soundness indicators for depository institutions

Financial soundness indicators: core and encouraged 2009		
Capital	Regulatory capital to risk-weighted assets	FSI 1
adequacy	Regulatory Tier 1 capital to risk-weighted assets	FSI 2
	Capital to assets	FSI 3
Asset quality	Non-performing loans net of provisions to capital	FSI 4
	Non-performing loans to total gross loans	FSI 5
	Geographical distribution of loans to total loans	FSI 6
	Sectoral distribution of loans to total loans	FSI 7
	Gross asset position in financial derivatives to capital	FSI 8
	Foreign-currency-denominated loans to total loans	FSI 9
	Large exposures to capital	FSI 10
Earnings and	Return on assets	FSI 11
profitability	Return on equity	FSI 12
	Interest margin to gross income	FSI 13
	Non-interest expenses to gross income	FSI 14
	Spread between reference lending and deposit rates	FSI 15
	Personnel expenses to non-interest expenses	FSI 16
Liquidity	Liquid assets to total assets (liquid asset ratio)	FSI 17
	Liquid assets to short-term liabilities	FSI 18
	Foreign-currency-denominated liabilities to total liabilities	FSI 19
	Customer deposits to total (non-interbank) loans	FSI 20
	Spread between highest and lowest interbank rate	FSI 21
Sensitivity to	Net open position in foreign exchange to capital	FSI 22
market	Gross liability position in financial derivatives to capital	FSI 23
risk	Trading income to total income	FSI 24

Source: IMF (2009).

These FSIs have been used for bank examinations in many countries for several decades to assess the financial condition of banks. Now that they are being collected on a monthly basis, they provide a logical basis for 'scoring' a bank and monitoring its financial condition from an off-site perspective.

4 BTB APPROACH: FSIS AND MONITORING BANK CONDITIONS

Although the IMF does provide accounting guidance and technical assistance support to developing countries, regulators ultimately must decide how to combine the FSIs to produce component and aggregate financial condition scores. As part of its technical assistance program the IMF has provided guidance to Sierra Leone, Tanzania, Kenya, Botswana, and a variety of other countries in Africa and the Caribbean that embrace a BTB approach to safety and soundness assessments based upon a piecewise linear relationship between a risk score and the values of individual FSIs. Figure 10.2 illustrates this procedure.

Increases in some FSIs are assumed to indicate an increase in risk (probability of loss in a subsequent period). In Figure 10.2, increases in non-performing loans net of provisions to total capital in period t produces an increase in the score and an increase in the probability of loss in the next period. By way of contrast, increases in other FSIs result in decreases in the score and risk, for example, regulatory capital to risk-weighted assets. As C/RWA increases, risks decrease. Mapping these with a piecewise linear function requires only two critical values for each FSI.

This choice of critical values may seem arbitrary but consider the Federal Deposit Insurance Corporation Improvement Act (FDICIA), 1991 which provided threshold levels for capital measures (technically FSIs). The critical levels that determine whether a bank is well capitalized, adequately capitalized, undercapitalized, and so on provide a 'step function' for risk assessment that reflects subjective judgments. Yet such judgments are reasonable benchmarks based on examination experience (see Table 10.2).

Returning to our discussion of Figure 10.2, the 'Critical Value 2' in the figure indicates either an upper or a lower limit threshold for a Very Risky Score = 5. Critical Value 1 represents a 'safe' FSI level (Score = 1). These two critical values must be chosen by the bank supervision department based upon experience, not unlike the critical ratios associated with the FDICIA critical levels for various capital ratios in Table 10.2. A complete set of 24 FSIs consequently therefore would require 48 parameters. A set of 13 FSIs would require only 26 parameters.

Barring additional information concerning how the values of the FSIs between the critical levels affect risk, a simple linear extrapolation provides a continuous piecewise linear function that maps FSI values into 'risk scores'.

Taking all the FSIs within a given CAMELS component, the supervision department assigns weights to each FSI to obtain a weighted average

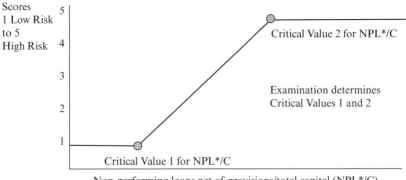

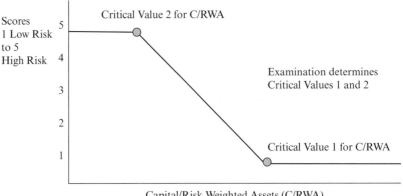

Figure 10.2   Illustration of piecewise linear risk mapping for FSIs

component score. For example, if FSIs 1, 2, and 3 in Table 10.2 constitute the three FSIs used to construct the C component of the CAMELS score, a weight of 1/3 applied to each could be used to construct a C rating. As an example, suppose FSI 1 had a 2.2 rating, FSI 2 had a 2.5 rating, and FSI 3 had a 2 rating. The C score becomes 1/3*2.2 + 1/3*2.5 + 1/3*2.0 = 2.3.

Following this same procedure for the A,M,E,L,S ratings, it is possible to obtain a complete set of scores for the component ratings. To link component ratings with aggregate ratings the BTB approach again employs a weighted average process. Consider an A rating of 3.0, an M rating of 2.2, an E rating of 3.1, an L rating of 2.5, and an S rating of 3.0. The aggregate CAMELS ratings can be calculated using equation (10.1):

Table 10.2 FDICIA risk-based capital requirements

Categories	Total risk-based capital ratio	Provisions*
1. Well capitalized	≥ 10%	None
2. Adequately capitalized	≥ 8%	No brokered deposits except with FDIC approval
3. Undercapitalized	≥ 6%	Suspend dividends, management fees, add capital, restrict growth, no brokered deposits
4. Significantly undercapitalized	< 6% and Tangible equity > 2%	Same as 3. Recapitalization
5. Critically undercapitalized	Tangible equity ≤ 2%	Same as 4. Receivership.

Note: * Partial listing of prompt corrective action (PCA) provisions.

Source: Gup and Lutton (2009).

Table 10.3 Weighted average CAMELS score

	Weights	'Score'	Sub-score
C	16.67%	2.3	0.38
A	16.67%	3.0	0.50
M	16.67%	2.2	0.37
E	16.67%	3.1	0.52
L	16.67%	2.5	0.42
S	16.67%	3.0	0.50
		CAMELS	2.68

CAMELS Score = $w1*(C = 2.3) + w2*(A = 3.0) + w3*(M = 2.2) + w4*(E = 3.1) + w5*(L = 2.5) + w6*(S = 3.0)$ (10.1)

Again, the weights reflect the supervision department's judgments. See Table 10.3 for a numerical example where each of the six components receives a weight of 1/6 (16.67 percent). The aggregate score becomes 2.68. BTB uses the same scoring process for each bank within a regulatory portfolio of banks.

5   BTB APPROACH: THE CENTRAL BANK OF KENYA

The Central Bank of Kenya (CBK) provides an example of how this procedure works. Each of the banks in Kenya is monitored using this weighted average monitoring process. See Table 10.4 for an illustration that depicts the scoring of a specific bank. CBK relies on a set of 13 FSIs to score each of its 44 commercial banks. The bank in question was monitored in May, 2009. Note the critical values and the component and aggregate scores obtained using the BTB approach.

In this case the supervision department did not compute an 'S' component in the on-site examinations, so that the aggregate score becomes a 'CAMEL' rating as opposed to a 'CAMELS' rating. In December 2008 the CAMEL score was 2.1 with $C = 3.5$, $A = 1.5$, $M = 2.4$, $E = 1.6$, and $L = 3.3$.

The scoring system may be used retrospectively to provide a time series of CAMEL scores for the bank in question. End-of-year scores appear in the table ranging from 2.0 to 2.4 over the previous 5 years. As the CAMEL rating increases and decreases over time, the regulator monitors the financial conditions of each bank under its regulatory authority. Although only yearly data appear in Table 10.4, monthly assessments are made as well to flag any deterioration in a bank's financial condition.

The procedure is remarkably simple and sufficiently flexible that new sets of FSIs may be introduced to complement the levels and ratios in the table. For example, trends, pre-commitments and projections of FSIs may be used to complement the set of FSIs that appear in the table. The CBK is considering such extensions.

6   BTB APPROACH: FROM ORDINAL RISK TO CARDINAL RISK ASSESSMENT

The bank in question that exhibits a CAMEL rating of 2.1 would be considered less risky than another bank with a CAMEL rating of 3 but more risky than a bank with a CAMEL rating of 2, but how much more or less risky?

The answer to this question requires that aggregate scores be mapped to an estimate of conditional probability of insolvency over a finite future period. In other words, 'What is the likelihood that a bank with a CAMEL rating of 2.1 would fail over the course of, say, the next two years under normal or stressful conditions?'. A panel dataset (pooled time series and cross-section) for banks with CAMEL ratings that subsequently failed or survived would supply such an answer if there had been a sufficiently long enough time series and historical incidence of failures. Alternatively, qualitative dependent variable models like logit or probit models provide such a link. In the case of countries with deep capital markets, distance to default models also provide such a link, but in countries like Kenya where data are more limited it is necessary to rely on experience of other countries with CAMELS systems and the experience of subsequent bank failures/insolvencies.

One simple approach is to employ a logistics function to map CAMEL(S) scores into estimates of the probability of insolvency. Probabilities must range between 0 and 1. Consider equation (10.2). In this case only 2 parameters ('*a*' and '*b*') can provide the required mapping. The parameter *b* is greater than 0 to indicate that higher CAMELS ratings indicate a higher probability of insolvency, holding all else constant:

$$\text{Pr(Insolvency)} = f(\text{CAMELS}) = e^{(a_t + b_t * \text{CAMELS})} / (1 + e^{(a_t + b_t * \text{CAMELS})}). \quad (10.2)$$

The values for a_t and b_t describe how the probability of insolvency over the next two years can change as a function of the CAMEL(S) assessment and because of the recursive construction process as a function of the FSIs. The subscript *t* for parameters *a* and *b* indicates that the values for these parameters can change over time with different economic conditions. For example, stressful conditions might result in a combination of *a* and *b* values that would result in a higher estimated likelihood of failure for a bank with any given CAMEL rating. The underlying S curve that results from equation (10.2) also permits banks in the mid-2 to mid-4 ratings to be more susceptible to external shocks such as higher unemployment or lower than average GDP growth than for banks with ratings outside that range. Figure 10.3 provides a visual example of this effect.

During a 2009 IMF technical assistance mission, the Central Bank of Kenya (CBK) used a version of equation (10.2) to estimate the probabilities of insolvency for its commercial banks under a variety of conditions. With the BTB system in place, CBK was able to estimate how changes in FSIs ultimately affected the estimated likelihood of insolvency. In addition, examiners can use the information available to work with banks to determine how much changes in capital, loan loss provisions, and sectoral loan portfolios might keep the probability of insolvency during stress to acceptable levels. Figure 10.3 provides a simple example of how CAMEL(S) ratings can reflect the estimated probabilities of insolvency under both normal and stressful conditions. The estimates for *a* and *b* were originally obtained using a variable coefficient procedure with cohort data for US banks over the 1985–92 period.[10]

Table 10.4 Example of BTB and CAMEL scores

Example of FSI ratings in Kenya off-site model	History 2004–2008					Critical FSI values		Piecewise linear coefficients	
	Dec-08	Dec-07	Dec-06	Dec-05	Dec-04	Critical FSI Value 2	Critical FSI Value 1	B0	B1
Capital adequacy	3.5	3.7	4.0	3.7	3.8				
Core capital/total deposits	3.5	3.4	3.6	3.4	3.4	7.0%	23.0%	6.8	−25.0
Core capital/RWA	3.4	3.5	3.7	3.4	3.5	7.5%	22.0%	7.1	−27.6
Total capital/RWA	3.4	4.1	4.7	4.3	4.4	11.0%	25.0%	8.1	−28.6
Liquidity	3.3	4.0	2.4	2.9	3.0				
Liquidity ratio	3.7	4.7	2.3	2.8	3.1	20.0%	45.0%	8.2	−16.0
Total loans/deposits	2.9	3.3	2.6	3.0	2.9	95.0%	70.0%	−10.2	16.0
Asset quality	1.5	1.4	2.1	2.9	2.1				
NPLs/total loans	1.1	1.0	1.8	2.4	2.0	40.0%	5.0%	0.4	11.4
(NPLs-prov)/total loans	1.0	1.0	1.3	2.4	1.4	20.0%	5.0%	−0.3	26.7
Provisions/NPLs	2.5	2.2	3.1	3.7	2.9	20.0%	80.0%	6.3	−6.7
NPAs/assets ratio	1.4	1.3	2.2	2.9	2.4	20.0%	2.0%	0.6	22.2
Management quality	2.4	2.3	2.3	2.5	1.9				
Overall M score	2.4	2.3	2.3	2.5	1.9				

Earnings								
Return on assets	1.6	1.4	1.3	1.4	1.4	1.0%	4.0%	6.3	−133.3
Return on equity	1.4	1.0	1.0	1.0	1.0	10.0%	40.0%	6.3	−13.3
Interest margin on earning assets	2.3	2.2	1.8	2.1	2.2	1.0%	12.0%	5.4	−36.4
Aggregate CAMEL (No 'S' component)	2.1	2.0	2.2	2.4	2.1				
Weights: C(0.3), A(0.1), M(0.2), E(0.1), L(0.3), S(0)								

Note: At this point, a critical component of BTB risk quantification has been completed.

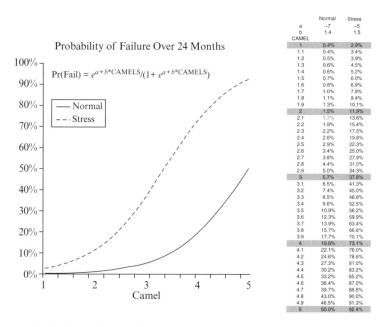

CAMEL	Normal $a = -7$, $b = 1.4$	Stress $a = -5$, $b = 1.5$
1	0.4%	2.9%
1.1	0.4%	3.4%
1.2	0.5%	3.9%
1.3	0.6%	4.5%
1.4	0.6%	5.2%
1.5	0.7%	6.0%
1.6	0.8%	6.9%
1.7	1.0%	7.9%
1.8	1.1%	9.4%
1.9	1.3%	10.1%
2	1.5%	11.9%
2.1	1.7%	13.6%
2.2	1.9%	15.4%
2.3	2.2%	17.5%
2.4	2.6%	19.8%
2.5	2.9%	22.3%
2.6	3.4%	25.0%
2.7	3.8%	27.9%
2.8	4.4%	31.0%
2.9	5.0%	34.3%
3	5.7%	37.8%
3.1	6.5%	41.3%
3.2	7.4%	45.0%
3.3	8.5%	48.8%
3.4	9.6%	52.5%
3.5	10.9%	56.2%
3.6	12.3%	59.9%
3.7	13.9%	63.4%
3.8	15.7%	66.8%
3.9	17.7%	70.1%
4	19.8%	73.1%
4.1	22.1%	76.0%
4.2	24.6%	78.6%
4.3	27.3%	81.0%
4.4	30.2%	83.2%
4.5	33.2%	85.2%
4.6	36.4%	87.0%
4.7	39.7%	88.6%
4.8	43.0%	90.0%
4.9	46.5%	91.3%
5	50.0%	92.4%

Probability of Failure Over 24 Months

$$\text{Pr(Fail)} = e^{a+b*\text{CAMELS}}/(1+ e^{a+b*\text{CAMELS}})$$

— Normal
--- Stress

Camel

Figure 10.3   Probability of insolvency and CAMEL score

Figure 10.3 provides both a graphical example and a table to compare the estimated cumulative probabilities of insolvency over a two-year period. Consider three banks with CAMEL ratings of 2.0, 2.1, and 3.0 respectively. Under 'normal' macroeconomic conditions (country-specific GDP growth, unemployment, inflation, and so on), the estimated probabilities of failure are 1.5, 1.7 and 5.7 percent, respectively, for the three banks. Under stressful conditions, these probabilities increase to 11.9, 13.6, and 37.8 percent, respectively, for the three banks. With such information, CBK examiners can estimate how changes in monthly FSIs affect changes in CAMEL components, CAMEL ratings, and estimated conditional probabilities of insolvency as well as monitoring changes in each of these metrics over time.

Stress testing, a critical part of financial stability assessments can be synthesized through the use of multipliers. See the following list for a capsule summary of the appropriate safety and soundness multipliers related to FSIs. Once the multipliers are estimated for the bank in question for a current time period, any change in an FSI produces changes in CAMELS components, aggregate CAMELS, and the Pr(Fail) in items numbered 1 through 4. In effect the list provides a matrix of 'stress tests':

1. $\Delta C/\Delta FSI$, $\Delta A/\Delta FSI$, $\Delta M/\Delta FSI$, $\Delta E/\Delta FSI$, $\Delta L/\Delta FSI$, $\Delta S/\Delta FSI$.
2. $\Delta CAMELS/\Delta C$, $\Delta CAMELS/\Delta A$, $\Delta CAMELS/\Delta M$, $\Delta CAMELS/\Delta E$, $\Delta CAMELS/\Delta L$, $\Delta CAMELS/\Delta S$.
3. ΔPr (Fail)/$\Delta CAMELS$.
4. ΔPr (Fail)/ΔFSI.
5. $\Delta FSI/\Delta t$.
6. $\Delta C/\Delta t$, $\Delta A/\Delta t$, $\Delta M/\Delta t$, $\Delta E/\Delta t$, $\Delta L/\Delta t$, $\Delta S/\Delta t$.
7. $\Delta CAMELS/\Delta t$.
8. ΔPr (Fail)/Δt.

It is easy to imagine how a list of regulated banks, like the 44 banks regulated by the CBK, may be compared with respect to components, aggregate ratings, probabilities of failure, and multipliers on a month-to-month basis and estimates of changes in risks become increasingly apparent.

Consequently the BTB approach readily provides a comparatively simple and straightforward early warning system that does not require complex models and more importantly it provides an approach that is consistent with informed bank supervision processes already in place in many developing countries.

7 CONCLUSIONS

Bank regulators in developing countries have taken note of the fact that more complex early warning systems and supervision by risk systems advocated in the post-Basel II environment, failed to provide adequate early warnings and underestimated risks, thereby contributing to a global financial crisis.

For the immediate future, regulators in developing countries have begun to reassess the need for estimating economic capital, estimating operation, market, and credit risk, and developing elaborate heat maps and qualitative risk matrices. Many countries have invested in improved data collection and off-site monitoring systems. By using information from the last on-site exam, current and historical off-site FSI information, and experience-based central bank supervision weights, regulators in developing countries have begun to consider alternatives to the more complex models and concepts advanced under the auspices of Basel II and SBR. One prominent alternative, referred to here as 'back to basics' (BTB) employs a comparatively simple weighted average scoring model with a probability of insolvency assessment to provide useful financial condition assessments on a bank-by-bank basis.

Working with such data and simple models, regulators have begun to recognize that it is possible to ensure consistency and integration of the on- and off-site evaluation processes. Ultimately risk management is best accomplished with information. In most countries with reasonable data systems, the programming and utilization of the BTB approach can be accomplished in terms of weeks, not months or years, in contrast to the economic capital and SBR systems.

The BTB, while conceptually simple, parametrically sparse, and less resource intensive, has its own inherent limitations. The critical values of the FSIs and weights are still subjective and require periodic testing and review. In addition, the assumption of independence across FSIs is unquestionably heroic, but the alternatives are so computationally challenging that they are beyond consideration at this time. Yet another limitation is the problem associated with extrapolating from the experience of one country to parameterize an early warning system for another country. Certainly, BTB has its own set of onerous assumptions.

Nevertheless BTB remains a prominent default option for those countries that have yet to experience bank and thrift failures like the US and for whom data are lacking. Better yet, BTB provides the possibility that regulators can learn from their mistakes and correct those mistakes by adopting new FSIs, critical values, and weights as the time and circumstances permit. For example, sector-specific information on non-performing loans could easily be included as a new FSI, well as trends and projections of last-period FSIs. Why depend solely upon last month's return on equity, when an objective reasonable projection of next month's return on equity under normal and stressful conditions is also available? Certainly every bank makes it own projections of FSIs as part of its strategic plans and decisions. It quantifies and prices risk. Regulators must do so as well. Why not collect and use bank projections as inputs in assessing bank risks?

The GFC has compelled regulators worldwide to expand their set of FSIs and improve regulatory risk assessments. BTB suggests that regulators will build on past regulatory successes and improved data. Rather than focus on complex models that replicate bank risk assessment tools and mimic bank decision making, regulators are likely to focus on building small models in keeping with the regulatory mandates to better assess and monitor the probability of insolvency. More likely than not, comparatively simple models with small forecasting errors will ultimately win out as risk metrics tools.

NOTES

*   The views represented in this chapter reflect those of the authors and should not be considered as representative of the Federal Housing Finance Agency.

1. See a collection of papers on this subject and the FSI website for the IMF Seminal papers include: Sundararajan et al. (2002); IMF (2003, 2004, 2009).
2. Staff of FDIC (2009).
3. Lopez (1999).
4. Berger and Flannery (1998); Cole and Gunther (1998); DeYoung et al. (1998).
5. Sahajwala and Van Den Bergh (2000).
6. Staff of FDIC (2009, Section 5000, Statements of Policy.
7. Under SBR, regulators seek to assess risk in four dimensions. *Quantity of risk* is the level or volume of risk that the bank faces and is characterized as low, moderate, or high. *Quality of risk management* is how well risks are identified, measured, controlled, and monitored and is characterized as strong, satisfactory, or weak. *Aggregate risk* is a summary judgment about the level of supervisory concern. It incorporates judgments about the quantity of risk and the quality of risk management (examiners weigh the relative importance of each). Examiners characterize such risk as low, moderate, or high. *Direction of risk* is the probable change in the aggregate level of risk over the next 12 months and is characterized as decreasing, stable, or increasing. Heat maps and 'risk matrices' with qualitative scores have become standard tools in the SBR culture. In Africa, few bank supervision departments have failed to adopt SBR.
8. See the Large Bank and Community Bank Comptroller's Handbooks, which feature a useful discussion of SBR and its implementation (Staff of OCC, 2010a and b).
9. IMF (2005).
10. Variations in the original specification and estimation of the model in equation (10.2) are contained in the following papers: Hiemstra (2000); Hiemstra and Jacques (2000); Hiemstra et al. (1997a, 1997b, 2001). Since 2005, versions of the model have been used to develop off-site early warning systems in Lesotho, Botswana, Kenya, Sierra Leone, and other African countries as well as selected countries in the Eastern Caribbean and Eastern Europe.

REFERENCES

Berger, A.N. and M.J. Flannery (1998), 'Comparing market and supervisory assessment of bank performance: who knows what when?', Finance and Economics Discussion Series 1998–32, Federal Reserve Board of Governors, Washington, DC.

Cole, R.A. and J.W. Gunther (1998), 'Predicting bank failures: a comparison of on- and off-site monitoring systems', *Journal of Financial Services Research*, **13**, 103–17.

DeYoung, R., M.J. Flannery, W.W. Lang and S.M. Sorescu (1998), 'The informational advantage of specialized monitors: the case of bank examiners', Working Paper 98–4, Federal Reserve Bank of Chicago, Chicago, IL.

Gup, B.E. and T. Lutton (2009), 'Potential effects of fair value accounting on US bank regulatory capital', *Journal of Applied Finance*, **19** (122), 38–48.

Hiemstra, S. (2000), 'Estimating, validating, and stimulating national bank failure probabilities, US Comptroller of the Currency, Draft Working Paper, January. Copies available at: Stephen.Hiemstra@fhfa.gov.

Hiemstra, S., and K.T. Jacques (2000), 'Contagion effects, macroeconomic conditions, and the design of regulatory capital standards', US Comptroller of the Currency, Draft Working Paper, November. Copies available at: Stephen. Hiemstra@fhfa.gov.

Hiemstra, S., K.T. Jacques and S. Kane (1997a), 'Implications from bank failure estimates for capital adequacy standards', US Comptroller of the Currency,

Draft Working Paper, September. Copies available at: Stephen.Hiemstra@fhfa. gov.

Hiemstra, S., K.T. Jacques and T. Lutton (2001), 'Measurement error: implications for monitoring the risk in national banks', US Comptroller of the Currency, Draft Working Paper, January. Copies available at: Stephen.Hiemstra@fhfa. gov.

Hiemstra, S., S. Kane, T.J. Lutton and P.A.V.B. Swamy (1997b), 'A new method of forecasting bank failures and insurance fund losses', US Comptroller of the Currency, Draft Working Paper, May 12. Copies available at: Stephen. Hiemstra@fhfa.gov.

International Monetary Fund (2003), 'Financial soundness indicators – background paper', prepared by the Staff of the Monetary and Financial Systems and Statistics Departments, approved by Carol S. Carson and Stefan Ingves, 14 May, available at: http://www.imf.org/external/np/sta/fsi/eng/2003/051403b.htm (accessed 8 June 2010).

International Monetary Fund (2004), 'Compilation guide on financial soundness indicators', Washington, DC, available at: http://www.imf.org/external/np/sta/ fsi/eng/2004/guide/index.htm.

International Monetary Fund (2005), 'Implementation of Basel II – implications for the World Bank and the IMF', Washington, DC, available at: http://www. imf.org/external/np/pp/eng/2005/072205.htm.

International Monetary Fund (2009), 'Financial soundness indicators (FSIs) and the IMF', Washington, DC, available at: http://www.imf.org/external/np/sta/fsi/ eng/fsi.htm.

Lopez, J. (1999), 'Using CAMELS ratings to monitor bank conditions', Federal Reserve Bank of San Francisco, *FRBSF Economic Letter* 99–19, June 11, available at: http://www.frbsf.org/econrsrch/wklyltr/wklyltr99/el99-19.html.

Lutton, T. (2009), 'Risk based supervision: market and operational risk', IMF Symposium, Joint Africa Institute, May, Tunis, Tunisia.

Sahajwala, R. and P. Van Den Bergh (2000), 'Supervisory assessments and early warning systems', Bank of International Assessments Working Paper 4, 2005.

Staff of FDIC (2009), 'FDIC Law, Regulations, Related Acts', Federal Deposit Insurance Corporation, available at: http://www.fdic.gov/regulations/laws/ rules/5000-900.html (accessed 8 June 2010).

Staff of OCC (2010a) *Comptroller of the Currency Administrator of Nation Banks, Large Bank Supervision, Comptroller's Handbook*, January, available at: http:// www.occ.treas.gov/handbook/lbs/.pdf (accessed 8 June 2010).

Staff of OCC (2010b), *Comptroller of the Currency Administrator of Nation Banks, Community Bank Supervision, Comptroller's Handbook*, Office of the Comptroller of the Currency, January, available at: http://www.occ.treas.gov/ handbook/cbs.pdf (accessed 8 June 2010).

Sundararajan, V., C. Enoch, A. San José, P. Hilbers, R. Krueger, M. Morettia and G. Slack (2002), 'Financial soundness indicators: analytical aspects and country practices', International Monetary Fund, Washington, DC, April 8.

11. Hedge funds and offshore financial centers: new challenges for the regulation of systemic risks

Navin Beekarry*

1 INTRODUCTION

Since the 1980s, the dual forces of globalization – deregulation and liberalization of capital – led to a complete transformation of finance,[1] with rapid and growing movement of capital across borders.[2] This transformation, identified with innovative and highly complex and obscure financial instruments, resulted in a restructuring of the international financial system, raising concerns among policy makers and regulators, about financial stability.[3] Hedge funds[4] and offshore financial centers (OFCs) provide appropriate lenses for assessing stability issues linked with this spectacular financial evolution. In fact, both have recently resurfaced on the global governance agenda as a result of concerns linked with their potential for financial instability. The impressive growth and increasing proliferation of hedge funds,[5] as a mainstream alternative investment vehicle, indicate that they are likely to constitute critical non-bank financial institutions although the implications for financial stability, of their role, activities, and impact on financial markets, remain relatively underexplored. In turn, this has triggered a debate about the need for more-stringent regulation seeking to forestall any future possibilities of financial instability and crisis. At the same time, OFCs have also witnessed surprising growth and importance[6] against conventional wisdom that deregulation of financial systems would eventually undermine the competitive rationale for OFCs.[7] Although stability issues related to OFCs have always been explained in terms of their weak, or absence of, regulatory frameworks and tax avoidance schemes, recent changes in their role and importance in the international capital markets have also given rise to new concerns about instability.[8] Not surprisingly, the shared characteristics of hedge funds and OFCs, such as rapid growth and activities, lack of transparency resulting due to secrecy and anonymity rules, absence of, or weak, regulation, and potential for criminal activities, raised concerns about their systemic risk implications, resulting in constant calls for more effective regulation and supervision.[9] This chapter examines the recent growth and importance of hedge funds and OFCs in capital markets, the extent to which OFCs, already operating under loose regulation, further facilitate hedge funds to move under the regulatory radar, and how their interaction potentially exacerbates systemic risks, and reinforces the case for stringent regulation.

The growth of hedge funds, as alternative investment vehicles, is due to their capacity to yield higher returns, relying on their flexibility to implement innovative strategies made possible by the absence of, or weak, regulation.[10] Their importance in financial markets is highlighted as providers of diversification and liquidity and the ultimate holders of risk in the dynamic and growing credit risk transfer markets.[11] For example, they benefit banks by reducing banks' credit risks by taking assets off of their balance sheets, and improving their liquidity by providing a market for their securitizations and other financing strategies.[12] Lack of transparency surrounding their activities makes it difficult, however, to quantify the extent of their role in the disintermediation of commercial banks' traditional lending, although, in the US, the Shared National Credit Program (SNCP) provides some understanding of their activities.[13] The recent rapid expansion of their investor base, identified with the rise of institutional investors such as pension funds and endowments, and attraction to the retail investor industry, investing in hedge funds, confirms their attraction as alternative investment vehicles.[14] However, anxiety has grown about the inclination of hedge funds to take large risks, often associated with high leverage, lack of transparency surrounding their activities, the amount of assets they manage, and their relationship with banks as intermediaries, factors which, although not necessarily of a systemic nature *per se*, can play a vital role in the transmission of systemic risks, causing contagion.[15] In addition, the growing 'retailization' of hedge funds,[16] has generated more concerns about consumer investment protection, drawing the regulators' and policy makers' attention.[17] Although consensus exists that hedge funds have not directly caused the recent market disruptions,[18] the recent financial crisis, with the collapse of the two Bear Stearns hedge funds, illustrates how they were at the origin of the crisis.[19] The near-collapse of Long Term Capital Management (LTCM) had already, in 1998, signaled the negative impact of hedge funds' activities on financial markets and financial institutions.[20]

The rapid increase and spread of capital flows across boundaries, facilitated by hedge funds, via OFCs, raises the critical issue of the soundness of a country's financial system, an essential component for economic growth, and macroeconomic and financial stability. While financial market development has contributed to economic growth across borders,[21] it is also true that financial weaknesses in one country can rapidly spill over across national borders.[22] Linkages between hedge funds and OFCs are key issues in financial market development and integration, and provide critical insights into possible systemic vulnerabilities.[23] The establishment and operations of hedge funds – already characterized by absence of, or lax, regulation and supervision – primarily domiciled in OFCs,[24] also with light regulatory treatment, secrecy rules, and favorable tax regimes, illustrate how the global reach of finance increasingly integrates economies and financial systems across borders, raising stability issues that cut across multiple jurisdictions.[25] Traditional approaches, therefore, offer limited insights into the relevance of the growth, importance, and implications, of OFCs, for the stability of today's international financial order. First, the definition of OFCs as small distant islands in the sun offering some advantageous tax outlets to onshore businesses, limits a thorough understanding of the types of jurisdictions involved in such offshore activities. Second, conventional wisdom's categorization of OFCs as peripheral outlets offering tax advantages and lax regulatory frameworks that allow for money laundering[26] obscures their growing role and importance in the internationalization of capital. A thorough understanding of OFCs in today's international order requires a paradigm shift, moving beyond the dual limitations, that captures the significance of the extent and types of capital market activities conducted through hedge funds, using OFCs which not only include distant small jurisdictions, but also advanced market economies such as the UK and the EU.[27] These developments provide new perspectives on related financial stability issues.

The potential of hedge funds and OFCs to undermine financial stability has fueled intense debate about failures in existing frameworks and the need to design more-stringent national and international regulation. The conventional approach relying on market discipline has been challenged for its failure to prevent or address the recent financial crisis,[28] leading policy makers, regulators, and academics to look for alternative models that would reduce the threat of systemic risks.[29] However, proposals for new and more-stringent regulation of hedge funds and OFCs have not been made without any resistance both in the US and the EU.[30] Sections 2 and 3 examine the growth and development of hedge funds and OFCs, followed by an analysis of their impact on systemic risks and financial stability (Section 4). In Section 5, the challenges that hedge funds and OFCs raise for regulation are examined, looking at the state of current and proposed regulation, at both national and international levels. A note of caution, however, relates to the data deficit that exists in relation to hedge funds and their activities which often renders any conclusive analysis definitive, as in all studies of hedge funds.[31] Section 6 concludes.

2   ORIGIN AND GROWTH OF HEDGE FUNDS[32]

There is no legal or standard definition of a hedge fund.[33] It is often described as an investment company, organized as a limited partnership administered by professional investment managers, whose funds are collected from wealthy investors, using high-risk techniques in the hope of yielding large profits. They date back to the 1940s[34] and have grown impressively over the past 10 years, despite the initial setback in the 1990s caused by the LTCM débâcle, which proved to be only a temporary setback to an accelerating long-term trend.[35] From a mere 150 in 1969, they grew to 800 hedge funds holding $75 billion in assets (1994) and, by the beginning of the century, to some 6,000 managing some $600 billion,[36] often engaged in derivative and other complex transactions and short-selling.[37] By the end of 2006, the global hedge-fund industry had 11,000 funds with about $1.43 trillon in assets under management.[38] However, because hedge funds are not required to register with any financial regulator or supervisor, these numbers can only be estimated.[39] Hedge funds are also dominant players in several markets and reportedly account for 18–22 percent of all trading on the New York Stock Exchange, and are here to stay.[40] Venture capital funds manage about $257 billion of assets, and private equity funds raised about $256 billion in 2008.[41] Legally, the assets of a hedge fund are separate from the portfolio management, which is directed by the hedge-fund advisor, who is typically also the general partner of the fund. The type of hedge-fund governance and strategy which is characterized by the separation of ownership and control, where the partners are silent investors and generally take no part in management activities[42] suggests that this organizational form may present complications in terms of determining ownership and tracing assets.[43] In addition, the recent governance activism of hedge funds whereby they use their voting power to influence the behavior of the institutions in which they invest, presents additional challenges.[44] These features of hedge funds, coupled with the possible impact of their liquidation, as revealed recently,[45] increases fears about related stability issues for the international financial system.

Innovative hedge-fund investment strategies, enjoying complete flexibility over their implementation and supported by the lack of regulation and supervision, led managers to look for minimum regulatory intervention and favorable tax treatment.[46] In addition, the absence of mandatory reporting, and advantages offered by offshore domicile, also with few information and disclosure requirements and regulation, contributed significantly to their attraction as a financial engine of growth and expansion.[47] This allowed for opaque and highly complex structures of their transactions with the potential to create excess risk-taking, as illustrated by their extensive use of leverage and short-selling. Because of their leverage, and their active trading and management styles,[48] hedge funds account for a much greater share in terms of market turnover, which explains in part why they have been important drivers of financial innovation and market liquidity, despite their relatively small size, and why their rising influence has generated concerns and interest.[49] Their ability to use innovative instruments and their special source of capital, using regulated financial institutions – including prime broker dealers and banks – that supply them with their overwhelming proportion of their available leverage, encouraged hedge funds to adopt more-adventurous investment strategies in the expectations of greater yields. Subsequently, banks also started setting up their own hedge funds providing similar services such as managers, custodian banks, prime brokers and investors.[50] However, the interaction of hedge funds with regulated financial institutions and intermediaries, for the provision of services, such as the extension of credit to the hedge fund, exposes the financial institution to counterparty credit risks, raising additional concerns.

Another distinctive feature which gained the attention of policy makers and regulators, albeit of recent origin, has been the considerable expansion of hedge funds' investor profile, moving from their traditional strategy of typically targeting only high net worth individuals and institutional investors, to official investment such as pension and retirement funds.[51] Governments are seeking higher returns through either investment by individuals as their choice of instrument or investment in hedge funds by institutions, whether private or public, that manage individuals' retirement savings.[52] The broadening of the investor class has happened as a result of relaxation of accreditation requirements to the extent that few limits if any exist on who can invest in hedge funds.[53] This growing 'retailization' of hedge funds, although they do not currently have significant exposures to hedge funds, has led policy makers to start considering investor protection with regard to future hedge-fund exposure by these investors.[54] During the last few years, hedge-fund returns have become more sensitive to a number of asset classes, suggesting that they are taking on more risks.[55] Changes in the investor base of hedge funds provide insights into the buildup of strengths and weaknesses in international financial markets.

3   OFFSHORE FINANCIAL CENTERS[56]

The definition of an OFC has always been problematic[57] relying on loose concepts such as tax havens or simply centers that provide financial services such as low or zero taxation; moderate or light financial regulation; and banking secrecy and anonymity to non-residents.[58] A common definition is one which includes 'jurisdictions with relatively large numbers of financial institutions engaged primarily in business with nonresidents'[59] and whose financial systems display external assets and liabilities out of proportion to domestic financial intermediation designed to finance domestic operations.[60] Relying on strict banking-secrecy rules, OFCs, such as Luxembourg, Switzerland and Singapore, have the advantage of providing foreign businesses and rich individuals with low or no taxes, political stability, business-friendly regulation and laws, and discretion, as most OFCs do not levy capital-gains or inheritance taxes.[61] Other OFCs, including many in the Caribbean, do not have any laws against tax evasion because they impose no income taxes.[62] Criticisms leveled against OFCs that they have a distorting effect, depriving onshore businesses of legitimate business, by using taxes to attract mobile financial capital without any 'real' business underpinning it, are disputed on the basis that foreign investors are attracted to OFCs because companies' subsidiaries in OFCs add value by providing important intermediate inputs used by its operations elsewhere, and by helping multinational companies (MNCs) lower their effective tax rates.[63] At origin, OFCs' association with tax evasion led to growing concerns about financial stability, and of the volume of capital located in such jurisdictions.[64]

Unbundling the complexities surrounding the interaction between hedge funds and OFCs requires a paradigm shift transcending the two limitations imposed by a conventional approach to OFCs. First, it is no longer possible to rely on the traditional and restrictive definition of OFCs as distant small tax haven islands generally providing ideal domiciles where it is relatively easy to set up and operate a hedge fund. A broader definition illustrates that the UK, EU countries, Switzerland and Luxembourg provide offshore regimes and channels for hedge funds, although both EU and UK hedge funds tend to be more concentrated offshore, albeit managed onshore.[65] Second, the popular image of OFCs as low levels of tax and regulatory regimes supported by secrecy rules facilitating money laundering and financing of terrorism, no longer provides a complete picture of the role and importance of OFCs in the present international financial structure. In fact, in the period following financial deregulation, the growth in the number of OFCs illustrates that they have started to develop into active and important players in more mainstream financial services, acting as critical mediation points in international capital markets.[66] It is the combined effects of this growth and impact of hedge funds and OFCs that led the global community to express concerns for the stability of the international financial system.[67]

OFCs can no longer be identified only as tax-free destinations for they have grown more relevant as financial centers hosting complex financial activities. Recent developments illustrate a new trend of OFCs' booming business[68] and close links with the internationalization of capital flows, making them an integral part in the functioning of international capital markets.[69] OFCs, often referred to as the middlemen of international financial transactions,[70] play a critical role in international portfolio flows across the globe,[71] moving somehow away from its traditional regulatory arbitrage functions, and raising issues of nationality and residence. Jersey, for example, which initially relied on its low-tax repository of cash to build up a sophisticated private-banking and trust business, has more recently moved into the corporate business of structured finance and the administration of investment funds.[72] IMF calculations suggest that OFCs' balance sheet role in cross-border transactions was something in the order of $4.6 trillion in 1999,[73] with around 50 percent being intermediated through OFCs, where they are often recycled.[74] The variety of offshore services such as special purpose investment vehicles, shell and brass-plate companies, offer financial services such as banking, insurance, and securities, provide financial channels, where nationality and recorded form of transactions can change very easily, without any change in their economic content.[75] Financial and nonfinancial corporations, registered in OFCs because of attractive incentives such as tax advantages and lower registration and establishment costs, increasingly resort to special purpose vehicles (SPVs) for securitization. In addition, most banks located in OFCs are branches or subsidiaries of international banks. This development provides alternative avenues for MNCs and other international investment institutions to diversify organizational forms.[76] This rapid growth, and variety, of international financial transactions due to international portfolio investment (IPI)[77] is illustrative of OFCs' new role, potentially leading to global imbalance. As business in OFCs develops, these jurisdictions no longer sit at the fringes of the global economy. The Cayman Islands hosts 8,000-plus hedge funds, more than half of the world's offshore hedge funds,[78] and is the world's fifth-largest banking centre, with $1.4 trillion in assets; the British Virgin Islands, home to almost 700,000 offshore companies, provides setting up and registration of hedge funds within a couple of days,[79] and Jersey's 46 banks, 1,055 investment funds and over 200 trusts administer over £700 billion in assets on the island. San Marino aspires to become a fully fledged financial center which offers light but firm regulation although it wants to avoid a reputation as a tax haven or a dubious destination to park questionable funds.[80] Singapore is trying to compete with Hong Kong as a home for hedge-fund investors and bankers by offering permanent residency in two years and a low-tax, business-friendly environment.[81] The Channel Islands, the Isle of Man, the Bahamas and the Caymans, apart from providing tax incentives during the 1970s, also acted as securities issuing centers and SPVs,[82] and collective investment schemes as well as host to insurance companies, pension funds and fund managers. This new development of OFCs, where hedge funds are usually incorporated,[83] albeit managed onshore, raises interesting challenges for stability issues, especially in the context of a series of events that triggered renewed regulatory interest about the implications of IPI for financial stability.[84]

4   SYSTEMIC RISKS: HEDGE FUNDS AND OFCS

The rapid growth of the hedge-fund industry and the active role of hedge funds in financial markets,[85] which far outweigh the importance of their size alone, continue to attract policy makers' attention, in view of their potential for undermining the stability of the international financial system. Systemic risk is not always easily defined,[86] although it can be referred to as negative externalities linked to an institution's failure, propagating contagion – causing other institutional failures – eventually negatively affecting the larger economy.[87] Destabilizing failures in markets and regulation, changes in financial sector structure, failure of risk management to keep up with financial innovation, and leveraged financial institutions taking on excessive risks without internalizing systemic risk, are examples of vulnerabilities that can potentially cause instability.[88] Systemic risk in hedge-fund investment can occur either directly with a wave of hedge-fund collapses, through fire sale of assets and subsequent disruption in asset prices, to eventual losses at systemically important counterparty institutions such as large prime brokers. Changes in hedge funds' international investor base, and their investment allocation behavior, are also critical for understanding the buildup of strengths and weaknesses in the international financial system.[89] Indirectly, the effect of forced hedge-fund liquidation on secondary market performance, in particular on rising volatility and the disappearance of liquidity, could impact on systemically important financial institutions whose assets are depreciated.

The impact of hedge funds, as a source of systemic risk, on the real economy, can be assessed in terms of symbiotic linkages with the financial sector and the economy, reflected through the role that financial intermediaries, such as banks, play in the provision of credit.[90] Discussions of this type of direct linkage from hedge funds to real economic activity through the banking system are common.[91] Such linkages to the real economy might occur through banks' direct exposures to hedge funds,[92] or disruptions to capital markets that hinder credit provision or allocation. Failure of a large individual or a group of hedge funds, serious mismanagement of exposures to hedge funds at an individual bank or banks, or the negative impact of hedge-fund activities on financial markets, can trigger financial instability,[93] when the spillover effect escalates on other channels leading to contagion.[94] Credit exposure to hedge funds may create externalities in the banking system and where the exposure represents a significant share of bank capital, a large shock to hedge funds could weaken banks and impair their ability to provide liquidity or credit. Given that commercial banks and securities firms are directly linked to hedge funds through their counterparty exposures, a bank's large exposure to a hedge fund that defaults or operates in markets where prices are falling rapidly, may reduce its ability or willingness to extend credit to deserving borrowers.[95] As a consequence of disruption of a bank's lending activity, due to insolvency or capital shocks, viable investment projects are deprived of funding and economic activity is reduced. A sudden decline in asset prices, triggered, for example, by the unwinding of a highly leveraged hedge fund, can reduce the value of that collateral, or generate liquidity risk and further price declines as investors sell into the falling market to meet margin calls. Bank lending, however, is not the only form of credit provision, and other forms such as capital markets are rising in relative importance.[96] The same rationale of market disruption is also applicable to capital market institutions, potentially limiting the provision of credit, with real economic effects. Hedge funds, in particular, are active traders and contribute to increased market efficiency and liquidity through their frequent trading and ability to exploit arbitrage opportunities. The potential for liquidation of a highly leveraged institution may lead to volatility and sharp asset price declines that heighten uncertainty about credit risk and disrupt the intermediation of credit.[97]

Over the years, and more recently during the credit crisis, repeated scandals associated with hedge funds' risky trading activities, and the serious impact on the real economy, have also prompted concerns about their potential for systemic instability. Although hedge fund scandals are not new,[98] it was the famous recent scandal of the Long-Term Capital Management (LTCM), a hedge fund that lost 90 percent of its $4.8 billion in 1998 as a result of its trading positions, that brought hedge funds to the surface of governance concerns. There is consensus that the recent financial and economic crisis originated with the implosion of two of Bear Stearns' hedge funds,[99] the Bear's Credit Strategies Master Fund and its sister Enhanced Master Fund, in 2007,[100] triggering the downturn, although, since 2006, questions have been raised as to whether Bear was using the funds to 'unload excessively risky or troubled assets' that it could not sell on.[101] Following the collapse of Bear, two years later, Lehman Brothers was liquidated, Merrill Lynch was rescued by Bank of America and the entire global economy has faced the worst recession for 70 years. The Madoff Ponzi scheme,[102] with its main hedge fund, the Ascot, followed by closures of other hedge funds,[103] confirm the linkages between hedge funds and massive financial fraud that can result in market meltdown. Various investors had, through various hedge funds, invested with Madoff.[104] The Madoff scheme revealed how the use of a legitimate broker-dealer business intermingled with a fraudulent hedge fund with the ultimate objective of diverting investors' money.[105] Amaranth[106] is another example where state pension funds were invested in a risky hedge fund.[107] However, there are strong indications that, albeit such scams and closures, hedge funds are here to stay with the top three prime brokers still controlling 62 percent of hedge-fund industry capital,[108] leading regulators to believe that contagion is likely to reemerge.[109] Three aspects of the LTCM case are interesting for understanding the role and importance of hedge funds for stability: the extent of the company's leverage, the extent of its use of derivatives, and the fact that leading banks lent to LTCM apparently without being well informed of either its activities or its other sources of financing.

Hedge funds and OFCs are also often portrayed as attractive channels for criminal activities as a result of the globalized financial economy which allows for capital to move around the globe instantly, providing openings for drug traffickers and money launderers and rogue nations in need of cash.[110] The other risk associated with OFCs is that market integrity may be compromised by financial crime such as money laundering. Concerns have been expressed about the huge growth in the use of hedge funds and OFCs for money laundering and financing of terrorism, raising systemic risk and financial stability concerns, due to illicit money being hidden away in islands with variable supervision.[111] Several instances illustrate the concerns.[112] The recent (2008) Stanford investigation into an $8 billion fraud is another illustration of the continued use of OFCs as offshore investment vehicles to defraud investors who invested their savings in Stanford's offshore schemes.[113] Enron's 700 companies in Cayman allowed its corrupt bosses to minimize taxes but also manufacture earnings. This is the underappreciated real cost of OFCs, rather than lost tax revenues.[114] Financial institutions' liquidity problems resulting from the credit crisis, compared to availability of huge amounts of illicit money (capital) ready to be injected into (rescue) financial institutions illustrate the high probability of money launderers seizing the opportunity presented by the crisis to develop new money laundering and financing of terrorism channels.[115]

Extensive use of leverage is considered to be one, if not the, most important feature of hedge funds that can trigger systemic risk, as recently highlighted by the FSF and the IMF in their analysis of the causes of the crisis.[116] Leverage constitutes the fire-power of hedge funds which, when combined with a rapid and focused trading style, allows hedge funds to have a much bigger impact on market turnover. Hedge funds can leverage themselves with very high multiples, either directly by borrowing from prime brokers, or indirectly through selling credit derivatives, making them especially vulnerable to a sudden decrease in market liquidity.[117] Moreover, there is a generalized view that hedge funds' leverage, in the aggregate, only keeps increasing.[118] The main problem, however, is posed by the lack of reporting requirements on hedge funds, which makes it very difficult to assess the extent of hedge funds' leverage, especially through their derivatives exposure.[119] One example of the type of risk associated with hedge funds is the sequence of negative events starting with losses on leveraged market positions where leveraged market risk can, if not supported by adequate liquidity reserves or borrowing capacity, lead to default on the fund's obligations to prime brokers and other financial institutions.[120]

Measuring illiquidity exposure in hedge funds is another central aspect of systemic risk,[121] directly related to hedge-fund failures and estimates of a fund's probability of liquidation[122] are critical for improving the stability of global financial markets. Hedge funds are typically viewed as being liquidity providers in the capital markets and are generally considered to help disperse risk more widely. However, generalized illiquidity plays an important part in general market collapse as the more illiquid the portfolio, the larger the price impact of a forced liquidation or fire sale, which erodes the bank's risk capital that much more quickly.[123] In the presence of leverage, the combination of relatively illiquid assets and short-term financing exposes the hedge fund to possibly significant liquidity risk. If many hedge funds or financial institutions become more highly correlated during times of distress and, as financial institutions are interrelated, the illiquidity crisis can cascade quickly into contagion, causing a global financial crisis. The collapse of LTCM in 1998, Bear Stearns, and Lehman Brothers in September 2008, made it clear that hedge-fund liquidations can be a significant source of systemic risk. The revelation about Madoff's hedge fund, Ascot Partners, being a major financial scam, raised fears about its impact on several hedge funds possibly going into liquidation.[124] In addition, concerns exist regarding risks associated with a decline in asset-market liquidity resulting from the failure or winding down of one or more major hedge funds. A particular concern is that, in illiquid markets, hedge funds may be forced to sell positions to meet margin requirements, driving down market prices. Because of such risks, supervisors focus on banks' ability to identify and mitigate the risks associated with a sharp decline in market liquidity.

Counterparty credit risk is the single most important risk for financial institutions in their interaction with hedge funds.[125] Although the transfer of risk from banks to hedge funds allows banks to better manage their credit risks, some concerns still remain. One is that this risk has not been transferred so much as transformed into counterparty credit exposure to the hedge fund. For example, in the purchase of credit protection on a loan via a credit default swap with a hedge fund, a bank would no longer bear direct credit risk to the original borrower but would instead have counterparty credit risk to the hedge fund. Assessing counterparty credit risk depends on the net exposure between two institutions which can change as either party may become the net debtor. Current exposure, the net exposure at current market values, or potential future exposure, which is the maximum amount to which an exposure could grow over a future time period, if markets move against the hedge fund, provide two ways of assessing counterparty credit risk.[126] Banks also 'stress' potential exposures to estimate how they may grow under adverse market conditions. Still, systemic concerns remain. In a crisis, interlocking credit exposures would be the key mechanism by which risks would be transmitted from one institution to another, potentially leading to a systemic situation. Excessive leverage and poor counterparty credit risk management practiced by banks and other creditors raised concerns that market players seeking to sell at once could have negatively affected asset prices across markets, indirectly affecting other market participants. Absence of data such as counterparty credit exposures, the net degree of leverage of hedge-fund managers and investors, and the gross amount of structured products involving hedge funds, renders any conclusive assessment of the magnitude of current systemic risk exposures with any degree of accuracy, almost impossible.

The assessment of potential systemic risks associated with financial flows arising out of financial activities of hedge funds located in OFCs is complicated by the strong growth of the hedge-fund industry and the increasing complexity of the instruments they trade in.[127] Offshore hedge funds, with many billions of dollars available to switch at short notice between markets, are often blamed for intensifying financial crises such as the 1997 Asian currency and stock market crash; but it is equally possible to argue that they have a smoothing effect on global financial volatility.[128] Three main concerns exist about hedge funds operating in OFCs:

existence of lightly supervised OFCs encourages regulatory arbitrage that may result in the establishment of rogue financial institutions; impediments to consolidated supervision in the OFCs result in supervisory gaps over important activities of a financial institution; and lack of information about the volume and type of activities conducted in the OFC. Offshore establishments provide alternatives to domestic financial institutions that are often subject to strict prudential regulations and high reserve requirements. Challenges associated with OFCs' ineffective financial supervision, strict bank and corporate secrecy rules that hinder investigation, arrangements that facilitate money laundering and other financial crimes, and loss of tax revenues onshore, allow hedge funds to escape the regulatory eyes, creating risks of some OFCs as a source of systemic problems nationally and globally.[129] Supervision concerns include weak licensing systems and know-your-customer requirements, which make it difficult for consolidated supervision by countries whose financial institutions have operations in OFCs. In the Asian crisis, large, undetected, and poorly accounted-for offshore funds contributed to credit expansion in the region, led to increasing exposures to liquidity, foreign exchange, and credit risks, and had systemic effects on the financial systems of individual countries concerned.[130] The turbulence in world bond markets in 1994, the Asian financial crisis of 1997, the demise of the world's largest hedge fund LTCM whose incorporation offshore did not prove to be an issue although concerns were expressed that any bankruptcy of LTCM would have been complicated by its offshore status, the recent collapse of the two hedge funds of Bear Stearns, which triggered the 2008 credit crisis, and the Stanford scandal, confirm the role played by hedge funds in OFCs through IPI transactions, perhaps compromising the efficiency of financial markets. It may happen that a large, leveraged and, in the worst case, insolvent offshore establishment, designed to escape the reach of supervisory authorities onshore, may disrupt the operation of its onshore affiliated bank. In other instances, offshore establishments may become substantially larger, in terms of assets and liabilities, than affiliated banks onshore. The exploitation by offshore banks of opportunities for regulatory arbitrage, may allow funds to be transferred that can be used to finance connected onshore activities, concentrating onshore risks in inadequately supervised offshore financial centers. Often, OFCs provide opportunities for complex corporate structures and relationships among various jurisdictions designed to impede supervision. 'Shell companies' that serve as registers for transactions arranged and managed from other jurisdictions, can be used to exacerbate the already complex coordination problems arising in normal cross-border banking where two supervisory authorities are involved.

Territoriality and residence issues associated with the emergence of 'brass-plate' companies, shell companies, international business companies (IBCs) and special purpose entities set up in OFCs, present further challenges for stability, as OFCs' structure can complicate tracing the exact origin and location of IPI, channeled through them.[131] These types of company, whose residence is determined by virtue of their registration in OFCs, are significant points in cross-border flows. The flexibility offered by OFCs complicates efforts to attribute investments to individual security holders, allowing funds to move under regulatory eyes. The significance of residence of hedge funds in OFCs lies in the impact of changes brought about in residence on the balance of payments accounting, where changing the registration of the companies to a different jurisdiction alters the direction of capital flows, even though no transaction of economic significance occurred.[132] In addition, a change in the form of transactions channeled through these OFCs alters balance of payments measures, although perhaps with no real change in economic relationships. In other words, the cross-border flows are recorded on the basis of the fund's registration as a nonresident from the investment, even though a majority of holders in the fund could conceivably be located in the same country as the asset being acquired. Pooled investments allow savings from different country residences, blurring the OFC residence criteria, and negating assumptions that holders in the fund have the same country attribution. Custodians, insurance companies, fund managers, trusts, pension funds and mutual funds as collective investment schemes are often not aware of the nationality of the security holder on whose behalf they are investing. Establishing the country attribution of a security issuer as well as finding the country attribution of a security holder becomes very problematic. Fierce competition for global financial business, on which OFCs depend, often raises concerns if the lower cost of financial services is achieved by lowering regulatory and supervisory standards. As OFCs provide financial services predominantly to nonresidents, the home countries' authorities are concerned about the impact, on their national economies, of OFCs' operations which are beyond their own country authorities' control. In addition, the lack or absence of reliable data on activities of OFCs hampers analysis, making it difficult to assess the risk that OFCs pose to international financial stability. With the growing integration of financial markets worldwide, problems in a financial institution located in an OFC can be transferred rapidly to markets elsewhere. Such characteristics of OFCs and hedge funds raise concerns about their potential risks to international financial stability. Consolidated supervision of the total operations of the bank by the home supervisor, with adequate regulatory and supervisory standards applied in OFCs, seems the most reliable way to reduce such risks.

5 NEW CHALLENGES FOR THE REGULATION OF HEDGE FUNDS AND OFCS

Concerns about hedge funds and OFCs' impact on financial stability have increased as their considerable growth and development[133] exposed potential shortcomings,[134] leading to controversy about whether existing regulatory frameworks are adequate to safeguard financial stability and protect hedge-fund investors, or whether new and more-stringent regulation is needed.[135] The debate about whether direct regulation of hedge funds,[136] and their investment advisors, or indirect regulation (market discipline) offer the best regulatory options for the future, has resurfaced. It is suggested that market discipline failed as the breakdown of regulatory and supervisory systems contributed to the recent financial débâcle.[137] Market oversight failed to stem excessive risk-taking or take into account the interconnectedness of the activities of regulated and nonregulated institutions and markets, perhaps due in part to fragmented regulatory structures and legal constraints on information sharing. The collapse of the two hedge funds of Bear Stearns, which fueled the credit crisis of 2007,[138] Lehman Brothers and AIG, demonstrated the failings of regulation and supervision of large and highly leveraged and substantially interconnected financial firms. Another example of market discipline's weakness is when the investment banks were allowed to leverage their capital more than 30 times.[139] In addition, the demand for more-stringent regulation of hedge funds is compounded by risks associated with the recent extension of its activities to retail investment, based on the 'social security' argument,[140] that regulation should protect the investing citizens' interest, relying on standards that integrate integrity, transparency, and competence criteria. As a result, the rationale for keeping hedge funds outside regulatory scrutiny because they target only 'high net worth' individuals, is no longer valid. It is even suggested that the state jeopardizes its social security obligations when it fails to properly regulate hedge funds in which it invests.[141] Regulators' attention is, therefore, expected to increase.[142] Recent proposals for the overhaul of financial regulation seek to address existing shortcomings, and restructure the two pillars of regulation and supervision for an efficient and safe financial system.[143] A well-balanced option combining elements of the direct and indirect approach seems to have gained favor.[144] However, regulating hedge funds and OFCs, has not been without its challenges.

The recent crisis has revealed the limits of current micro-prudential regulatory and supervisory approach characterized by weak financial institutions, inadequate bank regulation and supervision, and lack of transparency, and the assumption based on market fundamentalism, that in case of failures, financial institutions will always be bailed out.[145] The assumption was that if bank supervisors ensured an individual bank's safety, systemic stability would look after itself. Regulation and supervision focused on individual financial institutions and neglected the systemic and international implications of the actors of financial market participants. Market discipline relies on hedge-fund investors, creditors, and counterparties to reward well-managed hedge funds and to reduce their exposure to risky, poorly managed funds. Indirect regulation works on the assumption that the capacity of hedge funds to adversely affect systemic stability derives from their relationships with other financial intermediaries which are regulated counterparties.[146] There is, therefore, no need for a separate supervisory system for the hedge funds if supervisors of those intermediaries ensure that appropriate controls, such as oversight of the robustness of operational systems to exposures, and capital adequacy to cover risk in their interaction with hedge funds, are in place. Banks and other financial institutions are also sources of market discipline because they must perform credit assessments to rate a fund for its management, leverage, liquidity, and strategy, based on transparency, before providing financing or entering into derivatives transactions with hedge funds. These credit assessments should determine the amount of risk a bank will take when financing a hedge fund. However, this assumption that markets are self-correcting is challenged in the proposals for regulatory reforms for financial institutions, because in all cases the intervention of government saved the markets when they were in trouble,[147] and that banks can behave in a way that collectively undermines the system.[148] While markets are the best institutions for allocating private sector resources, their efficiency depends on rules that ensure the provision of sufficient information. But hedge funds are very reticent about sharing that kind of information, and are not usually required to do so by law as it is the responsibility of investors and counterparties to pressure them to improve their disclosures. Given that the contribution of hedge funds to market efficiency depends on their ability to generate and use proprietary information, any regulation compelling them to share that information limits their incentive to invest in information gathering. Nevertheless, rules that ensure greater transparency and disclosure are desirable to the regulation of the funds as they help discipline the risk-taking activities of funds, and provide markets with information about potential risks. The challenges of regulating hedge-fund activities, if only by requiring them to provide more information about their positions, especially because of links with OFCs, should not, however, be underestimated. If hedge funds are required to publish more information on their activities, the responsibility of reporting frequently on the aggregate movements in hedge-fund positions[149] and the impact on efficiency and stability of setting reporting requirements for hedge funds should be assessed.[150]

The disparate and dispersed nature of hedge-fund regulation, at both national and international levels, illustrates the ineffectiveness of and weakness in the indirect approach. At present, there is no common regulatory regime for hedge funds in the EU, although a number of member states have adopted national legislation.[151] In London, requirements by the regulator (the Financial Services Authority: FSA), for starting a hedge fund are so burdensome and require details on everything about the firm's compliance systems to its risk controls together with an annual report that, once established, the regulator can only use a relatively light-touch approach based on broad principles. In the US, regulation of the hedge-fund industry has always been difficult to enforce due to the dispersed and uncertain nature of the regulatory environment in which they operate.[152] Over a seven-year period, starting in 1933, the United States reshaped the regulation of the market structures for banking, securities, derivatives, and mortgage and asset management through key pieces of legislation[153] covering various financial sectors' issues, including systemic stability, regulatory reorganization, transparency, enhancing market integrity, and reducing conflicts of interest. Hedge funds have always benefited from greater flexibility under the provisions of the National Securities Markets Improvement Act of 1996, which allowed investment companies to act without registration, if their investors were 'qualified purchasers',[154] and from an exemption from regulatory requirements for collaterized debt obligations (CDOs) and commodity trading advisors (CTAs) offered only to highly accredited investors, most of whom are persons investing in hedge funds.[155]

The recent crisis has given rise to more voices for direct regulation of hedge funds and a substantially rule-based system.[156] The new consensus that has emerged on the re-regulation of the financial system is grounded in the concept of 'macro-prudential' regulation, the essence of which is that regulation should focus more on systemic risks instead of simply micro-supervision of individual banks. The perimeter of regulation needs to be expanded to encompass systemic institutions and markets that operate below the regulatory and supervisory radar.[157] The chief weapon in the macro-prudential armory is a capital regime for banks that curbs excessive credit growth.[158] The challenge is to design new rules and institutions, at both the individual institution and the macroeconomic levels, that reduce systemic risks, improve financial intermediation, and properly adjust the perimeter of regulation and supervision, without imposing unnecessary burdens. Integrating the direct and indirect–'the gripper approach'[159] – hedge-fund regulation has some merits whereby direct regulation would enable the consolidated exposure of the financial system *vis-à-vis* hedge funds to be highlighted by providing the necessary information to link any registered hedge fund with all of its brokers, relying on hedge funds' registration bearing in mind their OFC links, and collection of structural data. Extending disclosure would provide supervisors with enough information to determine which institutions are big or interconnected enough to create systemic risk.[160] On the other hand, indirect regulation would focus on systemic risk oversight directed primarily at the major banks providing funding, counterparty positions and transaction services to single hedge funds. The emphasis will be on monitoring counterparty risk management by prime brokers, including leverage ratios, and by looking after a sufficiently large capital base to cover the risks involved. Concerning funds domiciled in offshore centers, indirect regulation should factor in any risks emanating from counterparties not subject to direct oversight, a policy which will make the choice of offshore centers as the domicile for hedge funds less attractive.[161] The central question remains, however, whether counterparty credit risk management (CCRM), particularly by banks and securities firms, is sufficient to limit risk-taking of hedge funds and constrain systemic risk to socially efficient levels. Some have suggested that CCRM, as opposed to regulation, is the optimal way to control hedge-fund leverage and limit systemic vulnerabilities.[162]

At the national level, the leading economies such as London, the US and the EU have unveiled hedge-fund legislation in an attempt to reshape their patchy systems of financial services seeking to prevent a repeat of the 2007 financial crisis.[163] The European Commission has put forward an alternative investment directive that would force hedge funds and private equity firms to seek regulatory authorization, report their strategies and set aside capital against losses and to monitor and warn about threats to financial stability.[164] The EU directive would impose stark restrictions on hedge funds as it is also feared that hedge-fund short-selling destabilizes markets and opens avenues for market abuse.[165] A new system of financial supervisors will oversee individual banks and financial firms, with supervision of firms remaining with national supervisors.[166] The government of Germany, which is hostile towards hedge funds, placed hedge funds on the 2007 G8's agenda,[167] although the issue was never addressed by the G8. In the US, plans are moving forward to tighten the rules on everything from hedge funds and over-the-counter derivatives to mortgages and basic bank capital requirements.[168] Supported by the establishment of a consumer financial protection agency to regulate mortgages, and hedge funds and hedge-fund managers, the obligation to register with the Securities and Exchange Commission (SEC) and open their books to examination, will considerably increase disclosure, giving regulators a powerful microscope to probe into the secretive hedge-fund industry and help identify potential systemic threats.[169] It also aims to discourage excessive risk-taking among the biggest financial concerns and hedge funds found by regulators to be 'so large, leveraged or interconnected that they pose a threat to financial stability' will be subject to more stringent requirements for capital, liquidity and risk management. The proposals constitute a major departure from the *laissez-faire* focus on self-regulation of financial firms to one in which prudential measures aimed at improving the conduct of financial markets and addressing externalities that arise from large-scale risk-taking,[170] also prevents funds from moving offshore to escape registration.[171]

However, the issue about regulation of hedge funds is not without controversy, and the continued vehement opposition against regulation of hedge funds illustrates the complexity surrounding the issue. The involvement of several players in the game, including national governments, financial sectors and international organizations, complicates matters. The EU initiative to giving EU bodies any binding powers on supervision has not been without opposition. The German finance minister's attempts to push for an agreement on tightening regulation of hedge funds were quickly opposed, mainly by the US and UK governments, and watered down to mere calls for disclosure. The Labour government is largely defending the tripartite system it set up more than a decade ago, which divides power among the Bank of England, the Treasury and the FSA. Another argument against regulation has been the fear of increasing compliance burden, which 'far outweigh any benefits', building pressure from the views of institutional investors who are some of the biggest hedge-fund customers, arguing that the proposed rules would be unworkable.[172] The UK considers that the proposal is too intrusive and could trample on the independence of national supervisors, potentially harming parliament's sovereign rights over the use of public funds.[173] Concerns have also been expressed about the composition of the Economic and Social Research Council (ESRC), UK which should be independent from the European Central Bank (ECB).[174] Sweden's opposition to EU regulation of hedge funds is based on an exaggerated fear that hedge funds contain big systemic risks[175] and would impose unnecessary compliance burdens.[176] Criticisms are also based on opposition to regulation's one-size-fits-all approach.[177] In both the US and the EU, policy makers argue that hedge funds were not central to the crisis, but nevertheless welcome some minimal regulation aimed at protecting against the risks to the financial system.

The call for more-stringent regulation of hedge funds and OFCs is fully backed by the international community which has spared no effort to move forward on an agenda aimed at a complete overhaul of the existing international regulatory and supervisory framework of financial institutions, combining both the direct and indirect approaches.[178] As of 2008, a variety of international institutions and intergovernmental committees already address issues of prudential financial oversight.[179] Governments have also invested in designing rules and standards on the regulation of hedge funds and derivatives and often shared their conclusions with international bodies.[180] The work of the Financial Stability Forum (FSF)[181] on areas relevant to the potential systemic risks associated with hedge funds and OFCs is based on its worries about newer risks, such as the rapid growth of derivatives and hedge funds in OFCs.[182] The 2000 report provides an assessment of the financial stability issues and systemic risks posed by hedge funds, and set out a range of recommendations[183] to address the systemic risks posed by highly leveraged institutions, although it does not address the investor protection issues associated with institutional or retail investments in hedge funds.[184] It monitors and reports on progress and actions taken in respect of recommendations.[185] The Basel Committee on Banking Supervision (BCBS), probably the most prominent of the international public sector initiatives, issued, in 1999, a list of sound practices for banks' interactions with 'highly leveraged institutions' (HLIs). The BCBS's recent[186] proposals to raise capital requirements for certain complex structured credit products, to introduce additional capital charges for incremental risks in the trading book due to factors such as default, or changes in credit spread or in equity price, and to strengthen the capital treatment of liquidity facilities to off-balance-sheet conduits, provide viable options.[187] Pillar 2 of the Basel II framework can be used by supervisors to strengthen risk management practices by banks, sharpen banks' control of tail risks, and mitigate the buildup of excessive exposures and risk concentrations.[188] The International Organization of Securities Commission (IOSCO)[189] technical committee has set forth recommendations for hedge-fund regulation embodying a consistent global approach to addressing hedge-fund risk through risk-based regulatory oversight of hedge funds, focused particularly on systemically important and higher-risk hedge-fund managers.[190] As part of this regulation, hedge-fund managers should provide information to help regulators protect investors and monitor systemic risk and risks to hedge-fund counterparties.[191] The G20 Pittsburgh Summit Leaders' Statement of September 2009, to completely overhaul the financial regulatory system for banks and other financial firms, seeking to improve risk management, strengthen transparency, promote market integrity, establish supervisory colleges, reinforce international cooperation, and raise capital standard, is perhaps the strongest signal sent by perhaps the most important international forum responsible for international policy on financial stability issues, to address financial regulation at both national and international levels.[192] Against all odds that it would end up as a mere platform for countries and regions to win moral grounds on how to achieve regulatory reforms,[193] it succeeded in adopting 'a very blunt, transparent, simple, and inflexible rule about how much capital all financial institutions need, of what specific type, and enforc[ing] it at an international level'.[194]

Most of these initiatives recognize that it is very difficult to regulate hedge funds directly given the ease with which they can change their domicile with their operations based offshore, and avoid regulation. The potential risk posed by OFCs to financial systems have for some time been on the global agenda as part of the work of the FSF,[195] the IMF, FATF,[196] IOSCO, Basel, and the OECD, although some overlap exists on stability issues related to OFCs.[197] The FSF's report on OFCs indicates prudential and market integrity concerns stemming from factors in OFCs that impede effective supervision and impact on global financial stability.[198] In response to concerns about instability linked with OFCs, associated with their overwhelming volume of activity, the IMF has significantly stepped up its surveillance of OFCs in recent years to identify potential financial vulnerabilities, including those resulting from weak regulatory and supervisory systems.[199] The IMF's decision to integrate OFC assessment with the financial sector assessment program (FSAP)[200] illustrates an attempt to strengthen regulation and supervision of OFCs and improve compliance with relevant international standards.[201] International principles for banking regulation, which had already been set out by the Basel Accord in 1988, are based on the idea of 'consolidated supervision' in which a bank's home supervisor took responsibility for monitoring the risks of the entire bank. This called for cooperation from host regulators as many OFCs fell far short of this requirement. The FATF drew up 40+9 standards[202] for keeping money launderers and terrorists out of the financial system, including a ban on shell banks and a requirement that jurisdictions must know the true owners of all companies set up within their borders. Both bodies decided, separately, that the way to prod OFCs into action was to name and shame them.[203] Countries on these lists were often barred from doing business with banks and other financial institutions in the rich world or made subject to much more onerous disclosure requirements. In the US, recent legislation[204] was introduced in Congress as a result of pressures from senators who claimed that tax havens (small jurisdictions) draw offshore money through business-friendly rules and low (or no) taxes on nonresident business. The law will force states to identify the beneficial owners of corporations who have misused US corporations to hide illicit activity, including money laundering and tax fraud.[205] OFCs have started to be lawmakers' next target, as illustrated by the recent agreement between the US and Swiss governments over secret Swiss bank accounts held by US citizens.[206]

6 CONCLUSION

The recent credit crisis has brought to the surface of the global agenda the issue of hedge funds and offshore financial centers as a result of concerns expressed about their implications for the stability of the international financial order. The recent growth and complexities associated with hedge-fund activities through OFCs acting as hosts, combined with the lax regulatory systems for both, gave rise to such concerns. Concerns expressed about stability issues relate essentially to the absence of regulation and adequate supervision of both hedge funds and OFCs, which have the potential to lead to systemic risks spreading financial instability across regions. Such concerns have given rise to national and international efforts to improve the regulation of hedge funds and OFCs in an attempt to prevent future economic and financial calamities, relying on a new more rule-based approach, combining market discipline. Whether these new regulatory proposals will achieve the required objectives remains an open-ended question, although more in-depth analysis of the interaction between hedge funds and OFCs and their implications for regulatory design remains to be done.

NOTES

*   Research on this chapter began as part of my Visiting Scholarship at the Harvard Law School, during 2008–09, and was completed thereafter. My thanks go to Professor Howell E. Jackson, the James S. Reid, Jr. Professor of Law at the Harvard Law School, who advised me to work on the issue of OFCs; to Professor Benton E. Gup, Chair of Banking at the University of Alabama, for the opportunity to have the work published as part of this book; to Professor Arthur E. Wilmarth, Jr., Professor of Law at the George Washington University School of Law for his constant guidance and support; and to Åke Lonnberg and Eric Robert, ex-colleagues at the International Monetary Fund.

1.   Gup (2003, 2); Pazarbaşioğlu et al. (2007a, 7); Kose et al. (2007, 5); and 'A bigger world, a special report on globalization', *The Economist*, September 20, 2008, 4.
2.   Masson (2001, 14, 2007).
3.   Kern (2006, 14).
4.   A loose concept to include all investment companies, organized as limited partnerships, using high-risk techniques hoping for high-yield returns and whose funds are collected from wealthy investors, administered by professional investment managers, and, until recently, not widely available to the public.
5.   Interest in the explosive growth in hedge funds even led to the publication of a journal specifically addressing trading, legal and other derivatives, the *Journal of Derivatives and Hedge Funds* (JDHF) from May 2007, http://www.palgrave-journals.com/jdhf/index.html.
6.   'Places in the sun', *The Economist*, Special Report on Offshore Finance, February 22, 2007, 3, Economist.com, http://www.economist.com/specialreports/displaystory.cfm?story.
7.   Coates and Rafferty (2007, 42).
8.   Ibid., 39.

9. Existing literature always addresses hedge funds and OFCs in the light of these characteristics.
10. Eichengreen and Mathieson (1999, http://www.imf.org/external/pubs/ft/issues/issues 19/index.htm).
11. Blundell-Wignall (2007, 39).
12. Ibid., 43.
13. According to SNCP data, non-bank lenders (including hedge funds) have increased their holdings of syndicated loans in the United States from US$178 billion in 2002 to US$267 billion, or 14 percent of total credits, in 2006. The data also suggest that hedge funds have become significant holders of some of the riskiest assets in the financial system: between 2002 and 2006, non-bank lenders increased their holdings of classified credits from 27 to 51 percent of total classified credits, http://www.federalreserve.gov/newsevents/press/bcreg/20090924a.htm.
14. Caliari (2007) .
15. Issing et al. (2009, 5, http://www.ifk-cfs.de/index.php?id=1571).
16. Berzins et al. (2006, 2, http://www.fma.org/Barcelona/Papers/Berzins_BLT.pdf).
17. Garbaravicius and Dierick (2005, 5–8, http://www.ecb.int/pub/scientific/ops/date/html/opsall.en.html).
18. Cole et al. (2007).
19. Cox (2009); the Bear Stearns funds collapsed as billions of dollars of bets made on mortgage-backed bonds and collateralized debt obligations (CDOs) unraveled.
20. Gup, (1999); Markham (2006–07, 101); Ubide (June 2009, 5).
21. Kose et al. (2007, 5, 9); supra 1, 'A bigger world', 4.
22. Kern (2006, 24); Schinasi (2006, 3–8).
23. Financial System Soundness, A Factsheet, April 2009, http://www.imf.org/external/np/exr/facts/banking.htm.
24. Terhune (2005, 2, http://www.greencompany.com/HedgeFunds/OffShoreDosDonts Terhune.pdf). Hedge funds legally domiciled in an OFC hold around one-half of the hedge-fund assets reported by the TASS hedge-fund database, with the British Virgin Islands and the Cayman Islands being the most popular locations. Management of hedge funds is often conducted in or near major international financial centers such as London and New York, but the actual fund is registered in an OFC.
25. Coates and Rafferty (2007, 42).
26. Ibid., 7; Nick Coates and Mike Rafferty, 'Geographic patterns of recent international portfolio investment flows: confusing mess or conceptual confusion?', A Network Analysis of the IMF Coordinated International Portfolio Investment Surveys (CPIS) 2001 and 2002, http://www.departments.bucknell.edu/management/apfa/stockholm%20papers.htm.
27. Switzerland has long been a center for hedge funds – it is home to about 150 registered managers, most of them funds of hedge funds. Since its arrival in 1990s, London has emerged as the center of Europe's hedge-fund management industry, handling about two-thirds of a total $325 billion in funds under management (the funds themselves are held offshore, in tax havens like the Cayman Islands). New York City remains home to roughly double the number of hedge-fund managers as London. In 2005, Britain had the edge in performance, returning an average of 16.15 percent, almost twice the return of American funds. Estimates vary, but by one count Britain now has about 700 hedge-fund managers.
28. Wassim (2005); Kern (2006, 67).
29. Aglietta and Rigot (2009, http://www.cairn.info/resume.php?ID_ARTICLE=REL_751_0005).
30. See Section 5 of this chapter on 'New challenges for the regulation of hedge funds and OFCs', at p. 21.
31. Garbaravicius and Dierick (2005, 5).
32. For a useful introduction to the hedge-fund literature, see Eichengreen and Mathieson (1999, http://www.imf.org/external/pubs/ft/issues/issues19/index.htm).

33. The European Parliament uses the term 'sophisticated alternative investment vehicles' (SAIVs), which would also encompass other alternative investment funds that differ from conventional collective investments. The Basel Committee on Banking Supervision (BCBS) employs the term 'highly leveraged institutions' (HLIs), a label covering hedge funds as well as other institutions that are subject to very little or no direct regulatory oversight, have very limited disclosure requirements, and often take on significant leverage. The Multidisciplinary Working Group on Enhanced Disclosure (MWGED) prefers the term 'leveraged investment funds'.
34. A.W. Jones & Co., the first hedge-fund company founded in 1949 by A.W.Jones & Co., in Markham (2006–07, 20).
35. Cox (2009, 6).
36. Solomon (2006).
37. Ibid., 100.
38. Garbaravicius and Dierick (2005).
39. Coates and Rafferty (2009, 40).
40. In 2005, they accounted for 89 percent of the US trading volume in convertible bonds, 66 percent in distressed debt, 33 percent each for emerging markets bonds and leveraged loans, 20 percent of the speculative grade bond volume, and 38 percent in credit derivatives.
41. Donoghue (2009, 2, http://www.hedgefundslawblog.com/sec.supports-private-funds-transparency-act-2009).
42. *Goldstein v. SEC*, 451 F.3d 873, 877 (D.C. Cir. 2006, http://pacer.cadc.uscourts.gov/docs/common/opinions/200606/04-1434a.pdf).
43. Lehmann (2006), http://www.frbatlanta.org/invoke.cfm?objectid=9C10FFAE-5056-9F12-12A4BBAEA205CA5A&method=displaybody; Markham (2006–07, 17).
44. Crockett (2009, 16–19, https://www.imf.org/external/pubs/ft/fandd/2009/09/pdf/crockett.pdf).
45. The year 2008 was disastrous for hedge funds, lightly regulated investment pools as markets collapsed and investors withdrew money, triggering a cycle of forced selling that put more pressure on markets. The number of liquidations more than doubled the previous quarterly record of 344 set in the third quarter. In 2008 liquidations marked a 70 percent increase from the previous annual record set in 2005. Just in the Americas, more than 200 hedge funds or fund families shut down or began to liquidate in 2008. At their peak, these funds managed $84 billion in assets. A record 778 hedge funds liquidated during the fourth quarter, capping a year that saw financial markets melt down and investors yank $150 billion of their money at the end of 2008 (Hedge Fund Research Inc.). The ranks of hedge funds were more than decimated as 1,471 hedge funds closed down in 2008, or nearly 15 percent of all funds, HFR said. Of that figure, more than 275 hedge funds were liquidated in 2008, also a record. Meanwhile, 56 new funds were launched during the quarter, contributing to 659 that opened their doors throughout 2008. On a net basis, the total number of hedge funds fell by 8 percent to 9,284 in 2008.
46. Crockett April (2007, 20–23, http://www.banque-france.fr/gb/publications/telechar/rsf/2007/etud2_0407.pdf).
47. Blundell-Wignall 2007, 19).
48. Ibid., 22.
49. Chan et al. (2006, 50).
50. Garbaravicius and Dierick (2005, 5).
51. Caliari (2007, 52); Danielsson and Zigrand (2007). In some countries, a new category of investors with relatively modest financial means are now able to invest in them. In France, for example, hedge funds can now be accessed by individuals with a minimum of €10,000 (Prada, 2007, 130). In Germany, German investors can buy hedge funds from Deutsche Bank in units of less than €125 and UK regulators are considering reducing restrictions on marketing hedge funds to individuals (*Financial Times*, 2007).

Even regulated institutions such as mutual funds are increasing their investments in hedge funds (Daníelsson and Zigrand, 2007). Hedge funds now tap into a larger share of household savings that is channeled through institutional investors, such as funds of funds and pension funds. Governments are also increasingly investing their pension money in hedge funds, where in the US, the Securities and Exchange Commission (SEC) reports that about 20 percent of corporate and public pension plans were using hedge funds in 2002, up from 15 percent in 2001, and the trend is rising, http://www. coc.org/system/files/Regulation_of_HedgeFunds2007%5B1%5D.pdf.

52. Caliari (2007, 52); Daníelsson and Zigrand (2007, 31).
53. Ibid.
54. Lipsky (2007a, http://www.imf.org/external/np/speeches/2007/062007.htm).
55. Pazarbaşioğlu et al. (2007b, http://www.imf.org/external/pubs/ft/fandd/2007/03/pazar. htm).
56. This section and the next one rely on the proposition made by Coates and Rafferty (2007) regarding the new role of hedge funds in international markets and international financial flows.
57. Johnston et al. (2003, 32, https://www.imf.org/external/pubs/ft/fandd/2003/09/pdf/ darbar.pdf). The most practical definition characterizes OFCs as centers where the bulk of financial sector transactions on both sides of the balance sheet are where individuals or companies that are not residents of OFCs, where the transactions are initiated elsewhere, and where the majority of the institutions involved are controlled by non-residents, IMF (2000, http://www.imf.org/external/np/oshore/2000/eng/role. htm).
58. Ibid.
59. Ibid.: an OFC 'is a centre where the bulk of financial sector activity is offshore on both sides of the balance sheet (that is the counterparties of the majority of financial institutions liabilities and assets are non-residents) where transactions are initiated elsewhere, and where the majority of the institutions involved are controlled by non-residents'.
60. Ibid.
61. IMF (2008a, http://www.imf.org/external/np/pp/eng/2006/020806.pdf).
62. Offshore Financial Centers, 'The Assessment Program: A Progress Report', Prepared by the Monetary and Financial Department, approved by Ulrich Baumgartner, February 8, 2006.
63. Desai et al. (2005 http://www.people.hbs.edu/ffoley/havens.pdf) is a fascinating study looking at data on American multinational companies from 1982 to 1999; the economists found that tax havens boosted economic activity in nearby non-havens rather than diverting it.
64. 'Tax Havens Creating Turmoil', Evidence Submitted to the Treasury Committee of the House of Commons by Tax Justice Network, June 2008, estimates that tax revenues lost to OFCs exceed US$255 billion a year, although this is disputed; Senator Carl Levin has indicated that a study suggests that America loses up to $70 billion a year to tax havens. Ireland, considered to be a tax haven, in 2008 recovered almost €1 billion in unreported tax revenues from banks in the Channel Islands. South Africa reckons it is losing 64 billion rand ($8.8 billion) a year to tax havens, http://www. taxresearch.org.uk/Documents/CreatingTurmoil.pdf.
65. 'Offshore finance: on or off?' Special report on Offshore Finance, *The Economist*, February 22, 2007, Economist.com, 2, http://www.economist.com/specialreports/ displaystory.cfm?story; the Cayman Islands, the British Virgin Islands, Bermuda and the Bahamas are the most popular OFCs.
66. Coates and Rafferty (2007, 6); supra 6, 'Places in the sun', 3–5.
67. G8 Leaders' Declaration: Responsible Leadership for a Sustainable Future, July 8, 2009, http://www.g7.utoronto.ca/summit/2009laquila/index.html; G7 Chair's Summary, Heiligendamm, June 8, 2007; G20 Leaders' Statement, Pittsburgh Summit, September 24–25, 2009, http://www.g7.utoronto.ca/summit/2009laquila/index.html,

Pittsburgh, 7–16, http://www.pittsburghsummit.gov/mediacenter/129639.htm; aAlexander Kern; Kern (2001); Bosworth-Davies (2006); Jackson (2003).

68. Supra 6, 'Places in the sun', 3–6, http://www.economist.com/specialreports/display-story.cfm?story_id=E1_RGJVTRS.

69. Supra 26, Coates and Rafferty 'Geographic patterns'; Rose and Spiegel(2006, http://faculty.haas.berkeley.edu/arose/RevOFC.pdf. The Cayman Islands, for example, developed as an OFC due to its participation in the formation of euro–dollar markets in the 1970s and 1980s (Roberts, 1997). In 1968 the Asian dollar market developed in Singapore. By the 1970s, equities markets in Luxembourg became a focus for international investment as investors were exempted from any withholding tax (IMF, 2000, 5).

70. 'A survey of offshore finance: moving pieces', *The Economist*, Economist.com, February 22nd, 2007, see below.

71. Coates and Rafferty (2007).

72. Ibid.

73. Ibid.

74. Of this $4.6 trillion, $0.6 trillion passes through the Caribbean, $1.0 trillion through Asia, and most of the remaining $2.7 trillion is accounted for by London. Reporting of OFC transactions to the Bank for International Settlements (BIS) tends to be limited to major financial centers. Of the smaller OFCs like Bermuda, Liberia and Panama, most do not report to the BIS.

75. Johnston et al. (2003, 33).

76. Coates and Rafferty (2009, 39).

77. In the 1980s, balance of payments statisticians began to observe that a global financial imbalance had opened up of around US$40 billion (suggesting that global cross-border inflows of financial account liabilities were greater than reported outflows). This imbalance was not stable year to year, but took a sharp upward step in the early 1990s, reaching US$210 billion. For instance, the imbalance on global IPI amounted to US$170 billion in 1997 (IMF, 2003; Humphreys, 2003).

78. Supra 6, 'Places in the sun' 3–6; Franklin (2003, http://www0.gsb.columbia.edu/faculty/fedwards/papers/Edwards%20on%20Reg%20of%20Hedge%20Funds.pdf).

79. 'Offshore finance; what it takes to succeed', *The Economist*, February 22nd 2007; offshore holdings now run to $5–7 trillion, seven times as much as two decades ago and make up of 6–8 percent of worldwide investment under management. Canadian direct investment in OFCs increased eightfold within 10 years to US$75 billion, mostly in Caribbean countries. Of the Cayman Islands' $1.3 trillion in bank deposits, 93 percent are interbank bookings, http://www.economist.com/specialreports/display-story.cfm?story_id=E1_RGJVTRS.

80. 'San Marino, offshore, onshore', *The Economist*, March 18, 2007, Economist.com, http://www.economist.com/businessfinance/displayStory.cfm?story_id=E1_RRNDQVQ.

81. 'Offshore finance: rich pickings, how to defeat tax cheats', *The Economist*, February 22, 2007, Economist.com, http://www.economist.com/specialreports/displaystory.cfm?story_id=E1_RGJVTGT.

82. Bartram and Dufey (2001); The Netherlands and Netherlands Antilles, for instance, issue securities with an inexpensive administration and corporate legal system and no holding taxes on interest, dividends and capital gains. These OFCs are central to issuing special corporate vehicles that issue securities. SPVs are rapidly growing and can be used to issue shares, bonds, derivatives or raise capital in other ways, and can be international business corporations, which are basically shell and brass-plate companies where directors' identities can in some instances be concealed. SPVs are closely associated with securitization where the parent company transfers asset-backed securities to the SPV such as portfolio of mortgages, loans and receivables. The SPV then offers them as bonds to investors protected with underlying assets.

83. At end-2005 close to 70 percent of total (global) capital under management of the

hedge funds was domiciled offshore. The share of offshore-domiciled hedge-fund capital managed from Europe was even higher (close to 77 percent).

84. The turbulence in world bond markets in 1994, and the Asian financial crisis of 1997, and more recently, the 2008 credit crisis.
85. The ECB Financial Stability Review of June 2006 concerns relate to: (i) rising share of less liquid assets in hedge funds' investment portfolios; (ii) increasingly similar positioning of individual funds within broad investment strategies; and (iii) rising correlation not only within the same but also among differing strategies.
86. Schwarcz (2008). A 'systemic crisis' occurs when a shock affects 'a considerable number of financial institutions or markets in a strong sense, thereby severely impairing the general well-functioning (of an important part) of the financial system' (DeBandt and Hartmann, (2000); another description of a systemic event is a situation where 'shocks to one part of the financial system lead to shocks elsewhere, in turn impinging on the stability of the real economy' (Bordo et al., 1995, 31); and there is 'major damage to the financial system and the real economy' (p. 5). In our view, an essential feature of systemic risk is when financial shocks have the potential to lead to substantial, adverse effects on the *real* economy, for example, a reduction in productive investment due to the reduction in credit provision or a destabilization of economic activity. Indeed, it is the transmission of financial events to the real economy that is the defining feature of a systemic crisis, and which distinguishes it from a purely financial event (Counterparty Risk Management Policy Group, CRMPG, 2005).
87. Acharya. (2009a).
88. Mauro and Yafeh (2007, http://www.imf.org/esxternal/pubs/ft/fandd/2007/12/mauro.htm).
89. Supra 1, Pazarbaşioğlu et al., http://www.imf.org/external/pubs/ft/fandd/2007/03/pazar.htm
90. Wilmarth (2009, 966). The impact of the crisis saw five trillion dollars of Americans' household wealth evaporated in a matter of 3 months, and economic activity and trade around the world ground to a halt.
91. Federal Reserve Bank of New York (2007). While the magnitude of this exposure remains unclear, BIS estimates that banks' direct exposure to hedge funds has been growing proportionally with the hedge-fund industry itself. It should be noted, however, that banks' current exposures to hedge funds are heavily collateralized and the Financial Stability Forum (2007) estimates that both the current and potential exposure net of collateral of core firms to hedge funds is quite modest in the aggregate. Moreover, each bank has a clear self-interest to manage and mitigate the risk of these exposures.
92. Lipsky (2007b, http://www.imf.org/external/np/speeches/2007/073107a.htm).
93. Garbaravicius and Dierick (2005).
94. Mauro and Yafeh (2007, 8).
95. An externality is an impact of one party's action on others who are not directly involved in the transaction.
96. According to the US Flow of Funds, bank credit accounted for 39 percent of outstanding credit market instruments for nonfarm, nonfinancial corporations in 2005, down from 52 percent in 1985, which reflects the growing importance of alternative sources of credit such as corporate bonds and commercial paper.
97. Supra 42.
98. As far back as 1920, Charles Ponzi, an Italian immigrant, began advertising that he could make a 50 percent return for investors in only 45 days. In March of 1932, Ivar Kreuger, a Swedish businessman who had cooked the books of his match manufacturing business and forged $142 million of bonds, shot himself in the head. It was reported that he may have burned through $400 million of investor money by falsifying the accounts of 400 separate companies. Until Madoff came along, the Equity Funding scandal may have been the largest fraud in dollar terms in US history. A publicly held

company whose shares traded on the New York Stock Exchange, the top executives falsified 64,000 insurance policies that were used to report revenues of $2 billion.

99. Cox (2009); The Bear Stearns funds collapsed as billions of dollars of bets made on mortgage-backed bonds and CDOs unraveled, and no one wanted to buy them when the time came to try to sell some of the funds' subprime mortgages,

100. LTCM was a hedge fund that brought the financial world to its knees when it lost $4 billion trading exotic derivatives. It leveraged $4 billion into $100 billion in assets and the $100 billion became collateral for $1.2 *trillion* in derivatives exposure. Finally, when Russia defaulted on its bonds – many of which were LTCM owned – in 1998, this stirred up the world's financial markets in a way that caused many additional losing trades for LTCM. By the spring of 1998, LTCM was losing several hundred million dollars per day. By August 1998, LTCM had burned through almost all of its $4 billion in capital. With $1.2 trillion at risk, the economy could have been devastated if LTCM's losses continued to run its course. Finally, the Federal Reserve and Wall Street's largest investment banks decided to rescue LTCM. The banks ended up losing several hundred million dollars each.

101. James Quinn, US Business Editor, Telegraph.co.uk, August 20, 2009, http://www. telegraph.co.uk/finance/financetopics/financialcrisis/6061849/Case-will-throw-light-on-funds-before-Bear-Stearns-collapsed.html (Financial Stability *Forum*, 2000, 5). First, the East Asian financial crisis resulted in countries' concern about the impact that destabilizing activities of hedge funds in their markets would potentially disrupt their economies, (Brouwer, 2001, cited by Cornford, 2005). Some authors claimed that operations of macro hedge funds were an important source of instability in the region's financial markets in 1997–1998, (Fox, 1998; IMF, 2004, 146–8) although this contention has been questioned by others.

102. Bernie Madoff's $50 billion Ponzi Scheme; Robert Lenzner (http://www.forbes. com/2008/12/12/madoff-ponzi-hedge-pf-ii-in_rl_1212croesus_inl.html) was to be one of the first jailed investors of the 2008 market meltdown.

103. Citigroup's Old Lane Partners, once managing $4.4 billion, was closed in July 2008 and D.B. Zwirn shuttered his $4 billion Zwirn Special Opportunities fund amid a Securities and Exchange Commission's investigation and investor redemptions. Other major closures included Ospraie Management's flagship $3.8 billion commodities fund; two funds at Tontine Capital Management that had run $4 billion; two Highland Capital Management funds, which had $3.5 billion; and two Peloton Partners funds that had managed $3.5 billion, *Opalesque* (2009).

104. Lieff Cabraser Securities, 'Bernard L. Madoff Investment Securities LLC Financial Fraud'; such investors include Fairfield Greenwich Group, Tremont Capital Management, Ascot Partners and Maxam Capital Management, http://www.liefca-brasersecurities.com/cases/madoff.htm?gclid=CIfSofDnvJgCFRKAxgo.

105. Arvedlun (2009, http://www.ft.com/cms/s/2/89542248-9821-11de-8d3d-00144feabdc0, html).

106. In 2006, the regulation of hedge funds drew renewed attention following the US$6 billion loss by hedge-fund Amaranth and the 75 percent loss of its US$13 billion fixed income trading by hedge-fund Vega.

107. Rajan (2006, http://www.imf.org/external/np/speeches/2006/100506.htm).

108. Giannone (2008, joseph.giannone@thomsonreuters.com; +1 646 223 6184; Reuters Messaging: joseph.giannone.reuters.com@reuters.net). Among other findings, see Hedge Fund Research's conclusion that the biggest banks continue to had a grip on the prime brokerage business: the top three prime brokers still controlled 62 percent of hedge fund industry capital, http://www.hedgefundresearch.com/.

109. Mauro and Yafeh (2007, http://www.imf.org/external/pubs/ft/fandd/2007/12/mauro. htm).

110. Supra 6, 'Places in the sun', http://www.economist.com/specialreports/displaystory. cfm?storyid=E1RGJVTPJ.

111. Ibid., 1/6.

112. Ibid., 2/6. Abacha of Nigeria, Mohammed Suharto of Indonesia and Ferdin and Marcos of the Philippines illustrate corrupt leaders who have looted their countries helped by secrecy offered by some OFCs. Some of the money used in the 9/11 terrorist attacks was channeled through Dubai, now an established OFC. The accounting scams at Enron, Parmalat, and Tyco were made easy by complicated financial structures based in OFCs Tyco and Parmalat, both of which had thousands of subsidiaries offshore which their managers used not only to reduce their tax bills but also to loot the company.

113. 'The Stanford affair, an $8 billion scandal goes a long way *The Economist*, February 26, 2009 | PORT OF SPAIN, http://www.economist.com/world/americas/displaystory.cfm?story_id=13185500; 'Financial fraud, howzat!', February 18, 2009 | NEW YORK, From *The Economist* print edition, http://www.economist.com/businessfinance/displayStory.cfm?story_id=13136627.

114. 'Offshore finance: unintended consequences', *The Economist*, February 22, 2007, http://www.economist.com/specialreports/displaystory.cfm?story_id=E1_RGJVNPP.

115. Mark Heinrich, interview: 'Ample signs of mafia millions buoying banks', UN, 2009-02-09 (Reuters), 'Antonio Maria Costa, Executive Director of the U.N. Office on Drugs and Crime, warns that cash-rich mafia groups have been channeling funds into banks desperate to survive the global credit crisis', http://www.reuters.com/article/topNews/idUSTRE52A44I20090311. The United Nations claims that it has enough indication that in the second half of the 2008 crisis, liquidity was the banking system's main problem and that illicit money has been used to keep banks afloat in the global financial crisis. 'There were signs that some banks were rescued through 'interbank loans funded by money that originated from drug trade and other illegal activities' (Interview with Maria Costa, Executive Director of United Nations Office of Drugs and Crime, Vienna, reporting by Boris Groendahl, editing by Charles Dick), Austrian weekly Profil, Global Research, March 15, 2009, http://www.globalresearch.ca/index.php?context=va&aid=12718.

116. AIMA Breakfast Address on the Alternative Investment Fund Management Directive, HM Treasury, July 7, 2009, http://www.hm-treasury.gov.uk/speech. In their April 2008 analysis of the causes behind the current crisis, both the IMF (2008b) and the FSF (2008) highlighted the striking nature of the extent of leverage–the ratio of debt to equity–taken on by a wide range of institutions and the associated risks of a disorderly unwinding. 'Consultations I've had with prosecutors and law-enforcement officials around the world show there is ample evidence that the banking system's illiquidity is providing a unique opportunity for organized crime to launder their money', Costa told Reuters. 'Just about every financial centre can be characterized as part of the problem', 'You have the supply – an organized crime industry with enormous amounts of cash, estimated at $322 billion in 2005, not any more stored in banks – and the demand, a banking sector strapped for liquidity', said Costa. 'This is a supply- and demand-driven situation. Our intuition, based on logic, is now supported by ample evidence.' Asked where cases were occurring, he said: 'Traditionally, Europe and North America are the places where, as financial centers, most money would be laundered' (Supra 115, Heinrich interview).

117. Roubini (2007, Nouriel Roubini's Global EconoMonitor, http://www.rgemonitor.com/roubini-monitor/173905, 1–3); Tobias and Hyun Song Shin (2009).

118. A figure from 2004 indicated hedge fund leverage in the form of bank debt to be at an average of 141 percent (*Financial Times*, 2004). The Vice President of the European Central Bank claimed that 'the total leveraged assets of an individual hedge fund can sometimes be quite significant and comparable with the size of some systemically important banks' (Papademos, 2007, 115).

119. Ibid., 54, 109. According to one author (Noyer, 2007), effective leverage 'has become notoriously difficult to measure, due to the difficulty in capturing the effect of different layers of leverage, and in particular the leverage embedded in the most complex forms of credit derivatives'.

120. The credit crisis originating in mid-2007 with the failure by Bear Stearns, of its hedge

funds, is an example of an event that accelerated the recent severe financial market dislocation.

121. Chan et al. (2006, 49).
122. Garbaravicius and Dierick (2005).
123. Kambhu, et al. (2007, 14).
124. Garbaravicius and Dierick (2005).
125. Kambhu et al. (2007).
126. Garbaravicius and Dierick (2005).
127. Swire (2000, http://www.tax-news.com/archive/story/Financial_Stability_Forum_ Attacks_Offshore_Centres_xxxx373.html).
128. Eichengreen and Mathieson (1999).
129. IMF (2000, http://www.imf.org/external/np/oshore/2000/eng/role.htm).
130. Garbaravicius and Dierick (2005).
131. Coates and Rafferty (2007, 45–7).
132. Ibid.
133. Claire Smith, 'Is regulatory work the new fund formation for law firms?', *Hedge Fund Journal*, informing the hedge fund community, http://www.thehedgefundjournal. com/special-reports/hf-whos-who/is-regulatory-work-the-new-fund-formation-for-law-firms-.php.
134. G20 Leaders' Statement: Pittsburgh Summit, September 24–25, 2009, 7, http://www. pittsburghsummit.gov/mediacenter/129639.htm.
135. Markham (2006–07).
136. When dealing with externalities, we typically see direct regulation as the government explicitly limiting or supporting an activity based on the types of externalities it creates. So, in the case of pollution being a negative externality of creating electricity, the government may directly limit the amount of electricity that power plants are allowed to create in limiting the impact of the negative externality. On the other hand, some of the positive externalities associated with education are higher-income and more-informed voters; this gives the government an incentive to directly regulate how much education each citizen should receive. Econ port: Direct regulation: http://www.econport.org/ content/handbook/Externalities/Dealing-With-Externalities/Public-Sector-Solutions/ Direct-Regulation.html.
137. Wilmarth (2009, 971); Litan (2009); 'Two new issues for monitoring: hedge funds and energy trading', Global Financial Stability Report, *IMF Survey*, **33** (19), October 25, 2004, http://www.imf.org/external/pubs/ft/survey/so/2009/POL030609A.htm.
138. 'Two former Bear Stearns managers are indicted', *The Mortgage Reporter*, June 19, 2008, http://www.mortgagefraud.org/journal/2008/6/19/two-former-bear-stearns-managers-are-in.
139. Ibid., 3.
140. Caliari (2007, http://www.coc.org/system/files/Regulation_of_HedgeFunds2007% 5B1%5D.pdf).
141. Ibid., 53.
142. James Norris interviews Gus Pope, managing partner of Maples and Calder, *Hedge Fund Journal*, http://www.thehedgefundjournal.com/special-reports/hf-whos-who/ interview.php.
143. Supra 114.
144. Bernanke (2007, http://www.federalreserve.gov/newevents/speech/bernanke20007 0422).
145. Woodruff (2008, http://www.nybooks.com/articles/21352).
146. Berzins et al. (2006).
147. The international banking crisis of 1982, the bankruptcy of Continental Illinois in 1984, the failure of LTCM in 1998, and AIG in 2008.
148. Brunnermeier et al. (2009, http://www.voxeu.org/reports/Geneva11.pdf).
149. Fischer (1998, http://www.imf.org/external/np/speeches/1998/110998.htm).
150. Dodd (2007, http://www.imf.org/external/pubs/ft/fandd/2007/12/dodd.htm).

151. Garbaravicius and Dierick (2005).
152. MacKintosh (2008, http://us.ft.com/ftgateway/superpage.ft?news_id=fto03042008 2034521968).
153. In 1933, the Glass–Seagall Act separated commercial from investment banking activities; created the deposit insurance program and allowed greater branching by national banks; 1933 Securities Act: private funds typically avoid registration of their securities under the Securities Act of 1933 by conducting private placements, established disclosure requirements for issuing securities on public securities markets and established prohibitions against securities fraud and manipulation; 1934, the Securities Exchange Act created the Securities and Exchange Commission and authorized it for rule-making and enforcement; 1935, the (Omnibus) Banking Act reformed governance of the Federal Reserve and broadened its powers; 1936, the Commodity Exchange Act increased federal prohibitions against fraud and expanded them to manipulation; 1940, the Investment Company Act regulated companies that primarily invest in other companies such as mutual funds. including transactions between managers and any affiliate and set rules on corporate governance regarding executive management, board of directors, and trustees; private funds seek to qualify for one of two exceptions from regulation; 1940, the Investment Advisers Act required advisers to register, report, and keep records of their client relations; it also prohibited certain transactions and fee arrangements on the basis of conflict of interest, investment advisers who carry investment activities of private fund to private funds, often claim an exemption from registration under section 203(b) (3) of the Advisers Act, which is available to an adviser that has fewer than 15 clients and does not hold itself out generally to the public as an investment adviser.
    Hedge Fund Law Blog, SEC Supports Private Funds Transparency Act of 2009, July 20, 2009, Testimony Concerning Regulating. The SEC released a testimony from Andrew J. Donohue before the US Senate about the regulation of hedge funds and other private investment pools.
154. Pub.L.No. 104–290, sec.102, (18(b)(1)), 110 Stat, 3417–3418 (codified at 15 U.S.C. 77r(b)(1–2)(1998).
155. Initially required to register with the CFTC as CPOs), and CTAs, under the Commodity Exchange Act of 1936, in 1992; Ervin (2004).
156. Caliari (2007); de Larosiére, Jacques (2009).
157. IMF Survey online: 'Lessons from the crisis: IMF urges rethink of how to manage global systemic risk', March 6, 2009, 2, http://www.imf.org/external/pubs/ft/survey/so/2009/POL030609A.htm.
158. The concept was also roundly endorsed by the De Larosière Report (2009) to the European Union and in the Turner Review (FSA, 2009) in the UK.
    The effectiveness of macro-prudential regulation is a core assumption behind the capital proposals in the US Treasury (2009) white paper on financial regulation.
159. Bernanke (2007).
160. Caruana (2009, http://www.imf.org/external/pubs/ft/survey/so/2009/POL/030609A.htm; 2007, http://www.imf.org/external/np/speeches/2007/053007.htm).
161. Issing et al. (2009).
162. Most recently, PricewaterhouseCoopers Group (2008) concluded that 'market discipline most effectively addresses the systemic risks posed by private pools of capital'.
163. The Private Funds Transparency Act of 2009 would address the regulatory gap discussed above by eliminating Section 203(b)(3)'s de minimis exemption from the Advisers Act, resulting in investment advisers to private funds being required to register with the Commission. Investment adviser registration would be beneficial to investors and our markets in a several important ways Speech by SEC Staff: 'Regulating Hedge Funds and other Private Investment Pools' by Andrew J. Donohue Director, Division of Investment Management US Securities and Exchange Commission, New York, February 19 2010.
164. This will be a new body made up of central bank governors for all the member states

in the 27-country bloc, and chaired by the president of the European Central Bank, which will also provide working support.

165. FT.com, Editorial comment: 'Government's response like that of a rowdy drinker in a bar brawl', July 5, 2009, http://www.ft.com/cms/s/0/5bc508ba-698c-11de-bc9f-00144feabdc0.html.

166. By Nikki Tait in Brussels Published: September 23, 2009 13:23 | Last updated: September 23, 2009, Brussels unveils regulation reform plan, http://www.ft.com/cms/s/0/46d52e12-a834-11de-8305-00144feabdc0.html. Two-tier approach suggested by former French central banker Jacques de Larosière in February after he was called to advise on changes in the wake of the recent financial and economic turmoil.

167. Benoit and Tait (2009).

168. 'Obama Bill seeks to shine light on hedge funds', July 16, 2009, http://dealbook.blogs.nytimes.com/2009/07/16/obama-bill-seeks-to-shine-light-on-hedge-funds/; September 14, 2009, Remarks by the president on financial rescue and reform, Federal Hall, New York, http://www.hedgefundlawblog.com/obama-on-financial-reform.html.

169. Proposal for a Directive on Alternative Investment Funds, European Commission, Brussels, 30 April, 2009, COM(2009) 207 final, http://ec.europa.eu/internal_market/investment/docs/alternative_investments/fund_managers_proposal_en.pdf.

170. Dodd 2009, http://www.imf.org/external/pubs/ft/fandd/2009/09/pdf/dodd.pdf).

171. Supra 168, 'Obama Bill'.

172. Tait (2009a, http://www.ft.com/cms/s/0/550e7a6c-59db-11de-b687-00144feabdc0.html).

173. Benoit (2009).

174. Parker (2009, http://www/ft.com/cms/s/0/4af224ea-506f-11de-9530-00144feabdc0,s01 =1.html).

175. Milne (2009).

176. Barber (2009).

177. Tait (2009b).

178. Progress Report on the Actions to Promote Financial Regulatory Reform, Issued by the US Chair of the Pittsburgh G20, September 25 2009; the FSF has been converted into a Financial Stability Board, among other changes, http://www.pittsburghsummit.gov/mediacenter/129639.htm.

179. The most active have been committees or groups under the auspices of or associated with the Bank for International Settlements (BIS), especially the Basel Committee on Banking Supervision (BCBS). Supervision and regulation of securities and insurance have been discussed primarily in, respectively, the International Organization of Securities Commission (IOSCO) and the International Association of Insurance Supervisors (IAIS). Cross-border accounting issues are the domain of the International Accounting Standards Board (IASB). The IMF and the World Bank have limited monitoring responsibilities in these areas. An umbrella organization created in 1999, the Financial Stability Forum (FSF), provides some oversight and coordination among the institutions and committees.

180. Jackson (2007, 409, http://www.pennumbra.com/responses/02-2008/Jackson.pdf).

181. The FSF bringing together national authorities responsible for financial stability in significant international financial centers, international financial institutions, sector-specific international groupings of regulators and supervisors, and committees of central bank experts, underscores the importance of ongoing cooperation among financial authorities in taking forward these recommendations and in spreading good practices. Financial stability forum, Press release, 'FSF makes recommendations to address potential financial system risks relating to hedge funds', Ref no: 10/2007E.

182. 'Offshore finance: all together now', *The Economist*, February 22, 2007.

183. 1. Supervisors should act so that core intermediaries continue to strengthen their counterparty risk management practices; 2. Supervisors should work with core intermediaries to further improve their robustness to the potential erosion of market

liquidity; 3. Supervisors should explore and evaluate the extent to which developing more systematic and consistent data on core intermediaries' consolidated counterparty exposures to hedge funds would be an effective complement to existing supervisory efforts; 4. Counterparties and investors should act to strengthen the effectiveness of market discipline, including by obtaining accurate and timely portfolio valuations and risk information; 5. The global hedge fund industry should review and enhance existing sound practice benchmarks for hedge fund managers in the light of expectations for improved practices set out by the official and private sectors.

184. These reports are available at www.fsforum.org/publications/publication_21_25.html.

185. G8 Summit 2007, Heiligendamm, Summit Declaration (7 June 2007). In this context, we welcome the FSF's update of its 2000 Report on Highly Leveraged Institutions and support its recommendations.

186. BCBS (2008a and 2008b).

187. Issued by the Basel Committee in September 2008 (BCBS, 2008a).

188. Caruana and Narain (2008).

189. See http://www.iosco.org/.

190. Supra 157, 11.

191. Hamilton (2009, http://www.financialcrisisupdate.com/2009/04/iosco-recommends-hedge-fund-regulation-as-part-of-systemic-risk-oversight.html).

192. G20: Leaders' Statement, Pittsburgh Summit, September 24–25, 2009, Pittsburgh, 7–16, http://www.pittsburghsummit.gov/mediacenter/129639.htm.

193. Acharya (2009b, http://www.voxeu.org/index.php?q=node/3185).

194. Worby and Posen (2009, http://www.iie.com/publications/opeds/oped.cfm?Research ID=1297).

195. FSF Reviews its Offshore Financial Centers (OFCs) Initiative, Ref no: 7/2004E, April 5, 2004, http://www.financialstabilityboard.org/press/pr_040405.pdf.

196. The Financial Action Task Force List of Non-Cooperative Countries (NCCTs) also know as the FATF Blacklist, http://www.fatf-gafi.org/document/51/0,2340,en_322503 79_32236920_34297139_1_1_1,00.html.

197. 'Offshore finance: on or off?', Economist.com, February 22, 2007, http://www.economist.com/specialreports/displaystory.cfm?story_id=E1_RGJVTJJ.

198. Adams et al. (1999), prepared by a staff team led by Charles Adams, Donald J. Mathieson and Gary Schinasi.

199. Johnston et al. (2003); Supra 197, 'Offshore finance'.

200. The *Financial Sector Assessment Handbook* (IMF and World Bank, 2005) provides information for financial sector authorities on key issues and sound practices in the assessment of financial systems and in the design of policy responses.

201. IMF (2008a, 1/5, http://www.imf.org/external/np/sec/pn/208/pn0882.htm).

202. FATF International Standards against money laundering and the financing of terrorism, supra 196.

203. In 2000, the FSF put together a list of 42 jurisdictions that it defines as OFCs; the OECD in 2000 compiled a narrower list of 35 tax havens; and the FATF 23 'non-cooperative countries and territories'.

204. Coleman Levin, 'Obama Introduces Stop Tax Haven Abuse Act', http://levin.senate.gov/newsroom/release.cfm?id=269479.

205. 'The G20 and tax haven hypocrisy', March 26, 2009, http://www.economist.com/businessfinance/displayStory.cfm?story_id=13382279.

206. The US Internal Revenue Service's (IRS) agreement with the Swiss government and UBS AG will result in thousands of Americans who thought they had a secret Swiss bank account having their names and account details turned over to US tax authorities, Wall Street Journal, August 25, 2009.

REFERENCES

Acharya, Viral, V. (2009a) 'A theory of systemic risk and design of prudential bank regulation', Working Paper Series, Leonard Stern School of Business, New York University, Social Science Research Network, January, available at: http://papers.ssrn.com/so13/papers.cfm?abstract_id=236401.

Acharya, Viral, V. (2009b), 'Some steps in the right direction: a critical assessment of the de Larosiére report', VOX, March 4.

Adams, Charles, Donald Mathieson and Gary Schinasi (1999), 'Proposals for improved risk management transparency, and regulatory and supervisory reforms', in *International Capital Markets, Developments, Prospects and Key Policy Issues*, September, IMF, World Economic and financial surveys, available at: http://www.imf.org/external/pubs/ft/icm/1999/pdf/file10.pdf.

Aglietta, Michel and Sandra Rigot (2009), 'The regulation of hedge funds under the prism of the financial crisis', *Recherches économiques de Louvain*, **75** (1) 5–34.

Arvedlun, Erin (2009), 'How Bernard Madoff escaped detection', FT.com, September 4.

Barber, Tony (2009), 'Sweden rides to defence of hedge funds', FT.com, July 1.

Bartram, S. and G. Dufey (2001), 'International portfolio investment: theory and practice', *Financial Markets, Instruments*, Working Paper Series, faculty research, University of Michigan Business School, pp. 1–117.

Basel Committee on Banking Supervision (BCBS) (2008a), 'Liquidity: risk management and supervisory challenges', February.

Basel Committee on Banking Supervision (BCBS) (2008b), 'Basel Committee on Banking supervision announces steps to strengthen the resilience of the banking committee', April, available at: www.bis.org.

Benoit, Bertrand and Nikki Tait (2009), 'Berlin to back EU financial regulation plan', *Financial Times*, available at: http://www.ft.com/cmc/s/0/7e5b8432-5094-11de-9530-00144feabdc0.html (accessed 8 June 2010).

Bernanke, Ben, S. (2007), 'Financial regulation and the invisible hand', Speech at the New York University Law School, Board of Governors of the Federal Reserve System, April.

Berzins, Janis, Liu Crocker and Charles Trzcinka (2006), 'Hedge fund, mutual fund, and institutional fund conglomerates: risk and return choices for a sophisticated investor', Research Paper for Toronto CFA Society, December, available at: http://69.175.2.130/~finman/Barcelona/Papers/Berzins_BLT.pdf (accessed 8 June 2010).

Blundell-Wignall, Adrian (2007), 'An overview of hedge funds and structured products: issues in leverage and risk', *Financial Market Trends*, No. 92, Vol. 2007/1, 37–57.

Bordo, Michael D. Bruce Mizrach and Anna J. Schwartz (1995), 'Real versus pseudo-international systemic risk: some lessons from history', 21 National Bureau of Economic. Research Working Paper No. 5371.

Bosworth-Davies, Rowan (2006), 'Money laundering: towards an alternative interpretation – Chapter one', *Journal of Money Laundering*, **9** (4), 335–45.

Brunnermeier, Markus, Andrew Crockett, Charles Goodhart, Avinash D. Persaud and Hyun Shin (2009), 'The Fundamental Principles of Financial Regulation, Geneva Reports on the World Economy', Preliminary Conference Draft, ICMB International Center for Monetary and Banking Studies.

Caliari, Aldo (2007), 'Regulation of hedge funds: why is it a social security issue?', Social Watch, 52, Center of Concern, Washington, DC, September 14.

Caruana, Jaime, IMF (2007), 'Gobal financial market risk – who is responsible for what?', Keynote address at the Conference on Financial Stability, Heinrich Boll Foundation/German Association of Banks, Berlin, May 30.

Caruana, Jaime (2009), 'Lessons from the crisis, IMF urges rethink of how to manage global systemic risk', *IMF Survey Magazine*, March 6.

Caruana, Jaime and Aditya Narain (2008), 'Banking on more capital', Finance and Development, IMF, June, **45** (2).

Chan, Nicolas, Mila Getmansky, Shane M. Haas and Andrew W. Lo (2006), 'Do hedge funds increase systemic risk?', *Federal Reserve Bank of Atlanta Economic Review*, Fourth Quarter.

Coates, Nick and Mike Rafferty (2007), 'Offshore financial centers, hot money and hedge funds: a network analysis of international capital flows', in L. Assassi, A. Nesvetailova and D. Wigan (eds), *Global Finance in the New Century: Beyond Deregulation*, London: Macmillan, pp. 38–55.

Cole, Roger T., Greg Feldberg and David Lynch (2007), 'Hedge funds, credit risk transfer and financial stability', Banque de France, *Financial Stability Review*, Special Issue on Hedge Funds, No. 10, April.

Cornford, A. (2005), 'Book review of *Hedge Funds in Emerging Markets* by Gordon de Brouwer, Cambridge University Press, 2001', International Development Economics Associates, available at: http://networkideas.org/book/jul2004/bk10_FRC.htm (accessed 8 June 2010).

Counterparty Risk Management Policy Group II (2005), 'Toward Greater Financial Stability: A Private Sector Perspective', available at: http://www.crm policygroup.org/docs/CRMPG-II.

Cox, Hugo (2009), 'Hedge funds administration: lifting the veil', *Alpha Magazine*, April.

Crockett, Andrew (2007), 'The evolution and regulation of hedge funds', Banque de France, *Financial Stability Review*, Special Issue on Hedge Funds, No. 10, April.

Daníelsson, J. and J.P. Zigrand (2007), 'Regulating hedge funds', Banque de France, *Financial Stability Review*, Special Issue on Hedge Funds, No. 10, April.

De Bandt, Olivier and Philipp Hartmann (2000), 'Systemic Risk: a Survey'. European Central Bank, Working Paper Series 35 (November).

de Brouwer, G. (2001), *Hedge Funds in Emerging Markets*, Cambridge: Cambridge University Press.

de Larosiére, Jacques (2009), 'The High-Level Group on Financial Supervision in the EU', (de Larosière Report) Brussels, February 25.

Desai, Mihir, Fritz Foley and James R. Hines (2005), 'The demand for tax haven operations', Working Paper Series March, pp. 1–27.

Dodd, Randall (2007), 'Subprime: tentacles of a crisis', *Finance and Development*, December, pp. 15–19.

Dodd, Randall (2009), 'Overhauling the system', *Finance and Development*, September, pp. 32–4.

Donoghue, J. Andrew (2009), 'Testimony Concerning Regulating Hedge Funds and Other Private Investment Pools', in SEC Supports Private Funds Transparency Act of 2009, July 20.

Eichengreen, Barry and Donald Mathieson (1999), 'Hedge funds: what do we really know?', International Monetary Fund, Economic Issues, No. 19, September.

Ervin, Susan C. (2004), 'Letting go: the CFTC rethinks managed futures regulation', 24 *Futures and Derivatives Law Report*, 1.n.5 (May).

Federal Reserve Bank of New York (2007), 'Economic policy review', Staff Report, December, **13** (3), 1–18.

Financial Times (2007), 'Reporting standards for hedge funds must be raised', 12 January.

Financial Services Authority (FSA) (2009), 'The Turner review: a regulatory response to the global banking crisis', March, FSA, UK.

Financial Stability Forum (FSF) (2000), 'Report of the Working Group on Highly Leveraged Institutions', April.

Financial Stability Forum (FSF) (2007), 'Progress in Implementing the Recommendations of the FSF, Update Report on Highly Leveraged Institutions', 15 October.

Financial Stability Forum (FSF) (2008), 'Report of the Financial Stability Forum on enhancing market and institutional resilience', April 12.

Financial Times (2004), 'Hedge funds puzzle: should investors fear a crisis?', 28 July.

Fischer, Stanley (1998), 'Reforming the international monetary system', International Monetary Fund, David Finch Lecturé, Melbourne, November 9.

Fox, J. (1998), 'Did foreign investors cause Asian market problem?', *NBER Digest*, October.

Franklin, Edwards (2003), 'The regulation of hedge funds: financial stability and investor protection', Prepared for Conference on Hedge Funds Institute for Law and Finance / Deutsches Aktieninstitut e.V. Johann Wolfgang Goethe-Universitat, Frankfurt, May 22.

Garbaravicius, Thomas and Frank Dierick (2005), 'Hedge funds and their implications for financial stability', European Central Bank, Occasional Paper 34/ August.

Giannone, Joseph A. (2008), 'UPDATE 2–Meltdown, Madoff decimated hedge funds 08', Reuter Thomson.

Gup, E. Benton (1999), 'Preface', in Gup (ed.), *International Banking Crises, Large-Scale Failures, Massive Government Intervention*, Westpost, CT: Quorum Books.

Gup, E. Benton (2003), 'Creative destruction', in Gup (ed.), *The Future of Banking*, ch.1, London: Quorum Books.

Hamilton, James (2009), 'IOSCO recommends hedge fund regulation as part of systemic risk oversight', CCS Financial Crisis News Center, LL.M, April 17.

Humphries, Simon and Ben Norman (2003), 'A work programme in financial statistics –Monetary & Financial Statistics', Bank of England, April, available at: http://www.bankofengland.co.uk/statistics/ms/articles/artapr03.pdf.

International Monetary Fund (IMF) (2000), 'The Role of the IMF', Monetary and Exchange Affairs Department, IMF, Washington, DC, June 23.

International Monetary Fund (2004), *Global Financial Stability Report*, April, Washington, DC: IMF.

International Monetary Fund (IMF) (2008a), 'IMF Executive Board Integrates the Offshore Financial Center Assessment Program with the FSAP', Public Information Notice No. 08/82, July 9.

International Monetary Fund (IMF) (2008b), 'IMF world economic and financial surveys, global financial stability report containing systematic risks and restoring financial soundness', April 7.

International Monetary Fund (IMF) and World Bank (2005), *Financial Sector Assessment Handbook*, Washington, DC: IMF and World Bank, September.

Issing, Otmar, Jörg Asmussen, Jan Pieter Krahnen, Klaus Regling, Jens Weidmann and William White (2009), 'New Financial Order Recommendations' by the Issing Committee, Part II (March) Preparing G20 – London, April 2, White Paper, Center for Financial Studies, February 2.

Jackson, E. Howell (2007), 'The impact of enforcement: a reflection, in response to John C. Coffee, Jr., law and the market: the impact of enforcement', *University of Pennsylvania Law Review*, **156** (229).

Jackson, Jackie (2003), 'Reporting legitimacy after black listing by the Financial Action Task Force', *Journal of Money Laundering Control*, **7** (1), 38–49.

Johnston, Barry R., Salim M. Darbar and Mary G. Zephirin (2003), 'Assessing offshore: Filling the gap in global surveillance', *Finance and Development*, September,

Kern, Alexander (2001), 'The international action money laundering regime: the role of the financial action task force', *Journal of Money Laundering Control*, **4** (3), 231–48.

Kern, Alexander (2006), *Global Governance of Financial Systems: The International Regulation of Systemic Risk*, New York: Oxford University Press.

Kose, M. Ayhan, Eswar Prasad, Kenneth Rogoff and Shang-Jin Wei (2007), 'Beyond the blame game: the two faces of globalization in financial globalization – the impact on trade, policy, labor and capital flows', *Finance and Development*, March 5, 1–6.

Lehmann, Bruce N. (2006), 'Corporate governance and hedge fund management', *Economic Review*, (4), 81–91.

Lipsky, John (2007a), 'International Financial Markets – stability and transparency in the 21st century', Keynote speech by John Lipsky, First Deputy Managing Director, IMF, Social Democratic Party Caucus, Berlin, Germany, June 20.

Lipsky, John (2007b), 'The global economy and financial markets: where next?', Speech by John Lipsky, First Deputy Managing Director, IMF, Lowy Institute, Sydney, Australia, July 31.

Litan, Robert E. (2009), 'Where were the watchdogs? Systemic risk and the breakdown of financial governance', Testimony, March 4.

MacKintosh, James (2008), 'Hedge funds present dilemmas for regulators', *Financial Times*, March 5.

Markham, Jerry W. (2006–07), 'Mutual fund scandals: a comparative analysis of the role of corporate governance in the regulation of collective investments', Hein Online, *Hastings Business Law Journal*, **3** (67).

Masson, Paul (2001), 'Globalization: Facts and Figures', IMF Policy Discussion Paper 0, 14, Washington, DC.

Masson, Paul (2007), 'Globalization: the story behind the numbers', in *Financial Globalization: The Impact on Trade, Policy, Labor, and Capital Flows*, a compilation of articles from *Finance and Development*, April, 14–16.

Mauro, Paolo and Yishay Yafeh (2007), 'Financial crises of the future', *Finance and Development*, **44** (4), December 26–30.

Milne, Richard (2009), 'Fink warns on tough European restrictions', FT.com, July 6.

Noyer, C. (2007), 'Hedge Funds: what are the main issues?', *Financial Stability Review*, Special Issue on Hedge Funds, No. 10, April.

Opalesque (2009), 'Absolute return: American hedge fund closures total record $84bn in 2008 (more than quadruple the 2007 figure), Premium Alternatives News, 18 March, available at: http://www.opalesque.com/IndustryUpdates/67/Absolute_Return_American_hedge_fund_closures_total_record457.html.

Papademos, Lucas (2007), 'Financial integration in Europe', BIS Review 148/2007, 12 December, available at: http://www.bis.org/review/r070330h.pdf?noframes=1 (accessed 8 June 2010).

Parker, George (2009), 'Myners wary of Brussels scrutiny plan', FT.com, June 3.

Pazarbaşioğlu, Ceyla, Mangal Goswami and Jack Ree (2007a), 'The changing face of investors', *Finance and Development*, March, 28–32.

Pazarbaşioğlu, Ceyla, Daniel Hardy and Jack Ree (2007b), 'Changes in the international investor base and implications for financial stability', *Finance and Development*, **44** (1), March, 63–96.

Prada, Michel (2007), 'The world of hedge funds: prejudice and reality – the AMLs contribution to the alternative investment strategies, Bank de France, *Financial Stability Review*, Special Issue on Hedge Funds, No. 10, April.

PricewaterhouseCoopers Group (2008), 'Financial services regulatory highlights', **10** (2), February.

Rajan, Raghuram, G. (2006), 'Benign financial conditions, asset management, and political risks: trying to make sense of our times', address at the Conference on International Financial Stability: Cross Border Banking and National Regulation, Federal Reserve Bank of Chicago, October 5–6.

Roberts, Susan M. (1997), 'Small place, big money: the Cayman islands and the international financial system, *Trends Organized Crime*, **2** (3), March.

Rose, Andrew K. and Mark M. Spiegel (2006), 'Offshore financial centers: parasites or symbionts?', National Bureau of Economic Research Working Paper, Revised: April 4.

Roubini, Nouriel (2007), 'Credit derivatives, hedge funds and leverage ratios of 50: the credit house of cards', Nouriel Roubini's Global Econo-Monitor, January 20.

Schinasi, Garry J. (2006), *Safeguarding Financial Stability: Theory and Practice*, Washington, DC: International Monetary Fund.

Schwarcz, Steven L. (2008), 'Systemic risk', *Georgetown Law Journal*, **97** (1), Duke Law School Legal Studies Paper No. 163.

Solomon, Deborah (2006), 'Congress may let hedge funds manage more pension money', *Wall Street Journal*, July 28.

Swire, Mary (2000), 'Financial Stability Forum attacks offshore', Centers, Tax-news.com, Singapore, March.

Tait, Nikki (2009a), 'Alarm at EU's hedge fund rule plans', FT.com, June 15.

Tait, Nikki (2009b), 'Alternative funds score EU victory', FT.com, September 4.

Terhune, Hannah (2005), 'Offshore hedge funds: dos and don'ts', green TraderLaw.

Tobias, Adrian and Hyun Song Shin (2009), 'The shadow banking system: implications for financial regulation', Federal Reserve Bank of New York Staff Report No. 382, July.

Ubide, Angel (2009), 'Demystifying hedge funds', *Finance and Development*, **43** (2) June.

US Department of Treasury (2009), 'Financial regulatory reform: a new foundation – rebuilding financial supervision and regulation', white paper, September.

Wassim, N. Shahin (2005), 'De-listing from NCCTs and money laundering control measures: a banking regulation perspective', *Journal Money Laundering Control*, **8** (4), 320–27.

Wilmarth, Arthur E., Jr. (2009), 'The dark side of universal banking: financial conglomerates and the origins of the subprime financial crisis', *Connecticut Law Review*, **41** (14), May, 963–1050.

Woodruff, Judy (2008), 'The financial crisis: an interview with George Soros', in *The New York Review of Books*, **55** (8), May 15.

Worby, Adam and S. Posen (2009), 'Op-ed making capital rules', Peterson Institute for International Economics in Welt am Sonntag, September 16.

Index